UNDERSTANDING
DIVERSITY

THIRD EDITION

UNDERSTANDING
DIVERSITY

An Introduction

Fred L. Pincus
Bryan R. Ellis

LYNNE
RIENNER
PUBLISHERS

BOULDER
LONDON

Published in the United States of America in 2021 by
Lynne Rienner Publishers, Inc.
1800 30th Street, Suite 314, Boulder, Colorado 80301
www.rienner.com

and in the United Kingdom by
Lynne Rienner Publishers, Inc.
Gray's Inn House, 127 Clerkenwell Road, London EC1 5DB
www.eurospanbookstore.com/rienner

Library of Congress Cataloging-in-Publication Data
Names: Pincus, Fred L., author. | Ellis, Bryan R., 1984– author.
Title: Understanding diversity : an introduction / Fred L. Pincus and Bryan
    R. Ellis.
Description: 3rd Edition. | Boulder : Lynne Rienner Publishers, Inc, 2021.
    | Revised edition of Understanding diversity, 2011. | Includes
    bibliographical references and index. | Summary: "A thorough, accessible
    introduction to the issues and controversies surrounding concepts of
    class, race, ethnicity, gender, sexual orientation, and disability"—
    Provided by publisher.
Identifiers: LCCN 2021015776 | ISBN 9781626379534 (paperback)
Subjects: LCSH: Cultural pluralism. | Cultural pluralism—United States. |
    Minorities—United States. | Prejudices—United States. |
    Discrimination—United States. | United States—Social conditions—21st
    century.
Classification: LCC HM1271 .P56 2021 | DDC 305.800973—dc23
LC record available at https://lccn.loc.gov/2021015776

British Cataloguing in Publication Data
A Cataloguing in Publication record for this book
is available from the British Library.

Printed and bound in the United States of America

The paper used in this publication meets the requirements
of the American National Standard for Permanence of
Paper for Printed Library Materials Z39.48-1992.

5 4 3 2 1

Contents

Tables

Preface

Much has happened in US society since the publication of the second edition of *Understanding Diversity* in 2011. The election of President Donald Trump in 2016 marked the end of the relatively liberal administration of Barack Obama and ushered in four years of conservative policies that reversed many of those from the Obama administration. Trump's "zero-tolerance" approach to immigration and his harsh approach to social unrest caused widespread racial divisiveness. His hypocritical claims of "law and order" were demonstrated in the difference between his crackdown on antiracist protesters following the police's murder of George Floyd and his encouragement of White nationalists to illegally storm the US Capitol on January 6, 2021.

Early in 2020, the Covid-19 pandemic and resulting economic recession caused untold devastation for millions of Americans. By May 2021, more than 32 million Americans had been infected and more than 500,000 had died from Covid-19. Millions lost their jobs and fell into poverty. All of this will be discussed in appropriate chapters throughout the book.

Several other events are also noteworthy. The US Supreme Court ruled that same-sex marriage was legal in 2015, a major victory for the LGBTQ community. Yet, after the death of liberal Justice Ruth Bader Ginsburg in 2020, the Supreme Court has a six-to-three conservative majority that threatens the LGBTQ community, women's reproductive rights, and a number of other progressive issues.

All of these events indicate both progress and continuing problems. How far have we come, and how much farther do we have to go to achieve social equity? These are among the important questions addressed in this book.

This new edition reflects feedback from students and colleagues who used the second edition. In addition, Bryan R. Ellis has joined the project as coauthor. We both would like to thank Eric C. Grollman for reading several drafts of Chapter 6 and for making cogent criticisms and suggestions.

* * *

Fred Pincus had been teaching race and ethnic relations for twenty-seven years when he first became interested in the broader topic of diversity in 1996. He was never satisfied with the way he handled class and gender in his own teaching, and he did not confront LGBTQ issues or those concerning people with disabilities. He also began to realize that most undergraduates left the university without any exposure to African American studies, women's studies, or any other aspect of diversity. In 1999 he took over teaching a graduate course called Constructing Race, Class, and Gender; he included sexual orientation even though it wasn't in the course title.

For several years he worked with an interdisciplinary committee to design an introductory undergraduate course called Diversity and Pluralism: An Interdisciplinary Perspective. The course was originally team-taught by a pair of faculty who were "demographically different" and from different departments. This book grew out of the Diversity and Pluralism course.

Following Pincus's retirement, Bryan Ellis joined the University of Maryland, Baltimore County sociology faculty in 2016 and taught the Diversity and Pluralism course until 2019. In that course, he used the second edition of this book. His first inspiration for studying diversity came from his experiences as a youth. Growing up in Detroit, Michigan, when it was on the verge of bankruptcy, he noticed that both class and racial inequality were omnipresent. His second influence was his grandfather, Clemmont E. Vontress, who dedicated his life to studying diversity in the field of counseling psychology, for which he is acknowledged as a pioneer.

* * *

Pincus dedicates this book to his wife and intellectual partner, Natalie J. Sokoloff, also a retired sociologist. She has taught him about intersectionality and about life.

Ellis dedicates this book to Nicole Branch-Ellis, his wife and fellow sociologist, and to his two sons, Bryson and Dominic. May their futures be filled with possibility.

—Fred L. Pincus
Bryan R. Ellis

1

What Is Diversity?

Issues of population diversity in the United States are
filled with contradictions. A 2019 national survey of adults found that
more than three-quarters of them said it is "very good" or "somewhat
good" that the United States consists of people of many different races
and ethnicities (Horowitz 2019a). Nevertheless, the nation saw months
of protests after the killing of George Floyd, an unarmed Black man, by
a White Minneapolis police officer on May 25, 2020.

According to *Forbes* magazine, 614 billionaires resided in the
United States in 2020, the highest number ever (*Forbes* 2020). However, more than 39 million Americans were officially defined as poor
in 2019 (US Census Bureau 2020c).

Since 2010, five women justices (Sandra Day O'Connor, Ruth
Bader Ginsburg, Sonia Sotomayor, Elena Kagan, and Amy Coney Bar-
rett) have served on the US Supreme Court, the most in US history.
Still, women made only 82 cents for each dollar that a man made in
2019 (US Census Bureau 2020b).

We have more federal laws than ever to protect people with disabilities from workplace discrimination. Yet, 26,838 complaints were
filed with the Equal Employment Opportunity Commission (EEOC) in
2017 by people with disabilities (Equal Employment Opportunity Commission 2020a).

The US Supreme Court ruled in 2015 that same-sex marriage is
legal. Yet North Carolina and several other states prevent transgender
people from using bathrooms associated with their gender, and former
president Donald Trump reinstated the policy of banning transsexuals
from serving in the military.

Immigrants are essential workers in industries such as construction,
food services, hospitality, and meat processing and a 2019 poll showed

1

that 62 percent of Americans believe that immigrants "strengthen the country because of their hard work and talents" (Jones 2019). Trump, however, made restricting immigration a key policy in his presidency.

These are some of the many contradictions when considering diversity in the United States in the third decade of the twenty-first century. There is growing diversity along with increasing inequality. Is the glass half full or half empty? Addressing these issues is the goal of this book.

Despite all of the talk about diversity, most of us grow up in a world that seems fairly homogeneous. Our neighbors and schoolmates are generally from the same race and social class we are. Between 5 and 10 percent of the people in our neighborhoods are probably gay or lesbian, although many of us don't know who they are. People with disabilities make up 15 to 20 percent of the population.

Upon entering college—before, during, and after Covid-19—students often feel unaccustomed to diversity, especially those who live in campus residence halls. Suddenly, roommates or floormates can be of different races, ethnicities, and religious and economic backgrounds. Some are from different regions of the United States and even from different countries. The sounds of their voices, smells of their cooking, and visuals of their clothes and hairstyles are often unfamiliar. Men and women may live on the same floor. A gay person might live a few doors down or in the same suite. Sexual relations with the opposite sex (or with the same sex) are not supervised, and alcohol and drugs are everywhere.

When one walks around campus, one might see tables and signs promoting the women's union, Black Lives Matter, the LGBTQ support group, and international student organizations. You can take courses such as Black history, women's literature, and queer film studies.

On the one hand, this campus diversity might be exciting because there can be new and stimulating experiences every day. On the other hand, it can be disconcerting. Are people who speak Spanish talking about you? Is that gay person down the hall checking you out? Do you feel embarrassed that someone of the opposite sex sees you in your nightclothes or without makeup? Why are those guys down the hall so loud, or so quiet? That music is awful; how can they like it? Are those people going to rob you? Maybe you're uncomfortable seeing that girl in the wheelchair every morning. It's not always easy to be around people different from you.

For better or worse, *diversity* has become one of the buzzwords of the early twenty-first century. More than two-thirds of colleges and universities have diversity requirements in their curricula, and many have ethnic and women's studies programs. Several of the national college-rating publications contain diversity criteria or indicators. *U.S. News and World Report* has an index ranging from 0–1 showing the racial and ethnic diversity of each campus. The *Princeton Review* ranks schools in terms of LGBTQ friendliness, opportunities for race and class interaction, and the number of religious students.

Increasingly, large corporations have diversity departments that include recruiters, trainers, and troubleshooters. DiversityInc rates corporations on various aspects of diversity. Politicians and the media often extol the history of immigration to the United States, a pluralistic society characterized as a melting pot, a salad bowl, or a patchwork quilt.

There is another side to the diversity picture, however. Colleges and universities are accused of being too "politically correct" or "pandering" to people of color. The "cancel culture" is accused of censoring conservative ideas. Instructors often issue trigger warnings that the material covered could be traumatic to some students before they discuss controversial issues. Corporations are accused of hiring "unqualified" minorities and women to satisfy federal affirmative action guidelines. In the eyes of many White Americans, reverse discrimination against White males has replaced discrimination against people of color.

For decades before Trump was elected in 2016, many mainstream politicians and media commentators, especially conservatives, were concerned about how contemporary immigration is allegedly threatening the integrity of American culture and the English language.

Gay marriages are still controversial even though they are legal. Labor unions have been redefined as special-interest groups, and politicians who talk about growing economic inequality are often accused of fomenting class conflict, whereas corporations are thought to represent the interests of the entire country. Women have also been defined as a special-interest group, and pro-choice advocates have been called "baby killers." In contrast, antiabortionists and those who believe a woman's place is in the home are said to be protectors of "family values."

Defining Diversity

What is diversity? According to *Merriam-Webster's* (2020), **diversity** means "the condition of having or being composed of differing elements: variety; especially: the inclusion of different types of people (such as people of different races or cultures) in a group or organization."

Synonyms include "assortment, diverseness, heterogeneity, heterogeneousness, manifoldness, miscellaneousness, multifariousness, multiplicity, variety, variousness." This definition can apply to cultures, species, and a number of other topics. From a social science perspective, this definition is not helpful because it is much too broad.

Social scientists use the concept of diversity in at least four ways. **Counting diversity** refers to empirically enumerating differences within a given population. In a given country (or state, city, school, workplace), we can count the members of different races, ethnicities, religions, genders, and so on. A particular country can be described as relatively *homogeneous* if most people are of the same race (religion, ethnicity, etc.) or relatively *heterogeneous* if they are more diverse.

The 117th Congress, for example, took office in 2021 and had 27 percent female members and 23 percent people of color (Blazina and DeSilver 2021; Schaeffer 2021). Although these numbers are high relative to previous congressional classes, women and people of color are still underrepresented relative to the general population at 51 percent female and almost 30 percent people of color. Congress is still predominantly White and male. These numbers, of course, say nothing about *why* women and people of color are underrepresented in Congress.

Culture diversity refers to the importance of understanding and appreciating the cultural differences between groups. The focus here is on how rich and poor, White people and people of color, men and women, people with and without disabilities, and homosexuals and heterosexuals have different experiences, worldviews, modes of communication, behaviors, values, and belief systems. Those who use this definition of diversity tend to seek lower levels of discrimination and higher levels of inclusion so to even the playing field. Usually, the implicit assumption is that appropriate attitudinal changes can take place without large-scale structural changes in the economic and political systems.

Problems can arise when groups don't understand each other's cultures. White people, for example, sometimes wonder why Black people can use the "N word," whereas Whites are not supposed to. *Nigger,* of course, is a derogatory term White people have used for centuries as part of the systemic oppression of Black people. The word is now objectionable to most. *Some* Black people, however, have begun to use *nigga* as a term of endearment and a sign of ingroup solidarity. So, a Black person saying, "What's up, Nigga" to another Black person has a totally different meaning than if a White person said the same. Not understanding these cultural differences can lead to fraught interracial interactions.

Good-for-business diversity refers to the argument that businesses will be more profitable and government agencies and nonprofit organizations will be more efficient with diverse labor forces. Supporters of this definition would argue, for example, that a female car salesperson would be more effective than a male in selling cars to women customers. Along the same lines, a Hispanic police officer would do a better job than a White police officer in interacting with the Hispanic community. Not having diverse employees, according to this view, is simply bad for business.

Morgan Stanley, the huge investment bank, ran a full-page advertisement in the *New York Times* on August 18, 2020, posing the question "Can Gender Diversity Drive Bottom-Line Growth?" A smiling, young, White woman is identified as Jessica Alsford, head of global sustainability research. Her answer: "The trend line is clear: Over the past eight years, stocks in more diverse companies have outperformed their benchmarks. . . . The relationship between gender diversity and performance is likely to become more pervasive as women play increasingly prominent roles in the workplace, and in turn, the global economy." In short, Morgan Stanley is saying gender diversity leads to higher profits.

The website DiversityInc, founded in 1998, describes its mission as bringing "education and clarity to the business benefits of diversity." Each year it publishes a list of the top fifty US companies based on their successful diversity policies. "We have spent millions of dollars incorporating our methodology into SAS [software] and can positively correlate best practices, like senior-executive accountability, diversity councils, resource groups, and mentoring with specific results as expressed by human-capital and supplier-diversity results."

Finally, **conflict diversity** refers to understanding how different groups exist in a hierarchy of inequality in terms of power, privilege, and wealth. Scholars who use this definition emphasize the way in which dominant groups oppress subordinate groups who seek liberation, freedom, institutional change, and/or revolution. According to this perspective, calls to celebrate diversity within a fundamentally unjust system are insufficient; usually its proponents talk about dismantling the hierarchy.

For example, believers in conflict diversity would view heterosexuals as oppressing homosexuals through discriminatory laws, organizational practices, and individual behavior. They consider hate crimes against LGBTQ people an example of oppression.

Although these definitions are not always mutually exclusive, this book uses the conflict diversity definition described above. We will analyze the conflicts in the United States based on class, race, immigration, gender, sexual orientation, and disability in subsequent chapters.

The Study of Diversity

Studying group conflict within the population is nothing new. Sociologists and historians have been studying immigration and race relations for more than a century. W. E. B. DuBois and Robert Park conducted empirical studies in the late nineteenth and early twentieth centuries, and other scholars debated whether the appropriate metaphor for American racial and ethnic relations was the "melting pot," the "salad bowl," or "Anglo-conformity." Karl Marx and Max Weber wrote about class inequality in the nineteenth century. Both race relations and social stratification have for decades been recognized as legitimate sociological specializations. Although a few scholars had been studying male-female conflicts before the twentieth century, the social scientific study of gender inequality exploded in the 1960s, soon to be followed by a dramatic growth in the study of gays and lesbians and people with disabilities.

Black/African American studies programs began to develop in the late 1960s, with Hispanic, Asian, and Native American studies emerging as well. Women's studies programs were first institutionalized in the 1970s, followed by gay and lesbian studies. Working-class and disability studies came later.

Most of these earlier approaches, however, tended to focus on only one group or category at a time. Race relations, for example, tended to focus on racial differences without considering class and gender. Stratification studies tended to ignore gender and race. Almost all academic programs ignored sexual orientation and disabilities.

Eventually, increasing numbers of scholars, especially women, grew to understand the necessity of going beyond single categories because many people belong to more than one of these groups. Predominantly White socialist feminists began to use both class and gender in their analyses, and Black feminists began to incorporate class, gender, and race. Multiculturalists, especially in the field of education, crossed the boundaries of ethnicity, nationality, race, and religion.

Not until the late 1980s did social scientists began to systematically discuss class, gender, and race, and sexual orientation *together.* The first edition of Paula Rothenberg's *Race, Class, and Gender in the United States: An Integrated Study* (now in its eleventh edition) was published in 1988. The scholarly journal *Race, Gender, and Class* began publication in 1993. Even in specialty areas such as criminal justice, Barbara Price and Natalie Sokoloff used a class-gender-race approach in the second edition of their anthology *The Criminal Justice System and Women* (1996).

Theoretically, there is a variety of ways to understand conflict diversity. Some scholars take a single-issue approach and tend to see one aspect of diversity as more fundamental than all others. Marxists tend to emphasize class, feminists tend to emphasize gender, critical race theorists tend to emphasize race, and so forth. These scholars don't ignore other aspects of diversity, but they view society through the lens of their most fundamental concern.

Other scholars refuse to engage in debates about whether Hispanics are more oppressed than women or whether poor people are more oppressed than people with disabilities. Intersectionality theorists, a term coined by Kimberlé Crenshaw (1989), assert the existence of parallel systems of oppression (gender, race, sexual orientation, etc.) that sometimes reinforce each other and sometimes contradict each other. Although intersectionality proponents agree that no aspect of diversity is most fundamental, they also argue that in different contexts, different aspects of diversity are more important than others. In discussing rape, for example, gender is the most important factor, and poor women of color are the most vulnerable. In discussing the economic inequality endemic to capitalism, class is the most important, and Black and Hispanic men and women are overrepresented among the poor.

Levels of Analysis

Understanding conflict diversity is incredibly complex. After teaching about these issues for many years, we have come to realize there are no simple causes of, or solutions to, group conflict. In 1992, twenty-eight years before George Floyd was murdered by a White Minneapolis police officer, a jury acquitted the White police officers videotaped beating Rodney King, another Black man. A four-day uprising exploded in Los Angeles, resulting in 52 deaths, 8,000 injuries, 12,000 arrests, and $800 million in property damage. During the melee, a distraught King asked, "Why can't we just get along?" A simple question without a simple answer.

As with most social phenomena, it is necessary to look at group conflict using different levels of analysis. In the United States, we are used to *individualizing* group conflict and other social problems. It is also necessary to look at group conflict from the *structural* level by looking at the society in which the conflict takes place.

We can illustrate these two levels of analysis using the Me Too movement, which burst upon the national scene in 2017 when film producer Harvey Weinstein was accused by an actress of sexual assault. Dozens of other women subsequently accused Weinstein of similar crimes, followed by thousands of women with their own stories of sexual misconduct by hundreds of powerful men. Me Too was founded in 2006 but was little known before the Weinstein scandal.

At the individual level, we can ask why a specific man perpetrates sexual violence and what he gets from it. Similarly, we can ask why a specific woman did or did not report the violence to the police or some other authority. Are there personality measures that can predict whether a specific man will become a perpetrator? Finally, we would want to know how to help victims heal and how to prevent perpetrators from committing additional crimes.

It is also necessary to analyze sexual violence from the structural level by looking at the larger society. How do power differences and patriarchal culture influence sexual violence? How does the criminal justice system react to crimes of sexual violence? Are the dynamics of sexual violence different in different economic and racial communities? How can we prevent more sexual violence? These questions address the nature of the entire society, not just the individuals involved in a particular event.

To understand both the individual and structural levels of analysis, we must look at group conflict in an interdisciplinary way. We can't be limited by any one discipline.

The Covid-19 pandemic, which began in 2020, provides an excellent example. To understand the nature of the virus and to find treatments and vaccines, we need a broad range of scientists. Before treatments and vaccines were available, physicians, nurses, and other medical workers were exposed on the front lines in hospitals. Public health officials talked about how to mitigate the virus by wearing masks, washing hands, and social distancing.

Social scientists also had their roles. Psychologists tried to understand the resistance of some people to wearing masks. Sociologists looked at inequities in terms of who was more likely to get sick and die from the virus. Political scientists looked at why the Trump administration refused to develop a national plan to combat the virus. Economists studied the financial fallout from the pandemic, the worst since the Great Depression in the 1930s. Educators had to quickly adapt to online pedagogy because schools at all levels eliminated face-to-face instruction. Events such as the pandemic are multifaceted, and a variety of approaches is needed to confront it.

The need for an interdisciplinary and multilevel analysis puts a great burden on those of us who teach and write about diversity from a group conflict perspective. Most have been trained to look at social phenomena from only one discipline, so we must educate ourselves about intellectual approaches we didn't learn in graduate school. It is often difficult to find faculty to teach diversity courses because of the intellectual challenges these courses pose.

It also puts a great burden on students trying to understand the world in which they live. Many students enroll with the hope they will find an answer to Rodney King's question, "Why can't we just get along?" They find that the answer is much more complicated than they could have ever imagined.

The Rest of the Book

This book is intended to be a companion to one of the many anthologies that address class, race, ethnicity, gender, race, sexual orientation, and disability. The strength of anthologies is their breadth in providing descriptions and analyses of many different intersectional groups. They have articles on prejudice toward several different racial groups, not just Black people. There might be one article about discrimination against working-class White women and another about discrimination against middle-class Asian women. An article about the health problems of gay men could be contrasted with another about the process of going through a sex-change operation.

However, these same anthologies often do not provide a careful discussion of basic concepts or systematic comparisons between groups or up-to-date statistical data, as we intend to do in this short book.

Chapter 2 introduces some of the basic analytical concepts used in the study of diversity. Students also using one of the anthologies will benefit from having these concepts clearly defined in a single chapter. However, because social scientists don't always agree on these important concepts, the definitions in this book might not always be the same as the definitions in an anthology. One can find the key terms used in this book at the back of the book.

Chapters 3, 4, 5, 6, 7, and 8 will cover the issues of class, race, immigration, gender, sexual orientation and gender diversity, and disability, respectively. Each of these chapters:

1. show how the concepts discussed in Chapter 2 apply and introduce new concepts;
2. present descriptive statistics about differences in wealth, income, unemployment, education, occupation, and so on;
3. discuss the research on prejudice and ideology; and
4. discuss the research on discrimination and structure.

Chapter 9 addresses the issue of social change and emphasizes the importance of collective social action. We also provide a list of activist organizations students can join.

Some of the material might be unsettling. Students will no doubt agree with some things and strongly disagree with others. We encourage you to plunge in and keep an open mind. We invite you to question and challenge the issues discussed in this book. If you don't understand something, ask your instructor. If you disagree with something, ask your classmates what they think.

We also encourage you to disagree with your instructor and your classmates—in a respectful manner, of course. We hope your instructor has provided a safe and comfortable atmosphere in which to discuss some of these issues. Many of the students in our classes say it was the first time they were able to discuss diversity issues with people different from themselves. Pincus invited a lesbian speaker to one class to answer questions about sexual orientation; three students came out on that day. Another student told Pincus he was going to be absent for two weeks because he was going on a *hajj* (Islamic pilgrimage to Mecca). This student conducted a wonderful question-and-answer session with the class when he got back.

We encourage you to peruse news media with a new, critical perspective. When you watch television sit-coms, you will be able to see gender stereotyping. On crime shows, what are the economic and racial characteristics of the criminals, and how do they compare with those of the police and the lawyers? How are gays, lesbians, and people with disabilities presented, if at all?

Before moving on to the next chapter, consider that Donald Trump didn't want you to read this book or any other books on diversity. On September 22, 2020, Trump signed an executive order that criticized the entire field of diversity studies and training. The order prohibited federal agencies and all federal contractors from conducting diversity training that used concepts we discuss such as "systemic racism or sexism," "White privilege," and other "divisive concepts." Fortunately, President Biden overturned this policy on January 25, 2021.

As you go through the course, try to evaluate former President Trump's critique of diversity studies. We promise that by the end of the book, you will have a much different understanding of diversity and group conflict than you do now. Perhaps you will begin to look at the world in a different way. That's how change begins.

2

The Language
of Diversity

More than fifty years ago, when Fred Pincus enrolled in his first sociology class, the instructor said students would be learning "soc speak." By that, he meant they would be learning some of the terminology sociologists use to communicate with each other. Some in the class argued sociology was nothing but using jargon to describe what everyone already knows. Although this characterization of sociology is harsh, professional jargon sometimes makes it exceedingly difficult to understand what is being discussed.

All academics, including those who study diversity, have their own jargon, which makes it easier for them to communicate. Some of the concepts are shared by all members of a discipline and have common definitions. Other concepts are quite contentious, and people argue over their definitions. Sometimes there are arguments about whether the concepts are appropriate to use at all.

In this chapter, we'd like to introduce you to some of the important general concepts used in the study of diversity. We will concentrate on concepts that appear throughout the book. Some concepts, such as racism and sexism, we discuss in other chapters because they are both contentious and somewhat narrower in scope. The concepts appear in **boldface** as well as in the list of key terms at the back of the book.

Master Status

Two of the most basic concepts in sociology are status and role. **Status** refers to a position one holds or a category one occupies in a society. Each individual holds many positions and belongs to many categories. For example, a particular person can be a White, female, mother, sister, child, worker, neighbor, middle-aged person, suburbanite, flute player, and so on. Each of these has a culturally defined **role** that specifies expected behavior that goes along with a specific status. Teachers, for example, are supposed to help students learn certain content, treat students fairly, correct papers, issue grades, and so on. Students are supposed to attend class, study hard, and respect the teacher.

In a diverse society like ours, however, people don't always agree on the appropriate behavior associated with a particular status. For example, some would say "good" mothers are supposed to stay home and take care of children, whereas others would say good mothers can have jobs outside of the home. More importantly, within a particular culture, "appropriate" roles might look different at different levels of society. From a boss's perspective, for example, workers trying to organize a union might be viewed as troublemakers and be fired. From the workers' perspective, in contrast, organizing a union might be one of the few ways of trying to improve their lives.

Although we all occupy many different statuses, some are culturally defined as more important than others. A **master status** has a profound effect on one's life by dominating or overwhelming the other statuses one occupies (Rosenblum and Travis 2003, 33). In our society, master statuses include disability, class, ethnicity, gender, immigration status, race, and sexual orientation, among others. Age can also be viewed as a master status, but it will not be discussed in any depth in this book. These master statuses have a much stronger impact on our lives than, for example, being a friend or a chess player.

Master statuses are culturally determined, not a matter of individual choice. We know people, for example, whose religion is the most important part of their self-identity. In our country, however, social scientists don't usually view religion as a master status because it usually does not determine how one is perceived and treated by the larger society. In the Middle East, in contrast, religion would be considered a master status given the political and cultural conflicts in that area.

Some religions, such as Islam, have been viewed with great suspicion in the United States, and it has the potential to rise to the level of master status for those who practice it. At the beginning of the Trump administration, the president wanted to ban Muslims from entering the United States. Although he cited national security as the justification of this policy, many policymakers and ordinary citizens saw this as a gross violation of our country's commitment to freedom of religion. The president and his supporters were acting as if the Muslim/non-Muslim distinction was a master status. We will discuss the issue of anti-Muslim bias in Chapters 4 and 5.

Dominant and Subordinate Groups

Within each of the six master statuses we discuss, some groups have more power and influence than others. A **dominant group** is a social group that controls the political, economic, and cultural institutions in a society. In contrast, a **subordinate group** is a social group that lacks control of the political, economic, and cultural institutions in a society.

In terms of race in the United States, for example, White people make up the dominant group and people of color comprise the subordinate groups. Scholars of race relations have traditionally used the terms *majority group* and *minority group* to describe dominant and subordinate groups, respectively. People of color (non-White) in the United States are minority groups both numerically and in terms of power. However, if one applied this terminology to South Africa during apartheid, the White numerical minority was called the majority group because it had power, and the Black numerical majority was called the minority group. Because power is more important than numbers in studying diversity, we use the terms *dominant* and *subordinate*.

Native-born US citizens are the dominant group, whereas recent immigrants are the subordinate group. Naturalized American citizens fall somewhere in between.

In terms of gender, men are the dominant group and women the subordinate group. As we will see in later chapters, some people reject the male-female binary classification.

In terms of sexual orientation, heterosexuals are the dominant group. The subordinate group, however, is made up of a variety of groups that challenge traditional definitions of sexual orientation, including gays (male homosexuals), lesbians (female homosexuals), bisexuals (those sexually attracted to both males and females), trans-gendered people (whose gender identity is inconsistent with their biological makeup), and queer people, who do not want to be labeled with these terms. Collectively, this group is often referred to by the initials **LGBTQ**.

Finally, people with disabilities are the subordinate group relative to the nondisabled, the dominant group. We discuss labels such as "nondisabled" and "able-bodied" in Chapter 7.

It is also possible to discuss dominant and subordinate *class* groups, even though this is often not done by scholars who write about stratification. Although this is discussed more in Chapter 3, we call the wealthiest and most powerful 1 or 2 percent of the population the *dominant group*. The subordinate group consists of the large majority of the population who work for a living or who want to work and can't find jobs.

Social Construction

In discussing race and gender, most Americans assume there are biological differences between White people and other races and between men and women. This view, called **essentialism**, means reality exists independently of our perception of it; that is, real and important (essential) differences exist between categories of people (Rosenblum and Travis 2003, 33). Essentialists argue that biological factors differentiate heterosexuals and LGBTQ people and people with and without disabilities.

According to essentialists, then, racial groups can scientifically be differentiated by skin color, hair texture, facial shape, and other genetic characteristics. Men and women can be differentiated by primary and secondary sexual characteristics, hormones, body shape, and so on. People with disabilities have physical traits that differentiate them from everyone else. Finally, essentialists argue that homosexuals have some differences in their brains or some other genetic characteristic that predisposes them to be attracted to people of the same sex.

Advocates of the **social constructionist** perspective argue, in contrast, that reality cannot be separated from the way a culture makes sense of it—that meaning is "constructed" through social, political, legal, scientific, and other processes (Rosenblum and Travis 2003, 33). This refers to socially and culturally defined reasons people are assigned to being White, Black, Asian, or Native American that might have nothing to do with biological categories. For example, although some might say skin color is a defining characteristic, some people culturally defined as "Black" have lighter skin than some people culturally defined as "White." Should a person with an Asian mother and a Black father be defined as either Asian or Black, as opposed to being in a separate "mixed-race" category? Former president Barack Obama, whose father was Black and mother is White, is always described as either "Black" or "biracial" but never "White."

Racial categories are not real in a biological sense, but they are real in a social or cultural sense: people defined as White are treated differently from people defined as Black. We will discuss this in much more detail in Chapter 4.

Along the same lines, the distinction between male and female can be problematic among people who have both male and female or ambiguous sexual organs. What should we call someone genetically female who has a penis? What should we call someone born genetically male who has undergone a sex-change operation, or someone genetically female who presents like a man?

We usually try to fit people into one category or another, but the decisions are often arbitrary (see Chapter 6). The controversy over the sex of South African runner Caster Semenya is illustrative. After Semenya had won many important races as a woman, people challenged her sexual identity. Semenya was forced to undergo a series of tests, after which the International Amateur Athletic Federation finally ruled that she can continue to compete as a woman. The details of the test results were kept private. Here we have an athletic commission determining someone's gender.

Sexual orientation is also a problematic category to define. Most people would have no trouble saying a woman who has sexual relations with other women throughout her life is a homosexual/lesbian. However, what do we call a woman who occasionally has sex with women but is in a long-term heterosexual relationship? How about someone who was in a same-sex relationship for one year of his or her life but was otherwise heterosexual? Some people are attracted to people of the same sex but remain celibate. Our culture tries to force people into one or another category, but this has nothing to do with biology or with other essentialist criteria (see Chapter 7).

These same issues can also be raised in the area of abilities. Having a visual disability is certainly a biological impairment. However, Pincus's mother was defined as "legally blind" even though she still had some vision; the cutoff point for being legally blind is culturally determined. Also, the presence or absence of accommodations for visual impairment makes the difference between whether a given individual can perform a task. Having accessible computer software that "speaks" the written text permits a person with this disability to use a computer. Should this person still be considered disabled? (See Chapter 8.)

The essentialist/constructionist distinction can also be applied to the category of class. Although most people, including social scientists, don't equate class with any biological reality, there is still a widespread belief in the United States that terms such as *middle class* and *poor* actually refer to something essential, or real. Social scientists often quantify the percentage of the population in various classes. The United States is often called "a middle-class society."

In reality, these class labels are often arbitrary and vary from one social scientist to another. Marxists, for example, argue that most US citizens are *working class,* with the poor included as the lowest level of the working class. Others don't even use the term *working class* and refer to a *lower middle class* separate from the lower class, or poor. Some social scientists define the *upper class* as those in the top 10 percent of the income distribution, but they don't differentiate those who make $200 million per year from those who make $200,000. We discuss the social construction of class in more detail in Chapter 3.

Sometimes the concept of social construction is easier to see if we look at other countries. Throughout Latin America, for example, class is a more important distinction than race, even though lighter-skinned people are generally more economically privileged than darker-skinned people. Race is seen as a more continuous category in Latin America rather than the "either-or" category it is in the United States. We've had many Latin American students who hadn't even thought much about race in their own countries until they took our courses.

In Great Britain, a formal aristocracy based on family lineage still exists, though it has much less power than in the past. Eligibility for the House of Lords, one of the two houses of Parliament, is based on family background, though the House of Commons is responsible for most legislation. Although there are "high-society" lists in some major cities in the United States, we do not have a formal aristocracy.

The important point to take away from this discussion is that the master statuses and their subcategories are all socially constructed in each society. There is nothing real about them in either an essential or a biological sense.

Oppression

Some concepts, such as oppression, are frequently used in imprecise and rhetorical ways without being carefully defined. Often, an oppressed group is thought of as being extremely poor and/or living in a ruthless authoritarian police state filled with random acts of violence. The lack of a clear definition is most unfortunate in the study of diversity because the concept of oppression is central to understanding group conflict. After reviewing definitions put forward by a variety of writers, we have settled on the following definition, adapted from Blauner (1972): **oppression** is a dynamic process by which one segment of society achieves power and privilege through the control and exploitation of other groups burdened and pushed down into the lower levels of the social order.

Several important implications follow from this definition. First, because oppression involves power, only members of the dominant group can be oppressors, and only members of the subordinate groups can be oppressed. In the area of gender, for example, we can say women are oppressed because they are pushed down by the legal system, the economic system, and/or the family structure.

Many writers have observed that one of the difficulties men face is the inability to express emotions to women and to other men. Although this is a *limitation* that might prevent men from achieving their full potential, it is not an example of oppression because men tend to control most of the dominant social institutions (Frye 1983). Similarly, White people are not oppressed by racism even though their prejudiced attitudes might prevent them from forming friendships with people of color.

The term **exploitation** means the dominant group uses the subordinate group for its own ends, including gaining economic profit and maintaining a higher position in the social hierarchy. In the area of class oppression, for example, employers try to keep wages as low as possible so that their profits can be as high as possible. In the area of racial oppression, White people have used housing and educational segregation as a way of controlling the more desirable neighborhoods and schools. In the traditional, male-controlled family, men often have their meals cooked, their houses cleaned, and their children taken care of through the unpaid labor of their spouses.

The oppression and exploitation of LGBTQ people and people with disabilities are more social and cultural than economic. Because only heterosexual romantic/sexual relations are widely accepted, LGBTQ people are at the bottom of the social hierarchy and are often shunned, harassed, and physically brutalized. Similarly, people with disabilities are relegated to the bottom because they can't conform to the dominant, "able-bodied" norms of behavior. The thinking is that rather than making profits from the labor of people with disabilities, society must pay for their care, despite how many of them work.

Privilege

In a society characterized by oppression, some groups have more advantages than others. **Privilege** means members of some groups have something of value denied to others simply because of the groups they belong to; these unearned advantages give some groups a head start at a better life. Understanding this concept might be difficult, especially for those who are privileged.

In some cases, privileges are quite subtle—at least to those who have them. Heterosexuals, for example, assume it's okay for them to display a picture of their partner on their desk at work or to hold hands in a public place. LGBTQ people, in comparison, are often wary about displaying this type of public affection, often with good reason because of the risk of hate crimes, including murder.

A White customer in a store can usually assume those who work in the store believe she is there to purchase a product. Black customers, however, are often viewed with suspicion and are followed or watched by the store staff because they are assumed not to be legitimate customers.

In both of these examples, members of the dominant groups (i.e., heterosexual office workers and White store customers) are simply going about their business as usual. The problem is they usually don't realize that the very same behavior by members of subordinate groups (homosexual office workers and Black customers) is viewed quite differently. Business as usual for subordinate groups is not the same as for dominant groups.

In other cases, privilege is more egregious. Upper-income families, for example, usually can afford to live in a safe neighborhood and to send their children to high-quality schools. The children benefit because of the family into which they were born. Working-class and poor families have fewer options, and their children live in less safe neighborhoods and attend lower-quality schools. Similarly, men have a chance to compete for a number of high-status, well-paying jobs where the expectation is that the job will probably go to a male. Women, even if they are qualified, have much less of a chance in this competition.

Everyone should have the same opportunity to live in a safe area, attend a high-quality school, enter a fair competition for a job, hold hands with a loved one, and be assumed honest. These should be rights of living in the United States. The problem is the dominant groups have much greater access to these privileges than do the subordinate groups.

People without disabilities have the privilege of being able to use public buildings designed for them—stairs, doors that must be pushed open, standard-size toilet stalls, signs with no raised letters, and so forth. Although most such people take these things for granted, public buildings look much different to people with disabilities. Accommodations such as ramps, wider toilet stalls with handrails, and braille signs that make buildings more accessible have only been mandated since the passage of the Americans with Disabilities Act in 1990.

One of the most important privileges of the dominant group members is not having to know they are privileged in the first place. They assume, incorrectly, that everyone else has access to the same privileges they do. When Pincus was teaching his teenage son to drive, for example, he recalled reading an article about Black parents who had "the talk" with their children. One important lesson the Black teenagers learned was to keep their hands on the steering wheel if they were stopped by the police. This, hopefully, would reduce any accidental shootings by the police, who might think a Black driver was reaching for a weapon. The talk preceded the well-publicized police shooting of unarmed Blacks in 2020 by many decades.

Pincus never even dreamed of having the talk with his own White son about the police. Not surprisingly, members of the subordinate groups can more easily recognize the existence of privilege than members of the dominant group.

When we discuss privilege and oppression in the classroom, we often get two reactions from members of dominant groups. Some of the dominant group feel guilt or discomfort in learning they are privileged. They want to cast off their privilege to maintain their image of being a fair-minded person. Responding to these feelings, Allan Johnson argues that privilege and oppression are "rooted in a legacy we all inherited, and while we're here, it belongs to us. It isn't our fault. It wasn't caused by something we did or didn't do. But now that it's ours, it's up to us to decide how we're going to deal with it before we collectively pass it along to the generations that will follow ours" (2001, 15).

Other members of the privileged groups react with denial. A working-class White male student, for example, raises his hand and says, "I'm not privileged; I've had to fight for everything that I got." Often, this comment is followed by an angry but heartfelt story of someone from a poor family who had to struggle in life, including having to take out loans to pay for college. "And I had to do it without the benefits of affirmative action," he continues. Other White males (and some females) often nod in agreement, suggesting that the concept of race and gender privilege is a figment of our imagination.

Our response usually is to say that the student's story reflects *class* oppression, something we don't talk about much in our society. The student lacks *class* privilege even though he or she still has race and gender privilege. We in the United States often attribute economic oppression only to race because class remains largely invisible.

This illustrates another important point: people can be in the oppressor group with regard to one master status but in the oppressed group with regard to another. Our student still has some of the privileges of being White and male, but he lacks the privileges of being wealthy or middle income. Not all members of the oppressor group benefit in the same way, and not all members of the oppressed group are harmed in the same way. Sometimes this explanation neutralizes the students' anger somewhat, for they have gained a broader way to understand the complex reality of oppression and privilege.

One way to grasp the complexity of different kinds of privilege is shown in Table 2.1. Each category of privilege is trichotomized (i.e., separated into three parts). Those in the most privileged categories (i.e.,

Table 2.1   Rate Your Relative Privilege and Oppression by Diversity Category

Relative Privilege	Class	Race	Gender	Sexual Orientation	Disability Status
Most (2)	Capitalist	White	Male	Heterosexual	Nondisabled
Less (1)	Middle	Asian, Biracial	Female	Homosexual	Differently abled
Least (0)	Working	Black, Hispanic, Native American	Not clearly determined	Bisexual, Transgender	Disabled

Note: For each type of diversity category, circle the term that best describes you. To determine your relative level of privilege, give yourself a 2 each time you are in the "most" category, a 1 when you are in the "less" category, and a 0 when you are in the "least" category. Then, add up your total points. If your score is 10, you have the highest possible privilege. If your score is 0, you have the lowest possible privilege. Other scores fall somewhere in between the two extremes.

capitalist, White, male, heterosexual, nondisabled) receive two points for each privilege, for a total of ten points. Those in the least privileged categories (working class, non-Whites and non-Asians, those whose sex is not clearly determined, bisexual/transgendered people, and people with disabilities) receive zero points. Other combinations of privilege receive points in between zero and ten. Those with scores closer to ten have more privilege than those with scores closer to zero.

Of course, this method of assigning numbers to categories is overly simplistic and misses many of the nuances between categories. It also assumes that a zero in one category is equivalent to a zero in another. We are simply trying to illustrate the complexity of privilege across the different master statuses and its cumulative nature.

Using the discourse of oppression and privilege is really quite subversive in the United States. We often like to think of ourselves as a middle-class society gradually breaking down barriers of race and gender. The terms *post-race* and, less frequently, *post-gender* are used to describe this idealized view of the United States. Assimilation, inclusion, and upward mobility are the preferred discourse, not oppression, exploitation, and privilege.

This language is so controversial that in September 2020, former president Trump directed his director of the Office of Management and

Budget (OMB) to ban workshops that used this language. We discussed this in Chapter 1 (Vought 2020).

Culture, Attitudes, and Ideology

Diversity and group conflict also have important attitudinal components in terms of how different groups see each other. This is reflected in the culture as well as in how individuals think, feel, and believe. Privileged people, the dominant group in terms of power, usually have the ability to define nonprivileged people in an "us" versus "them" way. When a subordinate group is defined as the **"other,"** it is viewed as being unlike the dominant group in profoundly different, usually negative, ways. Groups that are "othered" are often seen as inferior, dangerous, or immoral. This is more charged than simply being seen as different.

This "othering" process is not inevitable when different groups come into contact with each other. Theoretically, the dominant racial group could view other groups as interesting curiosities rather than evil competitors. Men could view women as having different dispositions rather than as a weaker group to be dominated. *Different* does not have to mean inferior or threatening.

Groups defined as the "other" are usually stigmatized in a variety of ways. **Stigma** is an attribute for which someone is considered bad or unworthy because of the category to which he or she belongs. Being LGBTQ or a person with a disability is often viewed by many as grounds for social ostracism, no matter what else that person might have accomplished. In Nazi Germany, in fact, homosexuals were required to wear pink triangles to differentiate them from the rest of the population, just as Jews were required to wear yellow stars. In the present era, being on welfare is seen as a stigma.

Othering and stigmatization are both social processes that influence how given individuals might think. The same is true for **stereotypes**, cultural beliefs about a particular group that are usually exaggerated and distorted. Stereotypes are passed down from one generation to the next, often through the mass media.

Gay males, for example, are supposed to act feminine, and lesbians are thought to look masculine. These images are often promoted by television and movies even though only a minority of gays and lesbians fit this stereotype. Most LGBTQ people are indistinguishable from heterosexual men and women.

According to another stereotype, Blacks in our society are supposed to be naturally talented at basketball and football. Even though they are overrepresented in the National Basketball Association and the National Football League, it's safe to say most Black people, like most White people, have only average ability in these two sports.

These athletic stereotypes were brought home to Pincus when he was coaching his son's peewee league basketball team. Two Black boys were among the dozen children assigned to the team, and Pincus was thrilled for two reasons: he was happy the team was integrated, and he hoped the Black boys would raise the skill level of the team. The first child did not disappoint him; he was a tiny Michael Jordan. The second child, whom we'll call James, was a tall, broad-shouldered child who looked like the perfect center. The first time the ball was passed to him, James fumbled it, picked it up, fumbled it again, picked it up a third time, tucked it under his arm, and ran with it like a football player. He had no conception of dribbling, he couldn't jump, and he knew absolutely nothing about basketball. So much for the natural talent stereotype.

Hillary Clinton's unsuccessful presidential campaigns in 2008 and 2016 brought up a number of gender stereotypes. On the one hand, she was criticized for not being feminine enough—pantsuits, forceful speaking, and an aura of being aloof. On the other hand, the one time she confirmed the stereotype by shedding a tear during a speech, critics said this was proof she was too emotional to be president.

In addition to being inaccurate, stereotypes often portray the group in question in negative ways. Former president Trump promoted negative stereotypes of immigrants by referring to them as rapists, drug dealers, and criminals. The Black basketball player stereotype is part of a more general stereotype that Blacks can only excel physically, not intellectually. It also goes along with the "dumb athlete" stereotype.

In this othering, stigmatization, and stereotyping, the negative attitudes are part of a social process whereby the dominant group oppresses the subordinate group. The negative attitudes, in this view, act as justification for the political and economic oppression. In other words, the oppression causes the negative attitudes, not the other way around. The implication here is that it would be impossible to eliminate the negative attitudes until the oppression is eliminated.

Traditional social psychologists, however, often don't use this approach. Instead, they focus on the concept of **prejudice**, which generally refers to negative attitudes toward a specific group of people. This refers to what people think, feel, and believe. Although most of the research on prejudice has taken place in the context of studying racial and ethnic relations, the concept can also be applied to immigration, gender, sexual orientation, disabilities, and class. Although some preju- dice clearly incorporates cultural stereotypes, a variety of other inter- personal dynamics can be involved as causal factors.

The nature of prejudice can change over time, both in content and intensity. Some social scientists, for example, have argued that anti- Black prejudice on the part of White people has dropped dramatically in the years since the 1950s. They present evidence that White Americans are less supportive of segregation, are less likely to stereotype Black people, and are less likely to accept biological explanations of Black inferiority. Others counter that although this traditional prejudice has declined, it has been replaced by still quite intense "color-blind" preju- dice. We return to this argument in Chapter 4.

Although othering, stigmatization, and stereotyping tend to come from the dominant group against the subordinate group, prejudice can also be multidirectional. For example, Latinxs' anti-White attitudes or women's anti-male attitudes are just as prejudiced as the anti-Latinx attitudes held by Whites or the antifemale attitudes held by males. Whether one is worse than another is a more complex question.

Pejorative terms that dominant groups use against subordinate groups (e.g., nigger, welfare cheat) are much stronger and more demeaning than the other way around (e.g., Whitey, honky). Tim Wise (2002) suggests this is because dominant groups have the power to rein- force these pejorative terms with negative behavior, whereas subordi- nate groups don't. As we see in subsequent chapters, dominant-group prejudice toward subordinate groups tends to be much stronger than prejudice that goes in the other direction.

Negative attitudes about a particular group can also exist as part of an **ideology**, a body of ideas reflecting the social needs and aspirations of an individual group, class, or culture. There are several different bod- ies of ideas, for example, to explain why some people are successful in our society, whereas others are not. One view is that successful people worked hard to get to where they are. According to this view, individual effort can overcome barriers caused by adverse family circumstances or race/gender discrimination. A corollary of this view is the belief that most of those who are not successful didn't work hard enough.

A different explanation of success, which we might call the "oppressive society" perspective, is that those born into privileged posi- tions are the most likely to be successful because they control the dom- inant social institutions. A corollary of this view is that less-privileged people are usually held back by an unjust society, no matter how hard they work.

In a 2020 poll, most US citizens had beliefs closer to the oppressive-society view than to the hard-work view. Of those polled, 71 percent said people were poor "because they faced more obstacles in life than most other people," whereas 26 percent said that poor people didn't work as hard as most other people. When asked why a person is rich, 65 percent said they "had more advantages in life" and 33 percent said they worked harder (Pew Research Center 2020).

As we will see throughout the book, political party identification makes a difference in many attitudes. In the poverty question, for example, Democrats were much more likely than Republicans to select the "more obstacles" response. In the rich question, Democrats were more likely than Republicans to select the "more advantages" response.

Along the same lines, there are different views of the type of equality that should be guaranteed to each citizen. According to the equal opportunity perspective, all citizens should have the same right to compete in the marketplace by getting an education, selling their labor, investing their money, and so on. Presumably, policies that prevent individuals from competing because of their race or gender would be inconsistent with this equal opportunity perspective. However, there is no guarantee of equal results.

Suppose a corporation hired ten wealthy White males because they were viewed as the best candidates—that is, they beat out everyone else in a fair and competitive race. This would still be consistent with the equal opportunity perspective. According to this view, the United States is (or should be) a **meritocracy,** where the most skilled people have the better jobs and the least skilled people have the lowest-paying jobs, regardless of race, gender, age, and other factors.

An alternative perspective on equality could be called the "group rights" perspective. According to this view, dominant groups have unfair advantages in what might appear to be a fair race. For example, although subordinate group members have an abstract right to invest their money, most don't even have enough to live on, much less invest. A few subordinate group individuals might be successful, but most will be left behind. The solution, according to this perspective, is for the subordinate group to collectively demand that the structure of the competition be changed and/or that its members be given the chance to compensate for their lack of privilege.

Ideologies tend to reflect the interests of certain groups in society. The "hard-work" and "equal-opportunity" perspectives tend to support the positions of the dominant groups because they justify their dominance. In contrast, the "oppressive-society" and "group-rights" perspectives tend to be critical of the dominant groups and supportive of the right of subordinate groups to fight against oppression as groups, not just as individuals. The goal is to substantially reduce or eliminate the social and economic differences between different groups.

Within any given culture, some ideologies are so influential that they dominate all other ideologies. These dominant perspectives are called **hegemonic ideologies** because they are widely held by members of both dominant and subordinate groups. Hegemonic ideologies are often invoked by those in power trying to enact social policies. In our society, the "hard-work" and "equal-opportunity" perspectives are the hegemonic views of success and equality. Describing the United States as an oppressive society or invoking the idea of "group rights" is often viewed as un-American by politicians and business leaders. As you might have already guessed, this book attempts to counter hegemonic ideology.

Discrimination

Whereas prejudice refers to what people of one group think, feel, and believe about members of other groups, **discrimination** refers to actions that deny equal treatment to persons perceived to be members of some social category or group. To simplify things, prejudice is what people think, and discrimination is what people do. The following are all examples of discrimination: not renting an apartment to a welfare recipient who can pay the rent, not hiring an LGBTQ person who has the necessary job qualifications, not permitting a woman to join a social club when a comparable man would be admitted, not providing access ramps for people in wheelchairs, and not admitting a well-qualified Native American to a school.

Although the concept of discrimination seems straightforward, it is actually quite complex. First, there are different levels of discrimination; an individual landlord refusing to rent to a Latinx is not the same as a large bank refusing to grant mortgages to houses in Latinx communities. Second, the direction of the discrimination is also important. Is the dominant group discriminating against the subordinate group, or is it the other way around? Finally, there is the question of motivation or intentionality; if a particular policy is gender-blind in intent but negatively affects women more than men, is this discrimination?

Four different types of discrimination are outlined in Table 2.2. **Intentional individual discrimination** refers to the behavior of individual members of one group or category intended to have a differential

Table 2.2   Discrimination Typology

Level	Motivation	
	Intentional/Purposeful	Unintentional/Disparate Impact
Individual	Personal actions	Personal actions
Systemic	Explicit discriminatory policies	Unintended policy outcomes

and/or harmful effect on members of another group or category. Examples of this type of discrimination include attacking a gay person, not allowing a poor person in the corner store, refusing to rent an apartment to a Black person, and not hiring a qualified female to supervise male workers. These are all actions taken by individuals on their own intended to have a differential and/or harmful effect on members of subordinate groups.

Intentional individual discrimination can be multidirectional. In addition to dominant-group individual discrimination against members of the subordinate group, people in subordinate groups can practice individual discrimination against members of dominant groups or against other subordinate groups if they have the power. A Native American can attack a White person or a Black person. An LGBTQ landlord can refuse to rent an apartment to heterosexuals. A deaf person can refuse to associate with hearing people. A female employer can refuse to hire a male worker.

A poor person, however, couldn't prevent a rich person from entering his or her store because the poor person probably wouldn't own a store. This is an example of not having the resources to practice a particular type of discrimination. However, the poor person could yell at a rich person or attack that person. All of these examples are actions by one individual in one group against one individual in another group.

Unintentional individual discrimination refers to the behavior of individual members of one group or category that is not consciously intended to have a differential and/or harmful effect on members of another group or category but does have a disparate impact. K–12 teachers, for example, often call on boys more than girls in the classroom even though they might not be aware of it. Police officers might treat people of color more harshly because they are unaware of having internalized negative stereotypes about them; this is sometimes called implicit bias and can result in racial profiling (see Chapter 4).

Much discrimination, however, involves more than just individuals. **Intentional systemic discrimination** refers to the policies of dominant group institutions and the behavior of individuals who implement these policies and control these institutions intended to have a differential and/or harmful effect on subordinate groups. The terms *institutional* and *structural* are sometimes used to talk about what we have called *systemic discrimination.*

Laws that separated Black people and White people in the South from the late 1870s through the 1950s were an excellent example of intentional systemic discrimination. Another example would be the Catholic Church and Orthodox Judaism not permitting women to become priests and rabbis, respectively. The military's "Don't Ask, Don't Tell" policy, repealed in 2010, which prevented LGBTQ people from being publicly "out" is another example. A final example is a multinational corporation that refuses to provide accommodations for people with disabilities.

In all these cases, these policies are enacted by large, dominant group institutions and are intended to have a differential and/or harmful impact on subordinate groups. In most cases, intentional systemic discrimination is the dominant group acting against the subordinate group. Usually, the subordinate group doesn't have the power or resources to practice systemic discrimination against the dominant group, although it is still theoretically possible. For example, if Latinxs controlled a local government and refused to hire non-Latinxs as workers, this would be intentional systemic discrimination.

What about intentional systemic discrimination based on class? Clearly, the wealthy act in a variety of ways intended to have a differential and/or harmful impact on working people and the poor. Employers try to keep wages low to increase profits. They will abandon one city or even the entire country for another with a cheaper labor force. They don't want to be burdened by health and safety laws that protect workers. Walmart and many other corporations try to prevent workers from unionizing.

There's no question these things happen all the time, but is it *intentional systemic discrimination*? The basis of the capitalist economic system is for employers to do everything they can to increase their profits, including keeping their labor and production costs as low as possible. Workers often bear the brunt of these policies because they have less power than the employers. However, to describe these practices as "intentional systemic discrimination" would suggest that the capitalist system itself favors employers over employees—another subversive idea. We return to this issue in Chapter 3.

The fourth type of discrimination, **unintentional systemic discrimination**, refers to policies of dominant group institutions, and the behavior of the individuals who implement these policies and control these institutions, that do not intend to harm people because of their group membership but that have a differential and/or harmful effect (disparate impact) on subordinate groups. The policy *impact* is more important than the intent in this kind of discrimination.

Bank mortgage policies based on family income and assets tend to disadvantage non-Asian people of color because of their lower incomes. Tests of physical strength based solely on upper-body strength disadvantage women, who excel more in lower-body strength exercises. Providing fringe benefits only to married partners disadvantages gay couples, who couldn't get married until 2015. Having a management retreat at a nineteenth-century inn that is not handicapped accessible disadvantages managers with disabilities. Providing federal income tax cuts only to those with incomes disadvantage poor people who have such low incomes that they don't pay any income taxes, although they still pay more regressive sales taxes. All of these policies don't intend to disadvantage subordinate groups, but they do.

The Covid-19 pandemic provides some additional examples of unintentional systemic discrimination. Low-income people of color are less likely to have computers or internet access, so they can't avail themselves of learning when schools are closed. They are also less likely to have access to good health care, which means they have more underlying conditions that make them more susceptible to dying from the Covid-19 virus.

Another fascinating example of unintentional systemic discrimination comes from voice recognition software used in many computers and cell phones (Metz 2020). A recent study found that five major voice recognition systems misidentified words spoken by White speakers 19 percent of the time and Black speakers 35 percent of the time. The audio snippets were considered unreadable 2 percent of the time for Whites and 30 percent of the time for Blacks.

The reason for this discrepancy, according to the authors, is "in the way the systems are trained to recognize sound. The companies, it seems, are not training on enough data that represents African-American vernacular English." A company representative responded "We know the data has bias in it. . . . Humans have bias in them, our systems have bias in them. The question is: What do we do about it?" A similar problem exists in the way medical decisionmaking tools are designed (Kolata 2020).

For some policies that have disparate impacts on subordinate groups, people might disagree about where they would be placed in Table 2.2. Voter identification laws, where prospective voters must provide official identification cards, are an important example. Empirically, poor people of color are less likely to have these credentials for a variety of reasons, so voter ID laws disproportionately affect them.

Proponents of voter ID laws argue it is so important to protect against voting fraud that it is necessary to implement the laws regardless of their disparate impact. This would be an example of unintentional systemic discrimination if fraud protection was the main goal.

Opponents of voter ID laws, in contrast, say supporters are promoting the laws because they know the laws will dilute the voting strength of poor people of color. Supporters are just not being honest about their goals. This, then, would be an example of intentional systemic discrimination. Although we oppose voter ID laws (see Chapter 4), our main point here is to show that typology distinctions are sometimes messy.

Some diversity scholars, along with the US public, restrict the concept of discrimination to intentional actions and policies—intentional individual and systemic discrimination. We believe it is also useful to characterize unintentional actions and policies to highlight their negative impact. Good people implementing bad policies can be just as harmful as those who intentionally discriminate.

Unfortunately, scholars do not always agree on the definitions of prejudice, discrimination, and other important concepts. For example, it is common for scholars to speak of individual and systemic racism, sexism, and heterosexism rather than discrimination. Other scholars use racism, sexism, and heterosexism to describe prejudiced attitudes rather than discriminatory behavior. Still other scholars use these same terms to refer to a combination of prejudice and discrimination. The lack of consensus about these important concepts can cause a great deal of confusion and misunderstanding. As we proceed through the book, we carefully define these terms in their relevant chapters.

Politics and Political Labels

It is impossible to discuss the issue of diversity without also discussing politics. Most US citizens restrict the concept of politics to elections and what goes on in government. The only way people can participate in politics, according to this view, is to vote and to write letters to members of their legislatures. Although electoral politics is certainly important, this definition is too restrictive. We prefer to define **politics** as any collective action intended to support, influence, or change social policy or social structures.

With this broader definition, we can think of a whole range of activities that are political. Fighting for women's and LGBTQ studies programs on college campuses is political. International protests against the war in Afghanistan are political. Occupying Wall Street to protest economic inequality is political. Organizing a new union is political. Blocking traffic to protest police shootings of unarmed Black men and boys is political. Demanding sign-language interpreters for students with hearing impairment is political. Armed struggle, including terrorism, is also political, although it is often immoral and counterproductive.

Of course, the goals of political actions can be quite different. Antiabortion (sometimes called pro-life) demonstrations have different goals than pro-choice demonstrations. Pro–affirmative action and anti–affirmative action demonstrations also have different goals. Sometimes there are even political differences within movements such as Black Lives Matter and Me Too. The January 6, 2021, insurrection at the US Capitol was also political in that the White nationalist participants wanted to overturn Joe Biden's election victory.

This brings us to the often-used but not-well-defined labels of *conservative, liberal,* and *radical.* Most readers have heard these terms many times but are not sure what they mean except that conservatives are associated with the Republican Party and liberals with the Democratic Party. In the 2020 election, this was complicated by the lack of consensus in our society over these labels and their changing nature over time. In the following paragraphs, we do not provide crisp definitions as we have done with other concepts throughout this chapter. Instead, we outline some of the themes people who use these labels share and try to avoid caricaturing those perspectives with which we disagree.

Conservatives

People who call themselves *conservative* are pro-capitalist and believe that the market economy, free of unnecessary regulation, will result in the greatest good for the greatest number of people. This goes along with their belief in a weak federal government that leaves most decisions to state and local governments.

Economic conservatives emphasize limiting the federal government's role so that businesses can compete with each other to make more profits and create jobs, thereby strengthening the economy. Therefore, conservatives generally oppose strong federal regulations (e.g., civil rights, environmental protection, health and safety) and favor low taxes. They generally oppose increased federal spending for housing, job training, and schools, although they favor big spending on the military. They tend to subscribe to the "hard-work" and "equal-opportunity" ideologies mentioned earlier and argue that most poor people are economically worse off because of weak families and a lack of motivation, in part caused by an overly generous welfare system.

Social conservatives, although agreeing with much of the above, spend most of their energy promoting and protecting what they see as traditional family values. Former vice president Mike Pence is probably the best-known social conservative these days. They favor male-dominated nuclear families and are strongly opposed to abortion and LGBTQ rights. They are also in favor of bringing prayer and creationism back into schools, and they object to the concept of a strong separation between church and state. Many social conservatives identify themselves as evangelical Christian fundamentalists who believe in a literal interpretation of the New Testament.

Economic and social conservatives don't always agree on important issues. Some economic conservatives, such as Republican senators Susan Collins (R-ME) and Lisa Murkowsky (R-AK) are also pro-choice. Dick Cheney, who served as US secretary of defense and vice president in Republican administrations, has supported gay marriage as a result of having a lesbian daughter. Economic conservatives tend to argue that abortion and gay rights are private matters the federal government should not be involved in, just as it shouldn't be involved in the economy.

The election of Trump in 2016 coincided with the rise of a third type of conservatism we call *White nationalism* and some others call the *Alt Right*. This trend consists of White racist groups such as the Ku Klux Klan, Proud Boys, Boogaloo Boys, and various other neo-Nazi groups as well as the more "respectable" National Policy Institute and Breitbart News. In addition to incorporating the beliefs of economic and social conservatives, most of these White nationalists believe in White supremacy. They strongly object to the increasing immigration from Mexico, Central America, and South America and want to protect what they perceive as White culture from people of color, LGBTQ people, and Jews.

These White supremacist groups, of course, are not new and have existed as fringe political groups on the right for decades. They became part of Trump's base in the 2016 election and have tried to legitimize themselves by calling themselves *alt right*. Stephen Miller, Trump's policy adviser; Steve Bannon, former Trump adviser and head of Breitbart News; and Richard Spencer of the National Policy Institute are associated with this brand of conservatism. We discuss this further in Chapter 4.

Trump is difficult to label because he combines some aspects of each strand of conservatism and is inconsistent with many policy proposals. Consistently with economic conservatives, he supported reducing the role of the federal government and slashed taxes and regulations on corporations and the wealthy, arguing that this would create more jobs. This is the Trump version of trickle-down economics. Even so, he deviated from economic conservatives by creating huge budget deficits.

Trump also supported social conservatives by appointing three Supreme Court Justices likely to restrict abortion rights, and he reversed several regulations protecting transgender people. His personal behavior is inconsistent with evangelical values. Trump also views the White nationalist alt right as part of his base and rarely criticizes them, including those who participated in the January 6, 2021, insurrection.

Liberals

Liberals are also strongly pro-capitalist, a fact many conservative critics often ignore or distort. Liberals are different than conservatives because they have less faith in an unregulated market economy. They believe an unrestrained free market can generate serious problems (e.g., the 2008–2010 and 2020–2021 recessions, global warming, the massive oil spill in the Gulf of Mexico, etc.) and that the federal government must provide adequate regulations so that capitalism doesn't self-destruct. They also argue the federal government has an important role to play in education, health care, job training, and protecting the environment.

Liberals tend to be more supportive than conservatives when it comes to issues of civil rights, unions, programs for the poor, and so on. They tend to argue that poverty is caused by a lack of opportunity rather than lack of motivation. The goal of liberals is to have a fairer, more efficient form of capitalism.

Like conservatives, liberals hold a range of views. Progressive liberals such as Senator Elizabeth Warren (D-MA), Senator Bernie Sanders (I-VT), and Representative Alexandria Ocasio-Cortez (D-NY) tend to argue for somewhat more regulation and government spending to help poor and working people. They favored some kind of universal health insurance (Medicare for All) during the 2020 presidential campaign. Sanders identified as a *Democratic Socialist* and looked to Scandinavian countries as a model for government-sponsored programs in education, health care, and environmental protection. However, it is important to understand that Scandinavian countries are capitalist in that the overwhelming proportion of their economies are privately owned, as with the United States. The Scandinavian governmental social programs, however, are much more generous than those in the United States.

In contrast, more *centrist* liberals, such as President Joe Biden, Vice President Kamala Harris, former presidents Bill Clinton and Barack Obama, former secretary of state Hillary Clinton, and Speaker of the House Nancy Pelosi, tend to fall somewhere in between progressive liberals and economic conservatives. Bill Clinton, with the help of then-senator Biden, for example, signed the welfare reform act in 1996 that restricted recipients to only five years of welfare payments over the course of their lifetimes. The same is true for the Violent Crime Control and Law Enforcement Act of 1994, which during the 2020 campaign Biden admitted was a mistake.

During the health-care-reform debate in 2009, President Obama along with then-vice president Biden didn't permit any discussion of a single-payer system and didn't give people the opportunity to select a public plan as one choice among a variety of private plans included in the Affordable Care Act of 2010, also called Obamacare.

One source of conflict between progressive and centrist liberals arose in the 2019–2020 Democratic debates over health-care reform. Most centrists have wanted to improve Obamacare by providing a public option. Many progressive Democrats wanted to replace Obamacare with a broader health-care system called "single payer" or "Medicare for All." Trump, of course, wanted to abolish Obamacare and replace it with something else that he never explained.

To make things even more confusing, a number of anti-Trump conservatives supported Biden in the 2020 presidential election: Michael Steele (former chair of the Republican National Committee), Cindy McCain (wife of former senator and presidential candidate John McCain), Bill Kristol (a neoconservative), George Conway (Kellyanne Conway's husband and cofounder of the Lincoln Project), MSNBC commentators Joe Scarborough and Nicolle Wallace, *New York Times* columnist David Brooks, and more. They believe Trump is not a true conservative and is destructive to the country.

During the 2020 Covid-19 crisis, Trump and other conservatives borrowed a page from liberal doctrine by uniting with liberals to pass a $2.2 trillion stimulus package (Robert T. Stafford Disaster Relief and

Emergency Assistance Act) to save the economy from going into a depression. They were trying to save capitalism in the United States. However, the president was slow in mobilizing federal resources to confront the shortages of tests and equipment to confront the virus. He said the states should be the main actors, consistent with his view of limited government.

Former president George W. Bush, a conservative Republican, also deviated from traditional conservatism at the end of his term in 2008 when he pushed through the Targeted Asset Relief Program (TARP) to bail out the banks and insurance companies deemed "too big to fail" during the Great Recession. Bush noted this contradiction in a September 24, 2008, address to the nation:

> I'm a strong believer in free enterprise, so my natural instinct is to oppose government intervention. I believe companies that make bad decisions should be allowed to go out of business. Under normal circumstances, I would have followed this course. But these are not normal circumstances. The market is not functioning properly. There has been a widespread loss of confidence, and major sectors of America's financial system are at risk of shutting down. The government's top economic experts warn that, without immediate action by Congress, America could slip into a financial panic and a distressing scenario would unfold.

Radicals

Most discussions of political labels in the United States are restricted to discussing conservatives and liberals. The Pew Research Center for the People and the Press, for example, has an interesting website wherein you can answer a series of questions and be placed in one of nine different political categories (http://typology.people-press.org). However, there is no category to the left of "solid liberal."

Unlike conservatives and liberals, radicals are *anticapitalist* in that they see competition, private ownership of the means of production, and profit seeking as major causes of economic inequality and social injustice. Some radicals are socialists and want to see government ownership of the economy, economic and social planning, and genuine democratic civil institutions.

Other radicals want more of a "mixed economy" that would combine government ownership with a market economy and a more generous welfare state that would include some form of national health care, low-cost childcare, more extensive maternity/paternity leave, and so on.

Scandinavian countries are also seen as a model. This overlaps with the views of some progressive liberals.

Still other radicals are anarchists who reject large bureaucratic structures and want small, localized, collectively run institutions. All three varieties of radicals hold the "oppressive-society" and "group-rights" ideologies described earlier and believe that capitalism must be replaced with a more equitable form of economic organization.

The largest radical organization in the United States is the Democratic Socialists of America (see Chapter 9). Radical spokespeople include Noam Chomsky, Angela Davis, and Cornell West. Senator Bernie Sanders (D-VT) and Representative Alexandria Ocasio-Cortez fall somewhere between progressive liberal and radical.

These political distinctions are summarized in Table 2.3. On the right we include the three different types of conservatives. On the left we include radicals and two types of liberals. It is important to remember that the boundaries between the different categories are not hard and fast. To muddy the waters even further, not everyone agrees with our definitions. Trump, during the 2020 presidential campaign, often referred to Biden and Kamala Harris as "extreme socialists." We would call them centrist liberals.

A Note on Other Political Terminology

If all this isn't confusing enough, many radicals use the term *neoliberal* to criticize both conservatives and liberals. In the nineteenth century, the term *economic liberalism* referred to the belief in small government, business competition, low taxes, and low trade tariffs. In today's world, according to radicals, neoliberals extend this analysis to a more globalized economic system. Neoliberals argue that global capitalism and free trade benefit both rich and poor countries. Within individual countries, neoliberals want limited government, low taxes, and maximum competition in order to maximize profits. In other words, neoliberalism is

Table 2.3   Political Ideology in the United States, 2020

Left			Right		
Radical	Liberal (Democrats)		Conservative (Republicans)		
Marxist; Anarchist	Progressive; Democratic Socialist	Centrist	Economic	Social	White Nationalist; Alt Right

actually a form of what we have called economic conservatism. However, some centrist liberals can also be described as neoliberals.

Radicals are critical of neoliberalism. Although neoliberals argue their policies will benefit everyone, radicals say only rich countries will benefit, whereas poor countries will be hurt. More important, radicals argue that the business classes of both poor and rich countries will benefit more than the working classes (Navarro 2007).

Ironically, Trump also opposed much of neoliberal ideology with his America-first trade wars with China and other countries along with his opposition to the North Atlantic Treaty Organization (NATO). Rather than working with other industrialized nations, Trump preferred to go it alone. This drove some conservative Republicans to support the Biden/Harris team in 2020.

In 2020, radicals and liberals successfully united to defeat Trump. But our nation is still divided. During the Biden administration, there will certainly be clashes between progressive and centrist liberals as well as clashes between liberals and conservatives. Biden's American Rescue Plan, a liberal compromise, didn't receive a single Republican vote.

Senator Rand Paul (Kentucky) is a libertarian, a form of conservatism that seeks practically no government regulation on businesses and social programs in order to promote individual rights.

* * *

Congratulations. You have now made it through this introduction to diverspeak. In the rest of the book, we use these and other concepts to discuss race, immigration, class, gender, sexual orientation, and disability. For your convenience, we have included all the concepts in a list at the back of the book, so you can consult them when necessary.

3

Class:
The 1 Percent vs.
the 99 Percent

In most diversity anthologies, the section on class comes after the chapters on race and gender. We decided to discuss class *before* discussing the other issues because most US citizens aren't used to thinking in class terms. As we will demonstrate, class (i.e., access to income, wealth, and power) provides the context in which conflict over race, immigration, gender, sexual orientation, and disabilities exists.

When discussing economic inequality with our students, we find they are more comfortable and familiar with discussing racial and gender differences than with discussing class differences. This is in large part because the United States sees itself as a society without classes. This has been true since at least the 1830s (de Tocqueville 1994).

Although both race and gender are intimately connected with class, we don't emphasize these connections in this chapter (we discuss them extensively in Chapters 4, 5, and 6). By focusing more specifically on class in this chapter, our goal is to help students think in class terms, perhaps for the first time. It is important to recognize the pay and wealth difference between the top 1 percent and the bottom 99 percent and the income differences between various occupations such as CEO and truck driver, regardless of race and gender.

These differences have important implications. Let's start our conversation with the economic meltdown beginning in 2020 triggered by the global Covid-19 pandemic. The Household Pulse Survey (US Census Bureau 2020a) found that by the twelfth week of the pandemic, more than 50 percent of households indicated a loss in employment income since March 13, 2020, 40 percent indicated delayed medical care, more than 25 percent indicated that they had difficulty meeting housing costs, and 12 percent reported not having enough food. In contrast, US billionaire wealth totaled $850 billion, an increase of 28 percent between March and October 2020 (Collins 2020). Class makes a difference!

Terminology

The lack of consensus among social scientists about the nature of class makes it impossible to provide a definition with which everyone will agree. Dennis Gilbert, for example, defines class as "groups of families more or less equal in rank and differentiated from other families above and below them with regard to characteristics such as occupation, income, wealth, and prestige" (2008, 11). Although this definition has some value, disagreements over the meaning of "rank" and "differentiated" render this and other definitions of limited use. There is also disagreement about whether the US stratification system is a continuous one (i.e., there aren't clear distinctions between one class and another) or whether there are discrete classes.

In thinking about class, one of two economic indicators are often used. **Income** is the amount of money a family earns from wages and salaries, interest, dividends, rent, gifts, transfer payments (e.g., unemployment insurance and welfare payments), and capital gains (profits from the sale of assets). Generally, income refers to the money a family has coming in during a given year.

The federal government also collects data on **poverty**. The US Department of Agriculture publishes an emergency food budget each year for different-sized families; the larger the family, the larger the food budget. The government takes this figure and multiplies it by three; the product becomes the official poverty threshold. This official measure is contentious, and we discuss it further in the next section.

Wealth, in contrast to income, refers to the assets people own. In addition to assets such as houses, cars, and other personal property, wealth includes stocks, bonds, mutual funds, trust funds, business equity, and real estate. Usually, wealth is expressed as **net worth,** or the value of what you own minus the debts you owe.

The problem is that social scientists don't agree on how many classes there are or what they should be called. This division dates back to two important social theorists: Karl Marx and Max Weber. Marx defined class in terms of ownership of income-producing property such as factories and banks. The bourgeoisie, or members of the capitalist class, were the owners, whereas the proletariat, or members of the working class, sold their labor to the capitalists. Marx also talked about the petit bourgeoisie, or members of the middle class, which consisted of small business owners and self-employed professionals. Marx believed that the capitalist and working classes were in conflict with each other, with the petit bourgeoisie caught in the middle.

Weber defined class in terms of access to the market. Weber disagreed with Marx and maintained that higher-income workers had greater access to the market, that is, more money to spend on housing, education, health care, transportation, and other such goods and services. Therefore, although high-income workers might not own the means of production, they were distinct from their lower-earning working-class counterparts. They were, as we say today, middle class.

Following Weber's lead, using income as the proxy for class, one can imagine a vertical line whereby families with the lowest incomes are at the bottom and those with the highest incomes are at the top. The US Census Bureau routinely divides this income distribution into five quintiles (or fifths), each of which has the same number of families. Social scientists can then attach labels to these quintiles so that the lowest might be called the "lower class" or "poor." The highest might be called the "upper-middle class," and the middle three would be "the middle class." Both the divisions and the labels are arbitrary.

In the above example, there are three different classes—upper middle, middle, and lower. However, there could just as easily have been five; for example, lower class, working class, lower-middle class, upper-middle class, and upper class. Or the distribution could have been separated into deciles (tenths), each of which could have been given a label. In each case, there is no hard-and-fast distinction between one class and another, except that some have higher incomes than others. Usually the main distinction is between the poor and everyone else, and the latter are referred to as the middle class.

Using this continuous distribution approach minimizes the effect of those with the highest incomes. For example, in 2019, the top 5 percent of households had incomes of $270,000 and higher. If we call this the upper-middle class, it means that a family making $270,000 is in the same class as the family of the chief executive officer of a large corporation who makes millions. We discuss this further in the next section.

Sometimes occupational category is the key measure of social class, with professionals and managers being the upper-middle class and unskilled blue-collar and service workers being the lower class. Education can also be used as a measure of class, where people with advanced degrees make up the upper-middle class and high school dropouts make up the lower class. Finally, prestige (i.e., perceived social status) is sometimes used to measure class.

A variation of this theme is to create a measure of socioeconomic status (SES) by combining measures of income, occupation, and education into a single index. The simplest way to proceed is to take each of these three variables and dichotomize them, that is, split them into two. For income, those who earn more than the median income get a score of one, and those who earn less get a zero. For occupation, white-collar workers get a one, and manual laborers get a zero. For education, those who have more than a high school education get a one, and those with a high school education or less get a zero.

Using this method, everyone in the labor force gets a score from zero to three. For example, a college-educated corporate executive who earns more than the median income would get a score of three. A high school dropout who works as a janitor and earns less than the median income would get a score of zero. Because we have four levels of SES, we can attach labels to each level. The corporate executive at level three might be called "upper-middle class," whereas the janitor at level zero might be called "lower class." Although this is more sophisticated than using income alone, we still have a continuous distribution of SES scores with arbitrary labels attached to them.

A dramatically different approach to class is provided by neo-Marxists, who use the concepts of wealth and power to differentiate between classes. According to William Domhoff (n.d.), power is defined as who governs and who doesn't and about who wins and who loses (www.whorulesamerica.ucsc.edu). Contrary to the theory of pluralism, which asserts that various groups compete to exert influence on the government, Marxists tend to argue power is concentrated within a political elite or the capitalist class.

Economist Michael Zweig (2000), for example, argues that a small group of people (1 or 2 percent of the adult population) owns the means of production and have a lot of decisionmaking power in society. They are called the employer class, or the capitalist class. The majority of the population (62 percent) owns little and has scant decisionmaking power. This heterogeneous working class includes both blue-collar and white-collar workers and various levels of skill. The poor, according to Zweig, are considered the lowest level of the working class. The remaining 36 percent of the population is the middle class, which includes small business owners, freelance artists and writers, upper-level managers who are not wealthy, and highly paid athletes and entertainers.

In this neo-Marxist view, the capitalist class and the working class are in political and economic conflict with each other, with the middle class caught between them. Because the capitalist class makes its profits from the labor of the working class, the capitalists are always trying to push labor costs lower, whereas the workers are trying to gain more power to increase their incomes and control over the work process. Class is not only a descriptive category, as it is in the stratification perspective, but also it has important political ramifications.

Although other neo-Marxists agree with the concept of class conflict between the working class and capitalist class, they don't always agree on the number of classes that exist. Erik Olin Wright (1997), for example, has a twelve-class model in which he describes different subdivisions within the working and middle classes.

Class is more than economics. Sociologist Pierre Bourdieu wrote about social and cultural capital. He defined cultural capital as the strength of your networks. The more access you have to people with authority, power, and wealth, the more likely these people can get you jobs and give you access to other goods and services.

Cultural capital is the acquisition and understanding of education, values, beliefs, and behaviors that powerful people find valuable. Although it might be fun to play rock or to rap, these skills are less likely to get you into a prestigious music school that values jazz and classical music. It is fair to say, cultural and social capital have an impact on one's economic future.

Given these divergent and sometimes imprecise views, can we say class is a socially constructed concept? Is the social definition of class more important than its material essence? On the one hand, there certainly are different cultural definitions of class in terms of how many classes there are and what labels should be used. On the other hand, there appears to be something real about class because we can measure income, wealth, and other important variables, and we can see that some members of a population have a lot more of these than other members. It's also clear that people at the higher-class levels have more official (or institutional) power than those at the lower-class levels. The disagreements are about how class works and how it should be measured, not about whether it exists. There appears to be some essence of class even though there is no unity about what it is.

Another important concept is **social mobility**, which refers to individuals moving up or down in terms of their class level. The belief in upward mobility is an important part of mythology in the United States, encapsulated in the "log cabin to White House" journey of Abraham Lincoln or the often-touted rags to riches and riches to rags stories of professional athletes.

Sociologists talk about two types of mobility. **Intergenerational mobility** refers to a child's class position relative to the child's parents. Both Barack Obama and Bill Clinton came from modest backgrounds and were upwardly mobile relative to their parents. Donald Trump and George W. Bush, in contrast, were born into wealthy and powerful families, so they were not socially mobile.

Intragenerational mobility refers to the degree to which a young worker who enters the labor force can improve his or her class position within a single lifetime. This is the "stock clerk to CEO" version of upward mobility. Bill Gates was upwardly mobile in the intragenerational sense because he founded Microsoft as a small company and eventually became the richest man in the United States. We examine the extent of upward mobility in the next section.

Some diversity scholars characterize the economic inequality associated with capitalism as a form of *classism,* another one of those ill-defined concepts. Some see classism as a system of oppression that stigmatizes poor and working-class people and their cultures (Cyrus 2000, 6). Other writers define classism as prejudice and discrimination based on socioeconomic level or class (Blumenfeld and Raymond 2000, 25). In this view, class oppression is equivalent to racism, sexism, and heterosexism in terms of importance. We return to this issue later in this chapter.

Descriptive Statistics

Because there is no consensus on the definition of class, it is difficult to say who is in what class and how many people are in what class. However, it is not at all difficult to describe the degree of economic inequality that exists in the United States. The federal government collects a great deal of economic data, and we use some of it here. Get ready for some numbers. The distribution of income in 2019 is presented in Table 3.1. In the top of the table, all households are separated into quintiles, or five categories, with the same number of households in each. One-fifth, or 20 percent, of households earn between $0 and $28,084 annually. If we look at the combined income of these 26 million households and compare it with the combined income of all 128,579 million households in the country, we see that the poorest 20 percent of households have only 3.1 percent of the total income.

There are also 26 million households that earn more than $201,150, and they make up the richest 20 percent of all households. Their share of the total household income is a whopping 51.9 percent. Remember, there are the same number of households in the poorest and richest quintiles, but their shares of the total household income are dramatically different. The median household income, where half the households earn more and half the households earn less, was $68,703 in 2019.

Table 3.1   Distribution of Income of All Households, by Quintile, and Income of Highest-Paid CEOs, 2019

Income Quintile	Income Range	Percentage of Total Income
Poorest 20 percent	0–$28,084	3.1
Fourth 20 percent	$28,085–$53,503	8.3
Middle 20 percent	$53,504–$86,488	14.1
Second 20 percent	$86,488–$142,501	22.7
Top 20 percent	$201,150+	51.9
Top 5 percent	$270,002+	23.0

Highest Paid CEOs	Total Compensation	
400th	$12,403,336	
300th	$14,392,748	
200th	$17,235,108	
100th	$21,610,598	
1st (highest paid)	$280,621,552	

Sources: US Census Bureau 2019; American Federation of Labor–Congress of Industrial Organizations 2019.

Note: The poorest 20 percent of families had incomes below $28,084 and accounted for only 3.1 percent of total income. The highest paid CEO data is based on the S&P 500 index, and the total compensation measure includes salary, bonuses, value of stock awards, value of option awards, nonequity incentive plan compensation, change in pension value and deferred compensation earnings, and all other compensation.

Table 3.1 also shows that the top 5 percent of households, earning above $270,002 annually, account for 23 percent of the total income. Now, $270,000 is not a bad income, but it pales in comparison with some of the incomes of people in the top 1 percent of households. For example, the CEOs of the 500 largest corporations averaged $14.8 million in 2019 compared with the average production and nonsupervisory employees, who earned just $41,442. The CEO income was 356 times higher than the worker income. The top-paid CEO was Google's Sundar Pichai, whose 2019 income was $280 million, 1,085 times more than the income of average Google workers. At least 60 percent of CEO incomes derives from stock options and other perks (American Federation of Labor-Congress of Industrial Organizations 2019).

If we were to construct a graph of income with each inch representing $100,000 of income, a household with median income would be just over 0.5 inch above the floor. The beginning of the top 5 percent income bracket would be 2.8 inches off the floor. The average income of the top 500 CEOs would be 18 feet above the floor, somewhere on the second story of a building. Pichai's income would be 343 feet above the floor, the height of a thirty-story building.

In Table 3.2 we have rearranged the data to show changes in the aggregate income over time. In each column, we show the top 10 percent of households, the middle 40 percent, and the bottom 50 percent. Looking across the rows, you can see the share of aggregate income obtained by each of the three groups.

The aggregate share of income of the bottom 90 percent (middle 40 percent plus bottom 50 percent) declined between 1913 and 1940. In the post–World War II period (1950–1960), in contrast, the bottom 90 percent increased its share of the total income. During this period, there was a great boom in the middle class spurred by unionized factory jobs, suburban housing development, mass production and consumption, and changes to racial and gender policies.

Since 1970, the income share of the bottom 50 percent has declined. In 2019, the bottom 50 percent accounted for only 12.7 percent of the total income, less than the 15.3 percent they had in 1913.

The income share of the middle 40 percent has been declining since 1980. Its 40.5 percent income share in 2019 is less than its 1913 share of 42.4 percent.

These declines in the income shares for the bottom 90 percent are a result of the growing cost of housing, health care, and education; the relatively slow wage growth; the decline in labor union strength; and the increasing job loss because of globalization.

Conversely, the top 10 percent of households increased their share of total income from 35.8 percent in 1960 to 46.8 percent in 2019, higher than the 41.9 percent figure in 1913.

In other words, since the middle of the twentieth century, high-income earners have increased their share of the total income, whereas everyone else has experienced a decline. Income inequality was greater in 2020 than it was a century earlier.

The gap between the salaries of CEOs and average workers has been growing rapidly. According to Sarah Anderson and her colleagues (2008), CEOs made 42 times the salary of the average worker in 1980. By 2018, the CEOs on the Standard and Poor's 500 list made 361 times more than the average worker. Using a slightly different methodology, the Economic Policy Institute estimates that the CEO-worker income gap increased from 24 times the salary in 1967 to 320 times in 2019 (Mishel, Bernstein, and Allegretto 2005; Mishel and Kandra 2020). Whichever data you prefer, economic inequality is increasing at an alarming rate.

Table 3.2 Distribution of US Pretax Household Income (percent), 1913–2019

	1913	1920	1930	1940	1950	1960
Top 10 percent	41.9	43.2	45.2	47.8	39.3	35.8
Middle 40 percent	42.4	41.5	40.5	38.2	43.5	46.2
Bottom 50 percent	15.3	15.0	14.2	14.2	17.5	18.2

	1970	1980	1990	2000	2010	2019
Top 10 percent	34.4	34.7	38.9	44.0	45.8	46.8
Middle 40 percent	44.8	45.6	44.5	41.4	41.0	40.5
Bottom 50 percent	20.8	19.7	16.7	14.6	13.2	12.7

Source: World Inequality Database 2020.

While most people were struggling economically during the Covid-19 economic crisis, billionaires did just fine. From March 2020 to January 2021, the 600 US billionaires gained an additional $1.1 trillion in wealth, a 39 percent increase. During the same period, more than 73 million workers faced some unemployment, nearly 100,000 businesses permanently closed, and one in five renters reported being behind on their rent (Collins 2021). Economic inequality is growing.

One explanation is that the US Supreme Court over the past fifty years has upheld major decisions to benefit corporations and the wealthy, whereas the Court has eroded labor rights and consumer rights (Cohen 2020). One example of the lopsidedness in the caselaw is illustrated by the Trump administration's changes to the tax code. According to Johnston (2020), from DC Report, a nonprofit news organization that reports on governmental affairs, "for each dollar of increased income that you [99 percent] earned in 2018, each One-Percenter got $88 more income."

The official measure of **poverty** goes back to the 1960s, when President Lyndon B. Johnson declared a War on Poverty. At that time, the US government assumed that families spend about one-third of their income on food. So, the official poverty threshold was three times the Department of Agriculture's emergency food budget. But in 2012, the US Census Bureau introduced a supplemental measure of poverty, which considers not only food but also clothing, shelter, and utilities. We use the official measure even though it is contested.

A family's before-tax income includes wages, salaries, cash transfer payments such as welfare, social security, and unemployment insurance. Capital gains and losses (when you sell an asset) and the value of in-kind government services (e.g., food stamps, Medicaid, subsidized housing) are not included. This income is then compared with the official poverty threshold.

For a family of four including two children, the poverty threshold was $25,926 in 2019. This means that if the family income were less than $25,926, those four people would be counted as among the poor. A three-person family with two children has a lower threshold, and a family of five with three children has a higher threshold.

Using these calculations, 34 million people were counted as poor in 2019, or 10.5 percent of the population. It is likely that millions have slipped into poverty during the Covid-19 pandemic (Parolin, Curran, and Matsudaira et al. 2020).

Most poor adults work for at least part of the year. According to Michael Yates (2005), almost one-quarter of all workers had such low hourly wages that they would still be poor even if they had worked year round and full time in 2003.

Some have argued that this measure is too generous, *overestimating* the number of poor people. Most important, many conservatives argue that the value of noncash, in-kind government services (e.g., food stamps, subsidized housing, health care, etc.) should be *included as income*. They would also deduct income and payroll taxes and include the value of capital gains (of which the poor have virtually none). Keeping the same threshold levels, this revised measure eliminates more than 8 million people from the poverty count. These people have the same low incomes they had by the previous measure; they are just not counted as poor anymore.

When compared with Europe, the United States has higher income inequality. In Table 3.3, the top 10 percent accounts for a lower percentage of the total income in Europe than it does in the United States. The bottom 50 percent has a higher percentage of total income in Europe than it does in the United States. Sweden has the lowest level of income inequality of the four European countries. The gap between European CEOs and the average European worker is much smaller than it is in the United States (Kerbo 2009).

Mira Kamdar (2020), a Brooklyn, New York, native, explained why she left the United States to live in France. She said that although taxes are higher in France than in the United States, every citizen has greater access to health care, education, affordable housing, paid parental leave, and five weeks of annual paid vacation, all of which are seen as "rights, not pipe-dream privileges."

Table 3.3   **Distribution of Pretax National Income in Five Countries, 2017 (percent)**

Deciles	United States	United Kingdom	France	Germany	Sweden
Top 10 percent	46.8	35.5	33.0	36.8	29.8
Middle 40 percent	40.6	43.9	44.6	44.7	45.5
Bottom 50 percent	12.7	20.6	22.4	18.5	24.7
Total	100.0	100.0	100.0	100.0	100.0

Source: World Inequality Database 2020.
Note: The top 10 percent of families in the United States had 46.8 percent of the total income, while the top 10 percent in Sweden had 29.8 percent of the total income.

As bad as income inequality is, wealth inequality (what you own) is even worse. Table 3.4 shows the distribution of net worth in 1991 and 2017. More than 16 percent of households had a zero or negative net worth in 2017; that is, they owed more than they owned. At the other end of the spectrum, 22.4 percent of households had a net worth of $500,000 or more. The median net worth was about $104,000 in 2017.

When one compares the 1991 data with the 2017 data, it is clear that wealth inequality has gotten worse. The percentage of households with zero or negative net worth increased from 12.6 percent in 1991 to 16.2 percent in 2017. The number of households with a net worth of $500,000 or more also increased, from 3.5 percent in 1991 to 22.4 percent in 2017. The number of rich and poor have increased over this twenty-six-year period.

As we saw with income inequality, these data understate the true degree of wealth inequality. *Forbes,* the business magazine promoted as "the capitalist's tool," collects information each year on the 400 richest people in the United States. The "poorest" people on the *Forbes* 400 list in 2020 (a ten-way tie) each have a net worth of $2.1 billion. The net worth of the wealthiest person in the country, Jeff Bezos, was a whopping $179 *billion*, more than the $111 billion Bill Gates was worth.

If we were to make a wealth graph that began on the first floor of a building wherein each inch would represent $100,000 of net worth, the median family net worth would be less than one inch above the floor. The ten people with a $2.1 billion net worth would be 167 feet above the floor—about the height of a sixteen-story building. Jeff Bezos's net

Table 3.4   Distribution of Wealth (net worth) of All US Households in 1991 and 2017 and Net Worth of the Richest People in the United States in 2020

Net Worth	Percentage Distribution	
All US Households	1991	2017
0 or negative	12.6	16.2
$1–$4,999	14.2	8.1
$5,000–$9,999	6.5	3.6
$10,000–$24,999	11.2	6.2
$25,000–$49,999	12.2	6.3
$50,000–$99,999	15.1	8.9
$100,000–$249,999	17.6	15.8
$250,000–$499,999	7.0	12.5
$500,000+	3.5	22.4
Total	100.0	100.0

Richest 400 People in the United States, 2020	Rank of Person
$2.1 billion	391st (10-way tie)
$2.8 billion	299th (20-way tie)
$3.9 billion	197th (12-way tie)
$6.5 billion	95th (7-way tie)
$111 billion	2nd (Bill Gates)
$179 billion	Richest (Jeff Bezos)

Sources: US Census Bureau 2017a; Forbes 2020.
Note: In 2017, 8.1 percent of all households had a net worth between $1 and $4,999. The median net worth was $38,500 in 1991 and $104,000 in 2017. Jeff Bezos was the richest person in the United States with a net worth of $179 billion.

worth, in comparison, would be 14,000 *feet* high, about ten Empire State Buildings piled on top of each other!

The data show the limitations of the mainstream approach to class, which doesn't account for wealth and stops at the highest quintile or decile of income distribution. Someone with $500,000 in wealth can't be in the same class as someone with billions. The Marxist approach, with its emphasis on wealth, can easily incorporate these figures.

Finally, we look at some numbers about social mobility, or the extent to which people move up and down the stratification system. To understand how people's class origin affects their lives, we look at intergenerational mobility by comparing the current family wealth quintile of adult children with the past wealth quintile of their parents when the children were growing up (see Table 3.5). According to Max Weber's conception of life chances, individuals from wealthy and powerful families have greater access to power and wealth than individuals from poor or middle-class families, but there aren't any guarantees.

Of the children who grew up in the poorest wealth quintile, 35 percent found themselves in the poorest wealth quintile as adults (not mobile). Only 6.3 percent of the children who grew up in the richest wealth quintile found themselves in the poorest wealth quintile as adults (downwardly mobile).

In contrast, only 6.4 percent of the children who grew up in the poorest wealth quintile found themselves in the richest wealth quintile as adults (upwardly mobile). Of the children who grew up in the richest wealth quintile, 44.1 percent found themselves in the richest wealth quintile as adults (not mobile).

Although Table 3.5 shows both upward and downward mobility in terms of wealth, children are most likely to end up in the same or adjacent wealth quintile as adults as when they were children. Yet, research on the social mobility of members of the millennial generation find that they are not expected to surpass the living standards of their parents (Hout 2019, 30). If this trend continues unabated, it will be an unprecedented moment in US history. In general, parents' financial position has an important influence on the financial destination of their children.

Table 3.5   **Adult Children in Each Wealth Quintile Compared with Their Parents' Wealth Quintile in 2015 (percent)**

Parental Wealth Quintile	Adult Children's Wealth Quintile					
	Poorest	Second	Middle	Fourth	Richest	Total
Poorest	35.0	29.9	17.9	10.8	6.4	100
Second	26.0	26.6	23.5	13.8	10.2	100
Middle	22.2	20.7	22.2	22.8	12.2	100
Fourth	10.7	14.1	20.4	27.6	27.2	100
Richest	6.3	8.4	16.0	25.2	44.1	100

Source: Pfeffer and Killewald 2015.
Note: Wealth quintile in 2013 dollars. As the table indicates, 35 percent of children who grew up in the poorest quintile were in the same quintile as adults.

These data show that although upward and downward mobility of children in terms of wealth can happen, the best chance of being rich is being born into a wealthy family. In addition, most of the mobility consists of small steps between adjacent strata rather than big jumps from the bottom to the top. These findings are consistent with previous studies of social mobility. In addition, mobility rates in the United States are about the same as they are in other industrialized countries (Beeghley 2005; Kerbo 2009).

Most people in the United States believe that the path to upward mobility is through higher education. It's certainly true that the more education a person has, the higher his or her income. However, children from higher-income families tend to get more education than those from lower-income families. Table 3.6 shows that whereas 32.5 percent of the bachelor's degrees awarded in 2016 went to children from high-income families, only 8.4 percent went to children from low-income families. What is even more distressing is that the distribution has not changed much since 2008. To the degree that a college degree is important for upward mobility, higher education is reproducing inequality.

Although we often do not talk about this, there is class privilege—for example, the ways rich individuals bribe their way into opportunities and elite educational institutions, exposed by the 2019 college admissions scandal, which included actresses Lori Loughlin and Felicity Huffman and fifty-two other people. A number of these people paid fines and went to prison.

Although this was illegal, other forms of class privilege are perfectly legal. For example, "legacy admissions," an undiscussed form of

Table 3.6 **Distribution of Bachelor's Degree Recipients in 2008 and 2017 by Family Income Quintiles (as percentage of all recipients)**

Family Income Quintile	2008	2017
Lowest	7.2	8.4
Second	11.5	13.4
Middle	18.7	19.5
Fourth	25.9	26.2
Highest	36.6	32.5
Total	100.0	100.0

Source: US Census Bureau 2017b.
Note: As this table indicates, in 2017, 8.4 percent of children from families in the lowest-income quintile and 32.5 percent of the children from families in the highest-income quintile had received a bachelor's degree.

affirmative action for the wealthy, give applicants a boost if their parent attended the college, such as Harvard. According to a report in the *New York Times* (2017), "the median family income of a student from Harvard is $168,000, and 67 percent come from the top 20 percent."

Research also shows that Harvard has given strong preference for children of wealthy donors, such as Jared Kushner, admitted to Harvard after his father donated 2.5 million dollars (Rim 2018). In every form of capital (economic, social, and cultural), members of the upper class have an advantage, meaning more access and opportunities, than their middle-class and working-class counterparts. According to Markovits (2019), merit is a sham.

The *Economist* (2004), a mainstream British magazine, reviewed several studies and concluded that social mobility in the United States is declining:

> A growing body of evidence suggests that the meritocratic ideal is in trouble in America. Income inequality is growing to levels not seen since the Gilded Age, around the 1880s. But social mobility is not increasing at anything like the same pace; would-be Horatio Algers are finding it no easier to climb from rags to riches, while the children of the privileged have a greater chance of staying at the top of the social heap. The United States risks calcifying into a European-style class-based society.

It is also important to note that a lot of social mobility is a result of structural changes in the labor force. The number of people employed in farming has been declining for decades, so many of the children of farmers have to find nonfarm jobs. Also, white-collar occupations have been increasing faster than manual occupations, so that some of the children of manual workers are automatically pushed up in the occupational hierarchy.

United for a Fair Economy (2012) analyzed the family origins of those people on the 2011 *Forbes* richest 400 list. The organization used a baseball analogy of starting in the batters' box and ending up on home plate. It found that 21 percent of the *Forbes* 400 started out on home plate; that is, they inherited sufficient wealth to be on the list without doing anything (e.g., Forrest Mars Jr. and Bill Marriot). Also, 7 percent were born on third base—they inherited at least $50 million, so they had to work to increase their wealth in order to get on the list (e.g., Charles Butt and Charles Koch). And 11.5 percent were born on second base by inheriting a small company and/or wealth of more than $1 million (e.g., Donald Trump and Donald Schneider). Finally, 22 percent began on first base by being born into a prominent family but didn't inherit more than $1 million (e.g., Mark Zuckerberg, Bill Gates, and Louis Bacon). That left 35 percent who began in the batters' box, meaning that their families didn't have great wealth (e.g., Larry Ellison and Harold Hamm). However, even most of those who began in the batters' box did not come from poor or working-class families. If you want to be rich, your best chance is to be born into a rich family.

Attitudes and Ideology

In the United States, equality is defined as equal opportunity, the notion that all individuals and communities have equal access to buy goods and services, to earn money, to build wealth, and to achieve the American dream. In the 1950s, the American dream was redefined away from the pursuit of happiness to the pursuit of consumer goods. In the post–World War II period, people in the United States began to measure their success by the amount of income or wealth they obtained. Impoverished people or those who live paycheck to paycheck are considered failures.

To achieve status, one must pursue a job that has high earning potential so that one can engage in conspicuous consumption, that is, rather than consuming what one simply needs, we pursue and acquire luxury goods and services. We hold a certain self-esteem about who we are by how much we earn, own, and spend. But many great novelists such as F. Scott Fitzgerald and John Steinbeck have satirized US culture by showing the hollowness and the finite capacity of the American dream, and poet Langston Hughes famously called it "a dream deferred."

Most mainstream commentators argue that the United States is a middle-class society, implying that most of its citizens are middle class. As we saw in the previous section, however, there is no agreement on how class should be measured by objective standards.

The way people in the United States subjectively identify their own class position is highly dependent on how the question is asked. When asked to indicate whether they are in the upper, middle, or lower class, an overwhelming majority select "middle" (Ladd and Bowman 1998). The results are different, however, when they are given more options.

Table 3.7 shows results of two different national studies of the *subjective* measure of class. What's clear from these two measures is that few identify themselves as upper or lower class. Also, when given the option, a substantial proportion (30 percent and 44 percent, respectively) see themselves as working class. This has been true since at least the 1940s (Ladd and Bowman 1998).

Table 3.7   **Distribution of Social Class Identification in Two Studies (percent)**

Gallup (2016–2018)		General Social Survey (2018)	
Category	Percent	Category	Percent
Upper	2	Upper	3
Upper middle	16	Middle	44
Middle	43	Working	44
Working	30	Lower	9
Lower	9		
	100		100

Sources: Newport 2016, 2018; General Social Survey 2018.
Note: According to the 2018 General Social Survey data, 44 percent of the respondents believed they were in the working class. Gallup data are an aggregate of several surveys.

Another aspect of the middle-class society ethos is the connection between hard work and economic success. Ladd and Bowman show that this has been an enduring belief among most in the United States. In a 1952 survey, for example, respondents were asked the following: "Some people say there's not much opportunity in America today; that the average man doesn't have much chance to really get ahead. Others say there's plenty of opportunity, and anyone who works hard can go as far as he wants. How do you feel about this?" (quoted in Ladd and Bowman 1998, 54). Of the respondents, 87 percent said there was opportunity if people worked hard, and only 8 percent said there was little opportunity.

Unfortunately, the question was asked differently in different years. The *New York Times/CBS News* poll (2005) asked how important various qualities were for "getting ahead in life." Of the respondents, 87 percent said hard work was "essential" or "very important" for getting ahead. Having a good education was almost as important, at 85 percent. This was followed by having natural ability (71 percent), knowing the right people (48 percent), and coming from a wealthy family (44 percent).

The Great Recession might have caused some people to question this faith in hard work. According to a 2010 ABC/*Yahoo News* Poll, 42 percent of respondents said that the American dream of working hard to get ahead used to be true but is no longer. Half of the respondents said that the dream was still true. The high proportion who questioned the American dream alarmed many pundits, who felt that some of the cultural ties binding the country might be unraveling.

In 2020, a Pew survey changed the question again by asking why rich people are rich. This time, 65 percent of respondents said people are rich because of their advantages, whereas only 33 percent of people said riches accrued through hard work.

People in the United States also perceive the economy as being unfair. In 2018, 63 percent of US adults said the nation's economic system unfairly favored powerful interests, and only 33 percent of respondents agreed that the system is generally fair to most (Dunn 2018). In a 2019 Pew poll, 69 percent of respondents said the economy is helping wealthy people, whereas 64 percent said it is hurting the poor (Igielnik and Parker 2019). Of the respondents, 62 percent and 60 percent, respectively, agreed with the statements, "Some corporations don't pay their fair share of taxes" and "Some wealthy don't pay their fair share of taxes" (Pew Research Center 2017).

The flip side of the work-success question concerns explanations for poverty. The following question was put to national samples between 1964 and 1997: "In your opinion, which is more often to blame if a person is poor—lack of effort on his own part, or circumstances beyond his control?" (Ladd and Bowman 1998, 52). In 1964, two-thirds of the respondents thought lack of effort was either partially or completely the cause of poverty (Ladd and Bowman 1998). This is sometimes called "blaming the victim." By 1997, slightly more than half of the respondents still felt lack of effort was a partial or complete explanation of poverty, a substantial decline from 1964. In the Pew 2020 survey mentioned above, 71 percent of people said people were poor because of obstacles.

The blame-the-victim explanation of poverty is one of the enduring beliefs in US culture and social science. In the 1960s, anthropologist Oscar Lewis coined the phrase "culture of poverty." This term has gone through a variety of changes, with one of the more recent simply referring to *the cultural explanation of poverty* (Harrison 1992; Small, Harding, and Lamont 2010). The argument put forward by conservative scholars is that a substantial portion of poor people have cultural values, passed on from one generation to the next, that cause them to be noncompetitive in the modern labor force. The components of this culture are said to be living in the present rather than planning for the future (i.e., instant gratification rather than delayed gratification) and have feelings of powerlessness, broken families, confused gender roles, a proclivity for deviant behavior, and a dependence on welfare. According to this view, then, poverty results from the attitudes of poor people themselves, not from circumstances beyond their control. The solution is to change their culture, not to provide more opportunities. The assumption is that substantial opportunities are there for the taking.

Liberals and radicals tend to understand the causes of poverty in structural terms; that is, some communities are cut off from the American dream through segregation and economic disinvestment and, therefore, get left behind and trapped in poverty from one generation to the next. This is the case in coal mining towns and in impoverished cities (Harrington 1997; Wilson 2012). According to this view, poverty is a result of economic recession, racial and gender discrimination, globalization, and/or the actions of the capitalist class.

We can't help wondering if the skyrocketing unemployment rates caused by the Covid recession beginning in 2020, spiking to 14.7 percent by April 2020, will cause people to question the culture-of-poverty explanation. Clearly, the thrust of this book is inconsistent with the conservative culture of poverty analysis. Cultural differences cannot explain the growing income and wealth inequality we discussed earlier. But ideology is hard to change.

Despite these beliefs about the unfairness of economic inequality, Ladd and Bowman (1998) provide data showing that people in the United States disagree about whether and how the government should respond to income inequality. Using a seven-point scale, respondents were asked to use a score of one to indicate their belief that the government should reduce income differences by raising taxes on the wealthy and giving income assistance to the poor. A score of seven indicates the government should not concern itself with income inequality.

When the question was first asked in 1973, almost half (48 percent) said the government should try to reduce inequality, and less than one-quarter (22 percent) said it shouldn't. The remaining 27 percent were in between.

By 1996, however, things had changed dramatically. Only 28 percent said the government should decrease inequality, a substantial drop from 1973. In contrast, 20 percent said the government shouldn't decrease inequality, only a small drop from 1973. Half were now in the middle, a sharp rise from 1973. During the conservative 1990s, there was considerably less enthusiasm for government action to reduce inequality.

Not surprisingly, people from different income levels had different attitudes about government action. In 1996, low-income respondents were much more supportive of government action than were high-income respondents. From the 1970s to the 1990s, low-income respondents' support for government action remained stable, but high-income respondents' support dropped.

In 2010, people in the United States were still divided about how government benefits for poor people actually affect the poor. Of respondents to a national poll, 38 percent said such programs "encourage them to remain poor," whereas 47 percent said such programs "help them until they begin to stand on their own" (*New York Times/CBS News* 2010). However, in 2018, 60 percent of US adults respondents to a poll believed the government was not doing enough to help poor people (Pew Research Center 2018a).

In the winter of 2021, Congress passed President Biden's $1.9 trillion, wide-ranging American Rescue Plan to help individuals, state and local governments, and businesses that were hurt by the Covid-induced economic crisis. In spite of polls showing three-quarters of adults, including 60 percent of Republicans, supported the plan, not a single Republican senator or member of the House voted for the plan (Williams 2021).

The results of these national surveys did not show a US population united over the theme of a middle-class nation. What they did show was a population with differing viewpoints on the importance of hard work, merit, and the role of government, depending on where respondents were in the system of inequality.

Discrimination and Capitalism

Since the 1970s, the benefits of US capitalism for working people have been eroding as the rich have become wealthier. Although a variety of corporate scandals in the first two decades of the twenty-first century have hurt working people in various ways, the *legal* workings of capitalism are the larger problem.

One major problem of capitalism is its tendency to move toward *monopoly*. According to Dayen, "There are four major airlines; four major commercial banks; four major companies that deliver phone, wireless, cable, and internet services. One company controls most web searches; one company controls most social media; one company controls about half of all e-commerce" (2020, 2–3).

In Chapter 2, we defined discrimination as actions that deny equal treatment and access to persons perceived to be members of some social category or group. In the following chapters, we show how the dominant groups (i.e., White people, men, and heterosexuals) still practice intentional discrimination in terms of race, gender, and sexual orientation in a variety of ways (e.g., in employment, housing, education, etc.).

Sometimes this discrimination is at the individual level, and sometimes it is systemic. Sometimes it is illegal, and sometimes it isn't.

Although it is not usually defined as discrimination, when **monopoly capitalism** suppresses competition and rivals by limiting equal treatment and access, it functions like a kind of class-based systemic discrimination. It negatively affects the potential earnings of the middle and working classes, increases the price of consumer goods, and limits innovation, efficiency, and product diversity (Dayen 2020).

Even so, the concept of discrimination doesn't adequately describe the nature of class domination. Members of the capitalist class have power over those in other classes and can live in neighborhoods and go to restaurants working-class people can't, but this usually doesn't involve unequal treatment because of membership in a certain category, and there is usually nothing illegal about it. A secretary can't buy a home in Beverly Hills because he or she can't afford it. A restaurant can refuse service to people who can't pay its prices. Most families can't afford private schools, so they send their kids to public schools. A factory owner has the legal right to hire and fire workers and to boss them around. A wealthy political candidate can legally outspend a middle-class opponent by using millions of his or her own dollars to win an election. These and other unfair policies are built into the US capitalist system. The concept of discrimination doesn't capture the essence of this type of unfairness. Exploitation, in which the dominant group uses the subordinate group for its own ends, seems closer to the truth.

Increasingly, capitalism has become a global economic system. Private corporations and national governments have always tried to look outside their borders for raw materials, new markets, and cheap labor. This goes back to the seventeenth and eighteenth centuries, when European countries established colonies around the world.

With the development of rapid transportation, more sophisticated production techniques, and information technology, globalization has taken a great leap forward. Huge multinational corporations operate around the world, and their countries of origin have become less important. Corporations move their operations to areas of the world that offer cheaper labor, lower taxes, and fewer environmental regulations. Countries compete with each other in what some have called the race to the bottom, a system in which employers reduce cost by cutting jobs, hours, wages, and quality working conditions (Zweig 2000).

Sociologist Arne Kalleberg (2011) explains that since the 1970s, the US economy has moved increasingly toward precarious labor: temporary jobs with low wages, no benefits, and no unions. He argues the US economy is growing in bad jobs. A good example of this is the gig economy, based on short-term contracts or freelance work. Some scholars estimate that about a third of US workers are employed in the gig economy (Mulcahy 2016). Think of Uber and Lyft.

Although contract work and part-time employment was once mostly relegated to the low-wage sector, such as the fast-food industry, increasingly these jobs continue to expand into the professional sector. One example is faculty labor at universities. In 2014, PBS reported that now 70 percent of the college and university teaching force is made up of adjunct faculty (Fruscione 2014). The national average pay of an adjunct professor in the United States is estimated to be between $2,500 and $2,700 a course. If an adjunct professor taught a full teaching load, four courses a semester, he or she would earn around $20,000 a year, and research shows that about a quarter of part-time college faculty depend on public assistance (Gee 2017).

Globalization causes real problems for working people in the United States and other industrialized countries because of their relatively high wages compared with workers in the developing world. It's often cheaper for US companies to have their products assembled in developing countries and ship them to the United States than to pay US workers. It's impossible for US workers to compete with workers in China or India who make only a few dollars per day. According to some estimates, the United States lost as many as 1 million jobs to such outsourcing between 2000 and 2004.

This has resulted in a phenomenon known as "displaced workers." According to the US Bureau of Labor Statistics (2010), displaced workers are "persons 20 years of age and older who lost or left jobs because their plant or company closed or moved, there was insufficient work for them to do, or their position or shift was abolished." Between January 2017 and December 2019, the BLS estimates that as many as 6.3 million workers were displaced. Since the previous edition of this book, this number has substantially decreased, when it was estimated that roughly 15.4 million workers had been displaced, mostly because of the Great Recession.

The BLS then surveyed displaced workers who had been with their employer at least three years prior to displacement. At the time of the survey in January 2020, 70 percent of these workers had found new jobs. In a previous survey in January 2018, 66 percent of displaced workers had found new jobs. Of those reemployed in the 2010 survey, 65 percent were earning at least as much as they had been paid at their former job. In the 2018 survey, 51 percent earned at least as much as at the job they lost.

When most of us think of displaced workers, we probably think of factory workers in the steel, auto, rubber, or textile industries. But 15 percent were professional and business services, and 13 percent were in retail.

The Covid recession had a disastrous impact on jobs in the US economy. The economy lost 10 million jobs between February and November 2020. Labor force participation rates during this same period were down 2.3 percent for women and 1.3 percent for men. Unemployment peaked at 14.7 percent in April. In comparison, during the Great Recession in 2007–2009, unemployment never got higher than 9.9 percent (Handwerker et al., 2021).

Taking this a step further, Gould and Kandra (2021) found that most of the job loss occurred among low-wage workers in 2020. More than three-quarters of the jobs lost (7.9 million) were lost by those in the bottom wage quartile (i.e., those earning $13.49 per hour or less). At the other end of the spectrum, those in the highest wage quartile actually *gained* 981,000 jobs.

Increasing numbers of US corporations outsource some of their work to companies in Ireland, India, and other countries where they can pay lower wages. In India, the average manufacturing wage in 2005 was only ninety-one cents per hour. This was only 3 percent of the comparable labor cost in the United States (Sincavage, Haub, and Sharma 2010). Jobs in aircraft manufacturing, engineering, investment banking, and pharmaceuticals have also gone to India. IBM has reduced its US labor force by 31,000 and increased its Indian workforce to 51,000 ("Outsourcing Is Breaking Out of the Back Office" 2007).

Legal work is also being outsourced. In 2005, 40 US law firms had subsidiaries in India. By 2009 that number had grown to 140. Indian lawyers cannot advise US clients, but they can do much of the routine work that junior lawyers do. The billing cost is one-tenth to one-third of the cost of US lawyers (Timmons 2010).

The relentless search for lower labor costs to increase profits is costing working people good jobs. People in the United States often blame Chinese and Indian workers for "taking their jobs," but the profit-oriented corporations are truly to blame.

Globalization is also a contributing factor to the decline of labor unions in the United States. In 1955 more than one-third of the labor force belonged to a union. In 2020 that figure had plummeted to 10.3 percent (US Bureau of Labor Statistics 2020a). This is much lower than union membership in other countries in the industrialized world. More than one-fourth of Japanese workers and 42 percent of workers in England were unionized (Kerbo 2009; Zweig 2000). The decline in the US manufacturing industries, many of which were unionized, is one reason for the drop in union membership. Now, government workers, including teachers, are much more likely to be unionized (33.6 percent) than workers in the private sector (6.2 percent).

Without unions, working people cannot negotiate effectively with employers for higher wages, benefits, and better working conditions. Unions and working people fought for and won the eight-hour workday, the five-day work week, restrictions on child labor, health benefits, sick leave, vacation time, family leave, and other important benefits we often take for granted today. According to Yates (2005), unionized workers earn 15 percent more than nonunion workers after controlling for factors such as education, work experience, and age. The decline in unionization has contributed to the growth in income inequality. However, even unionized workers have had a difficult time holding on to hard-fought gains.

Monopoly capitalism and globalization affect the types of jobs available in the United States. According to public perception, high-skilled, high-paying jobs are displacing lower-skilled, low-paying jobs because of high-tech industries. The reality, as we shall see, is considerably more complex.

Every two or three years, the BLS revs up its computers and does a ten-year projection of which jobs will grow and which won't. The most recent projections are for the period 2019–2029. Table 3.8 shows the occupations expected to produce the most new jobs by 2029. Home-health aides top the list and are expected to add 1,159,000 new jobs by 2029. Fast-food and counter workers are second, with an expected growth of 461,000 new jobs, followed by cooks with a growth of 327,000 new jobs. Software developers and analysts (289,000) and registered nurses (222,000) follow in fourth and fifth place.

The categories that will add the most new jobs by 2029 are mostly low-paying and low-skilled jobs. In fact, half of the ten occupations expected to add the most new jobs by 2029 are in the lower two income quartiles, and four only require on-the-job training!

This is inconsistent with the popular view that low-paid, low-skilled jobs are declining. Where are the high-tech, well-paying jobs everyone has been talking about since the 1980s? Well, let's consider another list.

Table 3.9 shows the five fastest-growing jobs. Here we find occupations requiring somewhat higher skill and pay. Wind-turbine techni-

Table 3.8 Occupations Projected to Add the Most New Jobs, 2019–2029

Occupational Category	Employment in 2019 (thousands)	New Jobs Added by 2029 (thousands)	Percent Change	Quintiles[a]	Qualifications/ Training
Home health aides	3,440	1,159	34	5	Short-term OJT[b]
Fast food and counter workers	4,047	461	11	5	Short-term OJT
Cooks, restaurants	1,417	327	23	5	Various
Software developers and analysts	1,469	289	22	2	Bachelor's degree
Registered nurses	3,097	222	7	3	Bachelor's degree

Source: US Bureau of Labor Statistics 2020b.
Notes: a. Quintiles by income ranges in 2019 dollars: second is $86,489–$142,501; fifth is under $28,084.
b. On-the-job training.
As the table indicates, more than 3.4 million home health aides were employed in 2019. An additional 1,159,000 home aides are expected to be employed by 2029, a 34 percent increase. Home health aides are in the fifth (lowest) income quintile and require short-term on-the-job training.

cians, an occupation that employs only 7,000 people, is projected to increase by 61 percent. Nurse practitioners are projected to increase by 52 percent. Solar installers (51 percent), occupational therapy assistants (35 percent), and statisticians (35 percent) are also expected to grow rapidly. Three of these five occupations require some higher education and have somewhat higher pay than the ones in Table 3.8. Although seven of the ten fastest growing jobs require some higher education, home-health aides are also on the list. In fact, they are on both lists.

For those who find all of this confusing, let me explain. Table 3.8 identifies *large* occupations growing at *modest* rates. The current 4 million fast-food jobs are projected to increase by 461,000 new jobs by 2029, a growth rate of only 11 percent. In other words, it is a large occupation that is growing slowly. In contrast, Table 3.9 shows that the 7,000 people employed as wind-turbine technicians in 2019 are projected to add 4,000 jobs by 2029. This relatively small occupation is projected to expand by 61 percent, a rapid rate.

Table 3.9   Fastest-Growing Occupations, 2019–2029

Occupational Category	Employment in 2019 (thousands)	New Jobs Added by 2029 (thousands)	Percent Change	Quintiles[a]	Qualifications/ Training
Wind turbine technician	7	4	61	4	Long-term OJT[b]
Nurse practitioner	211	111	52	2	Master's degree
Solar photovoltaic installer	12	6	51	4	Moderate-term OJT
Occupational therapy assistants	47	16	35	3	Associate degree
Statisticians	43	14	35	2	Master's degree

Source: US Bureau of Labor Statistics 2020c.
Notes: a. Quintiles by income ranges in 2019 dollars: second is $86,489–$142,501; fifth is under $28,084.
b. On-the-job training.
As the table indicates, 7,000 wind turbine technicians were employed in 2019. An additional 4,000 wind turbine technicians are expected to be employed by 2029, a 61 percent increase. Wind turbine technicians have incomes in the fourth quintile and require long-term on-the-job training.

What does this mean? For the next decade or two, there will still be more openings for home-health aides and fast-food workers than for statisticians and nurse practitioners. A college degree in the right major increases one's chances of getting one of the better-paying jobs, but there are more college graduates than college-graduate-level jobs. This means that the job structure provides opportunities for upward mobility for some college graduates but restricts these opportunities for others.

The Walmart revolution, now coupled with the Amazon revolution of e-commerce, contributed to this occupational polarization (*Fortune* 2010). The statistics are astonishing. In 2020, Walmart had revenue of $559 billion, accounting for 9.5 percent of all retail sales in the United States. Amazon is closing fast with revenue of $386 billion and 9.2 percent of retail sales (PYMNTS 2021).

In 2020 Walmart ranked number one in the *Fortune* 500, and it had higher sales than Ford (number twelve), J. P. Morgan Chase (number seventeen), and Microsoft (number twenty-one) combined. Walmart had higher sales than the gross domestic products of most of the world's countries. In addition, Walmart had nearly $15 billion in profits in 2020 and is the number one private employer in the United States, with 2.3 million employees around the world.

The secret to Walmart's success is high volume and low labor costs, which result in low prices. Most Walmart employees work part time with no benefits. Walmart has agreed to increase the minimum wage of 165,000 US employees to $15 per hour, up from $11 per hour, and some other select job categories could see a salary increase from anywhere between $18 and $30 an hour, depending on the job type (Grothaus 2020).

Although these are positive changes, Walmart is aggressively anti-union. Early in the twentieth century, Henry Ford tried to keep wages low, but he understood that he had to pay his assembly-line workers sufficient wages so that they could buy the cars they produced. Walmart doesn't even pay enough for a family breadwinner to provide enough food for his or her family. Currently, Walmart pays its entry-level new hires only $11 per hour, which means if that new employee worked thirty-four hours per week, that employee would make less than $20,000 a year, which was below the poverty level for a family of four (Thomas 2021). This is an example of economic exploitation.

Walmart has such power that it suppresses wages in the communities where it has stores. Smaller chains find it difficult to compete with Walmart, and local businesses find it almost impossible. This same criticism has been levied at Amazon e-commerce practices; small businesses argue that Amazon prioritizes its products on its website, which they claim is unfair because it crushes competition. Walmart also drives hard bargains with the manufacturers of the products it sells. By insisting on the lowest possible prices, Walmart is practically forcing manufacturers to move to China and other low-wage countries. This, of course, means fewer jobs for US workers. To the extent that Walmart becomes the business model of the future, working people are in trouble.

In less than three decades, Amazon went from a new online bookstore to the leading e-commerce retailer in the world. Amazon is the number two corporation on the *Fortune* 500 list, behind Walmart. In twenty-one years, Amazon's stock rose 98,000 percent (Lane 2017). Amazon's success is tied to its online platform because without brick-and-mortar stores, it can reduce its costs, resulting in cheaper prices for shoppers.

Like Walmart, Amazon is not without opposition. Even though in 2018 the company agreed to raise the wages of its US employees to $15 per hour, the company has been criticized for evading taxes, for being antiunion, for having poor working conditions, and for monopolistic practices (Salinas 2018). In early 2021, Amazon workers in Bessemer, Alabama, lost their struggle to get Amazon to recognize its union.

* * *

We hope readers now feel more familiar with the current nature of class in the United States. Although we are a class-based society, we don't usually talk about class. As we stated at the beginning of this chapter, we have purposely stayed away from looking at how race, immigration, gender, and sexual orientation are intertwined with class. We made this decision because we wanted to emphasize class inequalities—the way income, wealth, and power are concentrated in the top strata of society compared with the limited wealth concentrated in the bottom, regardless of race and gender. If we removed racial minorities and women from the equation, the United States would still be an unequal, class-based society. In Chapter 4, however, we discuss race to show how class is integral to understanding racial conflict. We also show how race is integral to understanding class conflict.

4

Race, Ethnicity, and Discrimination

Racial conflict and inequality are still major issues facing the United States in the twenty-first century. Rather than disappearing, the problem has only become more complex. In 1903 W. E. B. Du Bois wrote, "The problem of the 20th Century is the problem of the color line" (1990, 3). In the twenty-first century, we face the "one step forward, two steps back" dilemma.

In 2008, the unthinkable happened: the election of the first Black president, Barack Obama, who brought hope to many with his message of change. Yet, Obama's election brought a backlash of White supremacy and xenophobic, Islamophobic, and anti-Semitic bigotry. The Tea Party movement preceded the election of President Donald J. Trump, but both reflected and encouraged White supremacy. More than half the country believed that Trump made race relations worse (Horowitz, Brown, and Cox 2019). The January 6, 2021, insurrection forecasts there might be a similar backlash to the election of Joe Biden and Kamala Harris (the first woman and person of color to become vice president).

In 2017, a White supremacist protest was organized in Charlottesville, Virginia, that left a White, female, antiracist protester dead. Trump neither condemned the protest nor the violence but defended the White nationalist group when he declared there were "fine people on both sides."

During the past two decades, many social scientists have challenged the Black-White binary as no longer being sufficient to understanding the complexity of race and racism in the twenty-first century. When Du Bois referred to the color line, he meant that the domination of White people over Black people was the fundamental issue. Native American genocide and land removal were largely ignored in our popular discourse on race.

The color line is different today. The Latinx (plural Latinxs) population has surpassed the Black population in the United States, and the Asian American population is growing rapidly. Projections suggest that if present trends continue, non-Latinx White people will cease to be the numerical majority by the 2050s.

Readers might wonder why it is necessary to talk about "non-Latinx White people" rather than just "White people." Are there also non-Latinx Black people or Asian Americans? What about people of mixed races? These questions underscore the ambiguous and interchangeable ways people self-identify and are labeled by the mainstream. Some groups choose to be defined by their race, some by their ethnicity, and others by their nationality.

To complicate the matter further, these labels can shift by geographical boundary. For example, when Bryan Ellis is home in the United States, he is known as African American; but when he traveled to Dakar, Senegal, in West Africa, he noticed the Senegalese paid closer attention to his nationality than they did to his skin tone. There he was American first.

In the twenty-first century, the nature of racial conflict has also changed. When Du Bois wrote his treatise on race, segregation was legal and lynching was commonplace in the South and in many other parts of the country. There was virtually no Black political representation at the state and federal levels. Since then, we have had Black and Latinx representation in Congress, a Black president, Black and Latinx Supreme Court justices, and a growing Black and Latinx middle class. Recognizing the many changes we have made over the past decades, some people have argued that we are in a "postracial" society, where race no longer matters.

In the social sciences, most research has not caught up to these changing demographics and new realities. They are stuck in the bipolar model of the past. But some contemporary analysts argue for a more comprehensive understanding of racialized oppression that includes the experiences and perspectives of all racial and ethnic groups. This nuanced approach to race is informed by the intersectionality theory pioneered by Black feminist scholars (see Chapter 6).

Before answering these and other questions, it is necessary to define some basic terms.

Terminology

Although many of us assume that we know what race means, it's really not so simple. Before proceeding, try writing out a definition, and you'll find out how complex it can be. For the purposes of this book, a **racial group** is a socially defined group who is perceived as having certain phenotypical characteristics that sets its members apart from those of other groups, often in invidious ways. The key aspect of this definition is that race is defined socially, not biologically determined.

Many people don't realize that most biologists and geneticists argue that race is not a biologically meaningful term. Of course, there are observable, phenotypical differences between some groups of people in terms of skin color, hair texture, and facial shapes. However, when one examines the genetic makeup of people from different races, there is more genetic variation within a given race than between races. In other words, the genes for skin color and for a few other observable characteristics are different, but nearly everything else is the same.

It's also impossible to tell where one race stops and another begins. Speaking in the excellent video *Race: The Power of an Illusion* (2003), evolutionary biologist Joseph Graves Jr. puts it this way:

> If we were to only look at people in the tropics and people in Norway, we would come to the conclusion that there is a group of people who have light skin and a group of people who have dark skin. But, if we were to walk from the tropics to Norway, what we would see is a continuous change in skin tones. At no point during that trip would we be able to say, "Oh, this is the place in which we go from the dark race to the light race."

Although race is not a valid biological concept, it is still a powerful cultural concept, especially in the United States. We *think* race is important, and we *treat* people in different ways according to the race we think they belong to. In other words, we have socially constructed racial categories even though they have no biological significance. Consequently, our approaches to race are often illogical and inconsistent.

In trying to determine who is Black, people in the United States have generally used the "one-drop" rule. People are considered Black if they have any Black ancestors, regardless of the color of their skin. In the past, this has been encoded into law. In more recent years, it's simply part of the culture. Some light-skinned people with Black ancestors can be "mistaken" for being White if no one knows the history of their family. This phenomenon of **passing** refers to a subordinate group member who does not reveal the stigmatized status he or she occupies. If the secret is revealed, the person previously defined as White, for example, is socially redefined as Black.

Most examples of passing involve members of subordinate racial groups making people think they are members of the dominant, White group. In 2015, however, the opposite of what usually happens took place. A woman of European ancestry, Racheal Dolezal, sparked a national debate about the definition of race when she was outed by her family of origin for passing as Black. Pictures of her as a young woman reveal a skin tone and hairstyle that resembles a light-skinned Black woman. When asked about her racial identity, she declared, "I identify as Black" and "transracial." Her critics maintain she is capitalizing on the lived experiences and struggles of Black women.

Contrast the one-drop rule with how people in the United States define Native Americans by their "blood quantum." If you have a Native American mother and a White father, you are considered "half Indian." If one of your grandparents was a Native American and the other three were not, you are one-fourth Indian. Individual nations can define the blood quantum level necessary for membership in their tribe. This can range from being half Indian to being one-fourth Indian to simply self-identifying as Indian. In contradistinction to the one-drop rule for Black people, Native Americans have to *prove* they are members of their nations. The federal government requires that people be at least one-fourth Indian to qualify for programs sponsored by the Bureau of Indian Affairs.

The census data on race are totally unscientific because they are based on people's self-identification. That is, individuals are asked to check one of the boxes to answer the question on race—White, Black, Asian American, Pacific Islander, Native American, or "Some Other Race." However, none of the boxes say "Hispanic" because the census defines being Hispanic (i.e., Latinx) as an ethnicity, not as a race. Respondents first are asked whether they are Hispanic and then are asked to indicate their race. This means Latinx people can be of any race.

An **ethnic group** is defined as a social group that has certain cultural characteristics that sets it off from other groups and whose members see themselves as having a common past. Language and culture, according to the census, are what set Latinx people off from other groups. Arab Americans would also be ethnic groups for the same reason.

This race-versus-ethnicity issue becomes both interesting and problematic in trying to answer a simple question like "What percentage of the population is White?" The top half of Table 4.1 presents the data using the five standard racial categories plus a mixed-race category. Out of the 327.2 million Americans in 2018, 236.2 million were White, which accounts for 72.2 percent of the population. Reading down the columns, we can see that 12.7 percent of the population was Black, 5.6

Table 4.1   Two Views of the Racial/Ethnic Distribution of the
US Population, 2018

Racial Group Plus Hispanic/Latinx	Number (millions)	Distribution (percent)
White	236.2	72.2
Black	42.0	12.7
American Indian/Alaska Native	2.8	0.9
Asian	18.4	5.6
Native Hawaiian/Pacific Islander	0.6	0.2
Two or more races	11.2	3.4
Some other race	16.2	5.0
Hispanic/Latinx[a]	60.0	18.3
Total	387.4	118.3

Racial/Ethnic Group		
Non-Hispanic/non-Latinx		
White	197.0	60.2
Black	40.3	12.3
American Indian/Alaska Native	2.1	0.7
Asian	18.1	5.6
Native Hawaiian/Pacific Islander	0.6	0.2
Some other race	0.8	0.3
Two or more races	8.3	2.5
Hispanic/Latinx[a]	60.0	18.3
Total	327.2	100.0

Source: US Census Bureau 2018b.
Note: a. Hispanics/Latinx can be of any race. There were 236.2 million White people in the United States accounting for 72.2 percent of the population. There were 197 million non-Latinx Whites in the United States accounting for 60.2 percent of the population.

percent was Asian American, 0.9 percent was Native American, 0.2 percent was Pacific Islander, 5.0 percent was some other race, and 3.4 percent was mixed race. In addition, 18.3 percent of the population was Latinx. If all these numbers are added together, they come out to 118.3 percent, and the total population comes to 387.4 million!

The problem is that because Latinx people can be of any race, they are counted twice. A White Latinx person would be counted once as White and once as Latinx. The categories are not mutually exclusive.

A second way to answer the question can be found in the bottom half of Table 4.1, which separates Latinx people and non-Latinx people.

In this case, there are 197 million non-Latinx White people, accounting for 60.2 percent of the population. The White category thus lost 39.2 million people placed in the Latinx category. The Black category also fell by 1.7 million. The total non-Latinx population was 267.2 million, or 82 percent of the population. The Latinx number (60 million, or 18.3 percent) is the same in both halves of the table. This time, the total adds up to 327.2 million and 100 percent. The categories in the lower half of Table 4.1 are mutually exclusive in that everyone is counted only once.

So, are White people 72.2 percent of the population, or 60.2 percent of the population? Actually, both are correct. If ethnicity is ignored, and all those who check the White box are counted, White people are 72.2 percent of the population. If only White people who are not also Latinx are counted, non-Latinx White people are 60.2 percent of the population. Sometimes federal officials use one number, and sometimes they use the other.

We will use the "non-Latinx White" category when the data are available because it's easier to see the advantages non-Latinx White people have in terms of income, occupation, and education. The gaps between non-Latinx White people and people of color are usually larger than the gaps between all White people and people of color.

But wait, there's more. Remember the "Some Other Race" category? In the 2010 census, 39 percent of Latinx people checked this box because they didn't think they fit into any of the standard race categories. In fact, most people who check "Some Other Race" are Latinx. Because some government agencies use the Modified Age/Race and Sex file (MARS), which doesn't include the "Other" category, census officials must reassign those who select "Some Other Race" to one of the standard categories. This creates many errors as well as a lot of extra work for the census officials.

To encourage Latinx people to select one of the standard racial categories, census officials considered eliminating the "Some Other Race" category for the 2010 census. This, in turn, provoked the following comment from Carlos Chardon, chair of the US Census Bureau's Hispanic Advisory Committee: "We don't fit into the categories that the Anglos want us to fit in. The census is trying to create a reality that doesn't exist" (Swarns 2004, A18). Thus, in the 2010 and 2020 censuses, people were able to check the "Some Other Race" option.

Prior to the 2000 census, there was a big controversy over how to deal with mixed-race people. For example, professional golfer Tiger Woods is usually described as Black even though he is half Asian American. After conservative southern senator Strom Thurmond died in

2003, a dark-skinned woman revealed that she was his daughter. In his youth, Thurmond had a relationship with one of his Black servants. His daughter, however, is always described as Black even though she is half White. The same is true for former president Obama.

In previous years, a person who is half Asian American and half Native American had to select only one box. Some biracial people argued for a separate "mixed-race" category on the 2000 census because those from more than one racial background share a variety of similar issues. The final decision, however, was to allow people to check more than one box. In fact, more than 8 million Americans made that choice. The issue of allowing a mixed-race box versus a multiple-race choice had absolutely nothing to do with biology.

In addition to language and national origin, an ethnic group can be characterized by religion, especially if it is not the dominant religion. The 3.5 million Muslims in the United States can be referred to as an ethnic group. It is important not to equate being Muslim with being Arab. The Arabic language and culture are prevalent in North Africa and the Middle East, but Iran and Turkey are not Arabic countries. The dominant language in Iran is Farsi, and the dominant language in Turkey is Turkish. However, these two countries are Muslim countries in terms of their dominant religion.

There are about 1.8 billion Muslims in the world, most of whom are not Arabs. There are more than 450 million Arabs in the world, most of whom are Muslim. To make matters even more confusing, half of the 3.7 million Arab Americans are Christian. On top of that, the census defines people from North Africa as White!

Jewish Americans are also an ethnic group, although there are important cultural differences among them. Ashkenazi Jews originally came from Central and Eastern Europe, whereas Sephardic Jews came from Spain and Northern Africa. The vernacular language for Ashkenazi Jews was Yiddish, and the vernacular for Sephardic Jews was Ladino. There are also differences in rituals and holiday celebrations.

Most Jewish people say they are religious and belong to one of the four major denominations—orthodox, conservative, reform, and reconstructionist. However, there are also many who define themselves as Jewish people culturally but who are not religious. In fact, 80 percent of Jewish people in Israel are secular. In the United States, there are two national secular Jewish organizations—the Congress of Secular Jewish Organizations and the Society for Humanist Judaism (Seid 2001).

Technically, Protestants and Catholics are also ethnic groups by virtue of their religions, but they are not usually referred to this way because Christianity is the dominant religion in the United States. Ethnicity usually refers to groups that are culturally different from the dominant group or groups.

Now we get to the really big concept—racism. Believe it or not, there is no commonly accepted definition of this widely used term. Some social scientists use the term synonymously with *prejudice* in terms of one person having a negative attitude about someone from another group. Others see racism as the same thing as *discrimination* (i.e., differential treatment). In an often-cited article, Robert Blauner (1992) argues for at least four additional uses of the term.

The most useful definition of **racism** is a system of power and oppression that provides, on the one hand, economic, political, or psychological advantages and privileges for the White (i.e., dominant) racial group, and, on the other hand, discrimination against and disadvantages for the non-White (i.e., subordinate) racial groups. When civil unrest exploded in 2020 after the killing of George Floyd by a Minneapolis police officer, *Merriam-Webster's Dictionary* changed its definition of racism to include systemic racism, congruent with the sociological definition provided here. The dictionary no longer acknowledges racism as *only* a belief or prejudice but now extends the definition to include "a political or social system founded on racism." This means you can use *Webster's* for your sociology papers and not fear you will receive a comment from your professor that says, "Use an academic definition and source."

Until sixty years ago, racial segregation was the law of the land. Whereas Fred Pincus was born in 1942, during the period of de jure (i.e., legal) segregation, Bryan Ellis was born in 1984, during the post-civil rights era. Ellis's paternal ancestors were enslaved in Kentucky before the Civil War. Both chattel slavery and Jim Crow policies were predicated on "the complex array of anti-black practices, the unjustly gained political-economic power of white people, the continuing economic and other resource inequalities along racial lines, and the white racist ideologies and attitudes created to maintain and rationalize white privilege and power" (Feagin 2000, 6). Thus, even though beliefs are the cornerstone of agency, racism doesn't just exist in the minds of individuals. Racist laws regulate our lives and influence our actions.

As we noted previously, racism extends beyond Black-White relations. Although Muslims and Jews are technically ethnic groups, anti-Semitism and Islamophobia are forms of discrimination akin to racism in which members of an ethnic group are targeted, singled out, and treated like racialized others. Whereas anti-Semitism is hostility or prejudice against Jews, Islamophobia is an exaggerated fear of Muslims.

Jewish people have been stereotyped in both biological and cultural terms. On the one hand, they have been framed as greedy bankers, media manipulators, and communists. On the other hand, they have been characterized as biologically inferior. Based on eugenics ideology and pseudoscience, during the reign of Adolf Hitler in Nazi Germany, they were forced into ghettos and concentration camps and suffered genocide.

Muslim Americans have been stereotyped as terrorists and targeted, racially profiled, and subjected to religious intolerance and hate-based violence in the United States. The United States has carried out several wars and conflicts in the Middle East, and the Trump administration barred people from certain majority-Muslim countries from entering the United States. In 2018, Jewish Americans reported 895 hate crimes and Muslim Americans reported 225 against them.

Although our definition of racism might seem straightforward, it has some important and controversial implications. Because racism involves power and oppression, it follows that only the dominant group can be racist. In the United States, this means that only White people can be racist. People of color cannot be racist because they don't have the power.

Many White people strenuously object to this argument, saying, "I know plenty of people of color who hate White people." True enough, some people of color are *prejudiced* against White people; however, people of color cannot be *racist* because they lack the collective power to oppress White people as a group. To complicate things further, though, Black writer Ibram X. Kendi (2019) argues that Black people who help to implement anti-Black policies should also be called racist.

Others have argued that "all White people are racist." If this means all White people are prejudiced, this is certainly not the case, as we discuss shortly. If it means all White people discriminate against people of color, this is also not the case. Many White people don't have the power to discriminate. If, however, this means all White people participate in an oppressive system that benefits them at the expense of people of color, this comes closer to the truth.

For instance, on May 25, 2020, a White woman, Amy Cooper, was caught on camera calling the police on Christian Cooper (no relation), a Black man watching birds in New York City's Central Park. He had asked her to obey the park rules and leash her dog. In her 911 call, she insisted she was being threatened by an African American man. She emphasized "African American man" to get a quick response from the police and to intimidate Christian Cooper. But she was fabricating the threat. Christian Cooper's cell phone video captured the whole incident, and the police didn't overreact.

This is an example of White privilege. An ordinary White person can use the system of racist oppression—in this case, Amy Cooper attempted to use the racial bias of law enforcement officers—to benefit themselves at the expense of Black people.

Members of another group of White people, however, committed to fighting against White racism, describe themselves as "antiracist" rather than "nonracists." They agree with the argument that all White people are racist in that they participate in a racist system, but they see themselves as trying to fight for a more equal world (Diangelo 2018; O'Brien 2001). We will discuss this position later in this chapter.

Finally, we encounter the issue of terminology for different racial and ethnic groups. Once again, there is no scientific answer here. Labels are contentious and change over time. The issue involves how groups are labeled by outsiders versus how groups refer to themselves. In politically mobilizing against oppression, subordinate groups often adopt new labels or redefine old ones.

For example, at various times in US history, both Black and White people considered it appropriate to call Black people "Colored" or "Negro." The National Association for the Advancement of Colored People (NAACP) was founded as an integrated antiracist organization in 1909. Martin Luther King Jr. used *Negro* in most of his speeches. Black people today reject both terms. In the 1960s, the term *Black* replaced *Negro*. That was followed by *Afro-American* and *African American*.

Whereas "Black" denotes a political identity rooted in solidarity with all people of African ancestry beyond national boundaries, African American denotes the experience of the US populace who trace their ancestry back to the continent of Africa and chattel slavery. This term was popularized by Jesse Jackson in the 1980s. As he explained then, "Black tells you about skin color and what side of town you live on. African-American evokes discussion of the world" (Wilkerson 1989).

In 2019, 64 percent of Black people said they had no preference between the labels Black and African American. The rest were evenly split between the two. This hadn't changed since 1991 (Saad 2020). Today, "most Black adults say race is central to their identity and feel connected to a broader Black community," according to a poll by the

Pew Research Center (Barroso 2020a). In this book, we will use the terms Black and African American interchangeably.

Then there is the issue of whether *Black* should be capitalized. More than a century ago, W. E. B. DuBois and the NAACP won the fight to capitalize the "N" in Negro. The same arguments have taken place regarding the "B" in Black. The *New York Times,* after a long internal debate, announced that it would begin capitalizing Black in June 2020.

Some Black people from Africa and the Caribbean prefer to call themselves Nigerian, Kenyan, Haitian, or Jamaican, reflecting their country of origin. By choosing their master status as their nation rather than their race, they attempt to shield themselves from the racism experienced by American-born Black people. African and Caribbean Black people sometimes cultivate their distinctive accents to make themselves more attractive to potential employers who might discriminate against American-born Black people. Although this strategy can have some short-term positive impact, the American-born children of immigrants usually lose their accents and are seen as African Americans.

What about pejorative terms such as *nigger, chink,* and *spic*? On the one hand, *nigger* has been such a powerful, negative term throughout US history that many people can't even say it out loud. Instead, they talk about "the N word." On the other hand, some Black people use the term *nigga* to refer affectionately to each other but would consider it offensive if White people used the same term. This is an example of a subordinate group taking a term of disapprobation and altering its meaning. Although this might be confusing to White people, it is most respectful to avoid saying *nigger* and *nigga* as well as any other pejorative racial terms (Akom 2000).

The term *Hispanic* was adopted by the US Congress in the 1970s to categorize a diaspora of people who share a common language: Spanish. Previously, Spanish-speaking populations in the United States usually referred to themselves by their country of origin; for example, Cuban, Guatemalan, or Mexican. *Latino* is a term preferred by some political activists. According to a 2019 Pew Research Center national poll of Spanish speakers in the United States, 61 percent preferred Hispanic and 29 percent preferred Latino (Noe-Bustamante et al. 2020). Also, Mexican Americans have sometimes adopted the label Chicano/Chicana since the 1960s.

Scholars and activists are increasingly using the term *Latinx* although only 4 percent saw this as the preferred term in the Pew study and less than one-quarter had heard of the term. The Spanish language has masculine and feminine words; Latina refers to women, whereas Latino refers to both men and the entire population (similar to *mankind*, a term the feminist movement fought hard to abolish). Latinx is more gender neutral, so we shall employ this term throughout the book.

The terms *Native American* and *American Indian* are both used to describe descendants of people indigenous to the United States. Some prefer to be called by their tribal names. Unfortunately we could not locate any recent polls to show preferences.

Prior to the 1960s, most people from Asia and the Pacific Islands referred to themselves by their or their ancestors' country of origin. During the 1960s, however, student activists started promoting the term *Asian* as a way of unifying people from this diverse diaspora for political purposes (Espiritu 1992). Sometimes, the letters AAPI are used to refer to Asian Americans and Pacific Islanders.

The issue of labeling might seem arbitrary to members of dominant groups, but it's not. Often, when a subordinate group is beginning to mobilize to fight oppression, its members' ability to label themselves is part of the process. When the Black Power movement split off from the civil rights movement in the 1960s, for example, activists insisted on being called "Black" rather than "Negro." Such a split often denotes a difference in approaches between activists.

Descriptive Statistics

Virtually all the data collected by the federal government show substantial economic inequalities between White people and people of color. Unemployment rates provide a good example. People are counted as unemployed if they don't have a job and are actively looking for work. Being in the labor force means that you are working or you are looking for work. People not looking for work are viewed as having dropped out of the labor force altogether and are not counted in the unemployment rate. The official unemployment rate is calculated as follows:

$$\frac{\text{no. looking for work}}{\text{no. working} + \text{no. looking for work}} = \text{\% unemployed}$$

Table 4.2 shows that unemployment rates in 2020 were substantially higher for Black and Latinx people (11.4 percent and 10.4 percent, respectively) than for White people and Asian Americans (7.3 percent and 8.7 percent, respectively). This same trend is true for both males and

Table 4.2 **Unemployment Rates for Sixteen-Year-Olds and Older in 2020 by Race, Latinx Origin, and Gender (percent)**

Race/Latinx	Male	Female	Both Genders	April Peak
White	7.0	7.6	7.3	13.8
Black	12.1	10.9	11.4	16.4
Asian	7.8	9.6	8.7	14.3
Latinx	9.7	11.4	10.4	18.5
Unemployment Ratio				
Black/White	1.7	1.4	1.6	1.2
Asian/White	1.1	1.3	1.2	1.0
Latinx/White	1.4	1.5	1.4	1.3

Source: US Bureau of Labor Statistics, 2021.

Note: As the table indicates, 7.0 percent of White males and 12.1 percent of Black males were unemployed in 2020. The Black male unemployment rate was 1.7 times higher than the White male rate. "April Peak" refers to unemployment in April 2020 at the peak of the Covid recession.

females of these groups. Due to the Covid recession, these rates are two- to three-times higher than they were in 2019. The last column in the table shows the data for April 2020 when unemployment was at its peak.

In the bottom half of Table 4.2, we compare the unemployment rates of people of color to those of White people. The Black unemployment rate for 2020 was 1.6 times higher than the White rate, a somewhat lower Black/White gap than has existed in the past. For several decades, Black unemployment has been close to double White unemployment, sometimes less and sometimes more. Latinx unemployment is 1.2 times higher than that of White people, and Asian American unemployment is 1.2 times higher than that of White people.

One common explanation for the difference in unemployment rates between White people and Asian Americans, on the one hand, and Black people and Latinx people, on the other hand, looks to education. Because low levels of education lead to high unemployment, and because Black and Latinx people tend to have less education than White people and Asian Americans, the argument goes, it's reasonable to expect differences in unemployment rates. An extension of this argument is that at the same level of education, unemployment rates for White, Black, Asian American, and Latinx people should be the same.

Table 4.3 allows us to examine this argument. When you read across the first four rows, you can see that for each racial group,

Table 4.3   Unemployment Rates of Twenty-Five-Year-Olds and Older in 2020 by Race, Latinx Origin, and Education (percent)

Race/Latinx	Didn't Finish High School	High School Graduate	Some College, No Degree	Associate Degree	Bachelor's Degree or Higher
White	10.5	8.0	7.5	6.5	4.6
Black	16.1	13.0	10.9	9.0	5.9
Asian	16.6	13.7	10.7	9.8	5.6
Latinx	11.2	10.1	9.0	8.7	6.5
Unemployment Ratio					
Black/white	1.5	1.6	1.5	1.4	1.3
Asian/white	1.6	1.7	1.4	1.5	1.2
Latinx/white	1.1	1.3	1.2	1.3	1.4

Source: US Bureau of Labor Statistics 2021.
Note: As the table indicates, 16.1 percent of Blacks and 10.5 percent of Whites who did not finish high school were unemployed. Among those who did not finish high school, the Black unemployment rate was 1.5 times higher than the White rate.

unemployment rates tend to decline as education increases. This is consistent with the argument that educational differences can explain racial differences in unemployment rates.

However, when you read down each column, you can also see that at all levels of education, White people are less likely to be unemployed than people of color. At the bachelor's degree and above level, for example, Black people are 1.3 times as likely to be unemployed as White people, and Latinx people are 1.4 times as likely to be unemployed as White people and Asian Americans are 1.2 times more likely to be unemployed than White people.

There are also important racial differences in the kinds of jobs people have. Table 4.4 looks at the distribution of different occupational categories in the United States in 2019. The best-paying and most skilled jobs are in the management and professional categories. Whereas 41.4 percent of White people and 55.1 percent of Asian Americans are in these two categories, only 31.9 percent of Black people and 23.4 percent of Latinx people are managers or professionals. In the lower-paid, lower-skilled service category, in contrast, we find only 15.9 percent of White workers and 15.8 percent of Asian American workers, compared with 23.8 percent of Black workers and 24.2 percent of Latinx workers. Clearly, Asian American and White

Table 4.4   Distribution of Employed Persons in 2019 by Occupation, Race, and Latinx Origin (percent)

Occupational Category	White	Black	Latinx	Asian
Management, business	18.1	11.7	10.1	18.5
Professional	23.3	20.2	13.3	36.6
Sales	10.2	9.0	9.4	8.2
Administrative support, office	11.1	13.3	11.2	8.8
Construction, extraction	2.9	3.1	10.9	1.3
Installation, maintenance, repair	3.3	2.3	3.6	1.6
Production	5.4	5.9	7.1	5.1
Transportation	5.9	10.4	8.3	4.0
Service	15.9	23.8	24.2	15.8
Farming, forestry, fishing	0.8	0.3	2.0	0.2
Total	100.0	100.0	100.0	100.0

Source: US Bureau of Labor Statistics 2020d.

Note: The table indicates, for example, that 18.1 percent of White people were employed in management and business jobs compared with only 11.7 percent of Black people.

workers are more likely to have higher-paying jobs than are Black and Latinx workers.

The high level of Asian Americans in managerial and professional jobs has led some conservative social scientists to refer to Asian Americans as the "model minority." This controversial concept charges that because Asian Americans can achieve this despite discrimination, neither Black nor Latinx people should need special policies such as affirmative action to help them succeed (D'Souza 1995). This denies the reality of systemic racism against non-Asian people of color.

Given these data, it is not unreasonable to expect that incomes for Black people and Latinx people would be substantially lower than incomes for White people and Asian Americans. Table 4.5 looks at the median incomes for all families in 2019. As predicted, Black ($58,518) and Latinx ($60,927) families earned roughly 60 percent of the income of White, non-Latinx families ($97,101) in 2019. Unfortunately, the Black/White family income gap has been fairly stable since 1959, before the apex of the civil rights movement.

Asian American families, in comparison, make about fifteen cents *more* for every dollar a White, non-Latinx family makes. However, it is important to understand the great variation among Asian American families. In 2015, for example, the median household income of Asian

**Table 4.5   Median Income of Families and Income Ratio in 2019 by
Race/Ethnicity and Family Type**

Race/Ethnicity	All Families	Married Couples	Male Head	Female Head
White, non-Latinx	$97,101	$108,261	$66,184	$49,221
Black	58,518	87,951	52,947	36,115
Asian	112,226	123,516	78,127	66,452
Latinx	60,927	73,166	56,568	37,891
Income Ratio				
Black/White	0.60	0.81	0.80	0.73
Asian/White	1.15	1.14	1.18	1.35
Latinx/White	0.63	0.67	0.85	0.77

Source: US Census Bureau 2019.
Note: As the table indicates, White, non-Latinx families had a median income of
$97,101, and Black families had a median income of $58,518; therefore, the median income
of Black families was 60 percent of the median income of White, non-Latinx families.

Indian families was $100,000, whereas the incomes of Burmese,
Nepalese, and Hmong families were less than $50,000 (Budiman, Cil-
luffo, and Ruiz 2019).

In trying to explain these income differences between racial groups,
many analysts point to differences in family structure. The percentage
of female-headed families (i.e., with no male living regularly in the
home) is much higher among Black people than White people. In 2018,
for example, 55 percent of Black mothers were living in families without a partner, compared with 26 percent of Latinx mothers, 16 percent
of White mothers, and 9 percent of Asian American mothers (US Census Bureau 2018a). Female-headed families have much lower incomes
than either male-headed families (i.e., with no female regularly living in
the home) or married-couple families in which either one or both of the
adults work. Presumably, these differences in family structure could
account for racial differences in income.

Table 4.5 controls for type of family. Reading across the rows,
married-couple families in each racial/ethnic group earn more than
male-headed families, who in turn earn more than female-headed families. Reading down the columns, however, White, non-Latinx families
for each family type earn more than Black and Latinx families. Asian
American families have higher incomes than White people. The high
Asian American family incomes are a result, in part, of having more
family members in the labor force.

The Black/White income gap declines somewhat after controlling for type of family, although when looking at all families, Black people made only 60 percent of what White families made. This same figure was 81 percent for Black married couples, 80 percent for Black male-headed families, and 73 percent for Black female-headed families. This trend for Latinx families is more mixed. Asian American/White comparisons, on the other hand, show *higher* gaps for female-headed families than for married-couple families. The important point to take away from these numbers is that family structure is only a *partial* explanation for racial differences in family income.

These same group differences can also be seen by looking at the incomes of year-round full-time workers in 2019. Table 4.6 shows that the White, non-Latinx median incomes are higher than the incomes of Black and Latinx people but lower than the incomes of Asian Americans. Latinx males made only 62 percent of the income of White males in 2019. Black males made 70 percent of the income of White males. Asian American males, in contrast, made 111 percent of the income of White people. A similar pattern occurred with racial differences in the incomes of women, though the racial gap for women was smaller than the racial gap for men.

Table 4.6 Median Income and Income Ratio of Year-Round Full-Time Workers, Aged Fifteen and Older in 2019 by Race/Ethnicity and Sex

Race/Ethnicity	Male	Female	Female/Male Income Ratio
White, non-Latinx	$65,282	$50,694	0.78
Black	45,590	40,214	0.88
Asian	71,760	58,051	0.81
Latinx	40,360	35,169	0.87
All workers	57,219	46,528	0.81
Income Ratio			
Black/White	0.70	0.79	
Asian/White	1.1	1.1	
Latinx/White	0.62	0.69	

Source: US Census Bureau 2020b.
Notes: As the table indicates, the median income for White, non-Latinx females was $50,694, which is 78 percent of the income of White men. Black women made 79 percent of the income of White women.

Table 4.6 also shows the gender gaps in income within a given race. The female-to-male income gap was highest among non-Latinx White people (0.78) and was lowest among Black people (0.88) and Latinx people (0.87), with Asian Americans falling in the middle (0.81). In other words, among non-Latinx White people, women earned only 78 cents for each dollar a man earned; but Latinx women earned 87 cents for each dollar a Latinx man earned. We will discuss gender differences in more detail in Chapter 6.

We can also look at the trends in racial income gaps over time, as illustrated in Table 4.7. Looking at the income ratio for Black people relative to non-Latinx White people, we can see that the income gap between Black and White men closed slightly from 1967 (0.65) to 2000 (0.78) and then widened again.

In contrast, the income gap between Latinx and White men actually increased between the early 1970s and 2018. The gap between Asian American men and White men has been small or nonexistent between 1990 and 2018.

Table 4.7   Median Income and Income Ratio of Year-Round Full-Time Workers, 1967–2018, by Race/Ethnicity and Sex

	Median Income				Income Ratios		
	Non-Latinx White	Black	Latinx	Asian American	Black/ White	Latinx/ White	Asian American/ White
Males							
1967	$7,396	$4,777	—	—	0.65	—	—
1970	9,223	6,368	8,885[a]	—	0.69	0.73[a]	—
1980	19,157	13,547	13,558	—	0.71	0.71	—
1990	28,881	21,114	19,136	26,765	0.73	0.66	0.93
2000	38,637	30,101	23,778	40,556	0.78	0.62	1.05
2010	54,653	37,724	31,843	52,505	0.69	0.58	0.96
2018	65,282	45,590	40,360	71,760	0.70	0.62	1.10
Females							
1967	4,279	3,194	—	—	0.75	—	—
1970	5,412	4,447	5,925[a]	—	0.82	0.84[a]	—
1980	11,277	10,672	9,679	—	0.95	0.86	—
1990	20,048	18,040	15,672	21,324	0.90	0.78	1.06
2000	28,243	25,089	20,659	30,475	0.89	0.73	1.08
2010	41,332	34,043	29,096	41,920	0.82	0.70	1.00
2018	50,694	40,214	35,169	58,051	0.79	0.69	1.10

Source: US Census Bureau 2020b.
Notes: a. Based on 1974 data. As the table indicates, in 2018, the Black male median income ($45,590) was 70 percent of the White, non-Latinx male median income ($65,282).

Looking at women's incomes, the Black/White gap declined substantially between 1967 and 1980 but then began to increase again. The Latinx/White gap for women, like that for men, grew since the early 1970s. Asian American women, however, continued to earn slightly more than White women. The income trends for Black and Latinx women were not encouraging.

Racial differences in wealth are even more unequal than the differences in income, mainly because wealth is accumulated and passed down generationally, especially through home ownership. Because of generations of housing discrimination and disinvestment in the form of redlining, African Americans have been cordoned off from wealth-building assets.

Table 4.8 shows that in 2019, White households had a median net worth of $188,200 compared with only $24,100 for Black households and $36,100 for Latinx households. This meant that the net worth of Black households was only 13 percent of that of White households, and Latinx households' net worth was only 19 percent of that of White households. Unfortunately, neither the 1984 data nor the 2019 data provide separate figures for Asian Americans.

Comparing wealth differences over time is often problematic because methodologies are not always the same. However, using government figures for 1984 and 2019, the racial gaps were still substantial even though they narrowed. Although everyone had more wealth in 2019, the relative differences between the groups changed only slightly. In 1984, for example, Black household wealth was only 9 percent of White wealth. In 2019 the gap had narrowed to 13 percent, still very large. This is because, as Thomas Piketty (2013) points out, wealth inequality is harder to reduce than income inequality. Wealth creates

Table 4.8   Median Net Worth of Households by Race/Ethnicity, 1984 and 2019

Race/Ethnicity	1984		2019	
	Net Worth	Wealth Ratio[a]	Net Worth	Wealth Ratio
White	$38,915	—	188,200	—
Black	3,342	0.09	24,100	0.13
Latinx	4,871	0.13	36,100	0.19

Sources: Shapiro, Meschede, and Sullivan 2010; data for 2019 come from Bhutta et al. 2020.

Notes: a. Black or Latinx wealth relative to White wealth. In 2019, for example, the median Black wealth was only 13 percent of the median White wealth.

more wealth, so those with greater wealth can use a smaller proportion of their portfolio for marketable goods and services and still have capital left over to pursue other wealth-building opportunities.

Unfortunately, the 2019 wealth data reinforce Piketty's pessimism. Whereas 30 percent of White people said that they had received an inheritance, only 10 percent of Black people and 7 percent of Latinx people said they received an inheritance. White homeownership rates were still much higher in 2019 than the rates for Black people and Latinx people.

It is also important to look at data on poverty. The official poverty threshold in 2019 was $26,172 for a family of four. Since the 1960s, the federal government has taken the Department of Agriculture's annual emergency food budget and multiplied it by three to get the poverty threshold. The actual threshold varies by both family size and number of children.

These data in Table 4.9 show that White people (14.2 million) make up the greatest number of the poor in the United States, followed by Latinx people (9.5 million), Black people (8.1 million), and Asian Americans (1.5 million). Why, then, do social scientists and policymakers see poverty as a greater problem for people of color than for White people?

The reason for this apparent contradiction is that non-Latinx White people make up such a large percentage of the total population. When we examine the poverty rate, the percentage of individuals who fall below the poverty threshold for each group, we find that Black people,

Table 4.9   Individuals Below the Poverty Level and US Poverty Rates in 2019 by Race/Ethnicity

Race/Ethnicity[a]	Number (thousands)	Poverty Rate (%)	People of Color/ White Ratio
White, Non-Latinx	14,152	7.3	
Latinx	9,545	15.7	2.2
Black	8,073	18.8	2.6
Asian	1,464	7.3	1.0
American Indian and Alaska Native[b]	681	27.0	3.7
Total	33,984	10.5	

Source: US Census Bureau 2020c.
Notes: a. Race/ethnicity refers to race alone, except for Latinx people, who can be any race.
b. A total of 681,207 American Indians and Alaska Natives were poor in 2019. Their poverty rate was 27 percent, which is 3.7 times higher than the White rate.

Latinx people, and Native Americans are disproportionately poor. In 2019, 7.3 percent of non-Latinx White people were poor, compared with 18.8 percent of Black people, 15.7 percent of Latinx people, and 7.3 percent of Asian Americans. Even though the White rate of poverty is relatively low, the absolute number of poor White people is large.

Poverty rates have fluctuated year by year, going down when the economy is expanding and increasing during recessions. Between May and September of the 2020 recession, for example, the number of poor people increased between 4 and 6 million people (DeParle 2020). This number would have been even higher if it weren't for the benefits provided by the CARES Act in March 2020.

We are especially interested in the relative differences in poverty rates for different racial groups. Specifically, is the gap in poverty rates between White people and people of color increasing, decreasing, or staying the same? Table 4.10 shows the poverty ratios between White people and people of color from 1980 to 2019. A ratio of more than 1.0 means that people of color had higher poverty rates than non-Latinx White people. A ratio of less than 1.0 means that White poverty was higher than that of people of color. From these data, we find that the Black-White and Latinx-White poverty ratios had decreased over time, meaning that the poverty gap was getting smaller. For instance, in 1980, the Black poverty rate was 3.6 times greater than the White poverty rate, but by 2019 it was only 2.6 times greater. The same trend was true for Latinx people. Asian American poverty remained the lowest among all people of color, declining from being 1.4 times greater than White poverty in 1990 to being 1.0 (i.e., parity) in 2019.

Table 4.10   Race and Ethnicity Poverty Ratios, 1980–2019

Year	Black/White	Latinx/White	Asian American/White
1980	3.6	2.8	—
1990	3.6	3.2	1.4
2000	3.0	2.9	1.4
2010	2.8	2.7	1.2
2019	2.6	2.2	1.0

Source: US Census Bureau 2020c.

Note: For the US Census, Asian American poverty data begin in 1987. To calculate the poverty ratio, we found the percentage of individuals living below the poverty threshold for each group and by decade and divided the poverty rate for people of color by the White poverty rate. According to the data in 2019, the Black poverty rate is 2.6 times greater than the White rate.

Does this represent progress? Although before Covid the United States made significant changes in the economics of poverty, in 2019 Black and Latinx poverty was more than double White poverty. There's still a long way to go. These tables show the complexity of race and poverty. Although poverty has racial undertones, it is a class issue that affects all people living in the United States.

There are also major differences in educational attainment by race and ethnicity. Table 4.11 shows that more than half of Asian Americans had a bachelor's degree or higher in 2019. Only 40 percent of non-Latinx White people, 26 percent of Black people, and 19 percent of Latinx people had bachelor's degrees or higher. At the other end of the spectrum, 31 percent of Latinx people did not finish high school, compared with 15 percent of Black people, 10 percent of Asian Americans, and 8 percent of non-Latinx White people.

In spite of the high level of education among Asian Americans as a group, there are great variations in educational attainment among Asian Americans. In 2015, for example, 72 percent of Asian Indians had at least a bachelor's degree or more compared with less than 20 percent of Bhutanese, Cambodians, Hmongs, and Laotians (Budiman, Cilluffo, and Ruiz 2019).

It is also important to look at trends in educational attainment. Data from the Department of Education show that the Black/White gap in

Table 4.11   Educational Attainment of the US Population Aged Twenty-Five and Older in 2019 by Race/Ethnicity (percent)

Highest Level of Education Reached	Non-Latinx White	Black	Latinx	Asian American
Eighth grade or less	1.4	3.2	15.4	5.0
Some high school	6.6	12.0	16.0	4.7
High school graduate	24.9	29.6	28.4	17.0
Some college	16	18.6	13.6	8.8
Associate degree	11.2	10.6	8.2	6.8
Bachelor's degree	25.0	16.6	13.1	33.3
Master's degree	11.2	7.7	4.4	17.5
PhD	2.3	1.1	0.7	4.9
Professional degree	1.7	0.7	0.6	2.4
Total	100	100	100	100

Source: US Census Bureau 2019.

Note: As the table indicates, 5 percent of Asian Americans and 15.4 percent of Latinx people did not go beyond the eighth grade.

education declined substantially since the 1940s. The Latinx/White gap, in comparison, increased slightly since 1980. The Department of Education doesn't track these data for Asian Americans.

Some of the racial gap in income can probably be explained by differences in educational attainment. What would happen if we controlled for education and then looked at racial differences in income? These data are presented in Table 4.12. There are a lot of numbers here so let us explain. Reading down the columns, we see that for each racial/ethnic group, a higher level of education results in higher incomes. This is true for both males (top half of the table) and females (bottom half). For example, White non-Latinx women who didn't finish high school made $26,202 while those who got a PhD made $100,450.

Reading across each row, we can compare the incomes of each racial/ethnic group at the same level of education. For example, compare the incomes of Black people, Asian Americans, and Latinx people to those of White, non-Latinx people at each level of education. For example, while White non-Latinx males with bachelor's degrees made $79,471, comparable Black males made only $52,545. So, Black males with bachelor's degrees made only 66 percent of what comparable White non-Latinx males made. We see that at every educational level, Black and Latinx people make lower incomes than non-Latinx White people. This is true for both males and females. Asian Americans also tend to make less than comparable non-Latinx White people, although they make as much or more than White people do in six of the sixteen comparisons, especially those with higher educations.

These data show continuing inequalities between White people and non–Asian American people of color. In spite of some dramatic closing of the gap in educational attainment and some minor improvements in the income and wealth gaps, economic inequality remains substantial. Asian Americans have exceeded White people in educational attainment and have come the closest to having parity with White people in terms of income. There is still a lot of work to be done.

Attitudes and Ideology

White people and people of color often have different perceptions of life in the United States, especially when it comes to issues of race and economics. Table 4.13 looks at the responses of White, Black, and Latinx adults during the Covid-19 pandemic and recession during the spring and early summer of 2020. When asked how different groups have been treated, White people are more likely than Black people to

88

Table 4.12 Median Income of Year-Round Full-Time Workers in 2018 by Race/Ethnicity, Sex, and Education

Education/ Sex	Median Income by Sex and Race/Ethnicity				Income Ratios		
	White, Non-Latinx	Black	Asian American	Latinx	Black/ White, Non-Latinx	Asian American/ White, Non-Latinx	Latinx/ White, Non-Latinx
Males							
Some high school	$40,636	$32,047	$29,976	$32,271	0.79	0.74	0.79
High school graduate	50,272	39,303	40,501	40,054	0.78	0.80	0.80
Some college	55,964	45,759	50,244	47,112	0.82	0.90	0.84
Associate degree	60,172	51,151	54,723	50,601	0.85	0.91	0.84
Bachelor's degree	79,421	52,545	81,390	56,432	0.66	1.02	0.71
Master's degree	100,270	75,166	102,483	87,841	0.75	1.02	0.88
PhD	120,934	73,591	120,374	—	0.61	0.99	—
First professional degree	140,108	—	150,784	92,082	—	1.08	.66
Females							
Some high school	$26,202	$24,854	$22,487	$24,009	0.95	0.86	0.92
High school graduate	36,289	30,668	30,364	29,919	0.84	0.84	0.82
Some college	40,296	36,146	41,196	38,113	0.90	1.02	0.94
Associate degree	43,334	37,187	42,009	39,897	0.86	0.97	0.92
Bachelor's degree	59,163	51,573	61,456	49,402	0.87	1.04	0.83
Master's degree	66,834	62,403	80,865	60,244	0.93	1.21	0.90
PhD	100,450	81,650	100,253	—	0.81	1.0	—
First professional degree	102,094	80,050	121,620	—	0.78	1.20	—

Source: US Census Bureau 2020d.
Note: With a bachelor's degree, for example, White females made $59,163 and Black females made $51,573. This means among those with a bachelor's degree, Black females' income was 87 percent of White females' income.

Table 4.13   White, Black, and Latinx Adult Responses to Treatment of Diverse Groups, 2020 (percent agreeing)

Questions	Race/Ethnicity of Respondent		
	White	Black	Latinx
Very/somewhat satisfied about the treatment of different groups			
Blacks	41	21	—
Latinxs	45	26	—
Asians	65	49	—
Arabs	47	34	
Immigrants	43	21	—
My life is thriving	55	48	52
Economic system in the United States is rigged in favor of certain groups	61	81	65
It would be very/somewhat difficult to pay an unexpected expense of $250	42	58	54

Sources: Brenan 2020; Witters 2020; Nguyen 2020.
Note: 41 percent of Whites and 21 percent of Blacks are satisfied with how Blacks are treated.

say they were very or somewhat satisfied. For example, 41 percent of Black people and 21 percent of White people said they were satisfied with how Black people are treated. Unfortunately, the survey did not ask for the opinions of Latinx respondents.

More than half (55 percent) of White respondents felt that their lives were "thriving" compared with 48 percent of Black people and 53 percent of Latinx people. Black and Latinx people were significantly more likely than White people to say that it would be difficult to pay an unexpected $250 expense.

Six in ten White people felt that the economic system was rigged, compared with 81 percent of Black people and 65 percent of Latinx people. Respondents' support for certain presidential candidates had a major impact on answers to this question. Whereas only one-third of Trump supporters said the economic system was rigged, 86 percent of Biden supporters said it was rigged.

White people were also more likely than Black people to have confidence in major institutions in the United States. What follows are some examples of White versus Black respondents' differences in how confident they were: presidency (47 percent versus 13 percent); US

Supreme Court (44 percent versus 27 percent); criminal justice system (24 percent versus 11 percent); and police (56 percent versus 19 percent). One of the few institutions in which Black people showed more confidence than White people was Congress (11 percent versus 15 percent). However, more significant was the low ratings both groups gave to Congress (Jones 2020).

The overall picture from these data is that Black people were having a harder time than White people during this pandemic/recession and had less confidence in major institutions. Black people were also less satisfied than White people about how different racial and ethnic groups have been treated. When data for Latinx attitudes were available, they fell between those for White and Black people.

Traditional Prejudice

There has been a long tradition in the fields of sociology and social psychology of studying racial prejudice. Until recently, most of the studies addressed the issue of White prejudice toward Black people.

The *traditional prejudice* of the past involved White belief in Black biological inferiority and White support of formal racial separation/segregation. Typical measures of traditional prejudice might have asked respondents to agree or disagree with the following statements:

"There should be laws against racial intermarriage."

"Black people and White people should not attend the same schools."

"As a race, Black people are less intelligent than White people."

Most of us would acknowledge that agreeing with these statements would indicate that the respondent was prejudiced.

Most studies have shown that whereas a majority of White people would have agreed with these statements in the 1950s and 1960s, a smaller percentage still agreed with them in the decades after the 1960s. For example, 94 percent of White people disapproved of marriage between Black people and White people in 1958; only 4 percent approved (Carroll 2007). In 2013, however, 84 percent of White people approved of interracial marriage (Newport 2013). The same trend has been shown with many studies of racial stereotypes.

There are several different interpretations of these findings. On the one hand, it's possible traditional prejudice among the White population has, indeed, declined dramatically. Sociologists Daniel J. Hopkins and Samantha Washington (2020) found that anti-Black and anti-Latinx prejudice expressed by White people *declined* after Trump was elected. Members of White supremacist groups such as the Ku Klux Klan (KKK), neo-Nazis, the Proud Boys, and the Oath Keepers were the exception. Sixty percent of Americans believed White supremacists are a growing threat in the United States (Hawkins et al. 2018).

On the other hand, it's possible White people still believe these things but won't say so to an interviewer because it is no longer the socially desirable response. The Pew Research Center found respondents are more likely to acknowledge discrimination on the telephone than on internet surveys (Keeter 2015). Although social desirability is an important factor, we think prejudice against people of color has become much more complicated.

New Prejudice

Many White people today hold other negative and/or distorted attitudes toward Black people and other people of color. Many social scientists argue that since the 1970s, a new form of anti-Black prejudice has replaced the traditional form. This *new prejudice* (often referred to as *new racism*) goes under a variety of different labels—symbolic racism, modern racism, aversive racism, laissez-faire racism, color-blind racism, and social dominance orientation (Feagin 2010; Jones 1997). Although there are some differences between them, discussions of the new prejudice have certain factors in common:

1. A rejection of traditional prejudice and seeing oneself as non-prejudiced
2. A rejection of legal discrimination
3. The belief that racial discrimination is a thing of the past
4. The belief that Black culture causes Black inequality
5. A negative attitude toward Black people based on fear, resentment, and/or ambivalence, usually expressed indirectly

Measures of the new prejudice might include the following statements:

"Black people are getting too demanding in their push for equal rights."

"Discrimination against Black people is no longer a problem."

"Over the past few years, the government and the news media have shown more respect to Black people than they deserve."

"Black people would be more successful if they worked harder."

There is some evidence that a sizeable segment of the White population has attitudes consistent with this concept of a new prejudice. In a Pew Research Center study, for example, respondents were asked how much progress the country has made in giving Black people equal rights with those of White people (Horowitz et al. 2020). In Table 4.14, six in ten White people said the country had gone too far or had been about right. In contrast, 86 percent of Black people and more than half of Latinx people and Asian Americans said the country hadn't gone far enough.

Furthermore, fewer than one-fifth of Republicans said the country hadn't gone far enough, whereas more than one-fourth said the country had gone too far. These findings are consistent with the concept of new prejudice in that only a minority of White people and Republicans don't think more has to be done for Black people to have equal rights.

In another question, Pew asked the sample whether too much, too little, or about the right amount of attention was being paid to race and racial issues (see Table 4.15). White people were twice as likely to say

Table 4.14   In 2020, When It Comes to Giving Black People Equal Rights with White People, Our Country Has . . . (percent)

Type of Respondent	Not Gone Far Enough	Been About Right	Gone Too Far	Total
White	39	42	18	100
Black	86	5	6	100
Latinx	57	28	13	100
Asian American	56	28	15	100
Democrat	78	16	5	100
Republican	17	55	26	100

Source: Horowitz et al. 2020.
Note: 39 percent of Whites and 86 percent of Blacks said our country hasn't gone far enough.

Table 4.15   There Is _____ Attention Paid to Race and Racial Issues in Our Country These Days (percent)

Type of Respondent	Too Much	About the Right Amount of	Too Little	Total
White	51	22	26	100
Black	12	14	73	100
Latinx	30	21	46	100
Asian American	32	33	35	100
White Democrat	14	34	52	100
White Republican	76	17	7	100

Source: Horowitz et al. 2020.
Note: 51 percent of Whites and 12 percent of Blacks say our country pays too much attention to race.

too much attention, compared with too little attention, was being paid to race. Republicans were ten times more likely to say too much attention was being paid to race as compared with too little attention. Black people, on the other hand, were six times more likely to say too little attention was being paid to race than too much.

Those White people who said the country has gone too far, too much attention was being paid to race, and White people were victims of reverse discrimination had attitudes consistent with the new prejudice. They wouldn't use pejorative terms to describe people of color, but they seemed to be saying "Enough, already. We're the real victims. Leave us alone."

A National Public Radio (NPR) poll reported that more than half (55 percent) of White people believed that White people were discriminated against. A much smaller number believed they, personally, had experienced discrimination in employment (19 percent), in pay or promotion (13 percent), or in college (11 percent) (Gonyea 2017).

Some social scientists, especially conservatives, reject the idea of a new prejudice. Traditional prejudice is the only valid type, according to conservatives, and it has diminished (Sneiderman and Carmines 1997). They also see the new prejudice as a misguided liberal attempt to equate conservative ideology with anti-Black attitudes (Roth 1994). According to this argument, it is possible to oppose policies such as affirmative action for philosophical and political reasons without being prejudiced.

Implicit Prejudice
A growing number of social scientists argue that because of stronger social norms *against* being prejudiced, many White people are not even aware they hold such beliefs. *Implicit prejudice* refers to unconscious beliefs not measurable by traditional interviews or questionnaires. Several measures, using electronics and computers, have been developed to measure these unconscious beliefs; though they are too complicated to be discussed here, readers can go to www.implicit.harvard.edu and take the Implicit Association Test for themselves.

The Pew Research Center gave the implicit bias test to Black people and White people and found that members of each race showed a preference for people of their own race (Morin 2015). The same was true in a test of Asian Americans and White people. Although this probably comes as no surprise to anyone, it remains to be seen if implicit bias is a valid concept. It is well known, however, that most people can't help but absorb some of the racist culture in which we live in the United States.

Regardless of the type of prejudice, most social scientists would agree that prejudice involves a set of negative attitudes held by individuals.

People learn these attitudes from families, peer groups, media, schools, and other social institutions. Social psychologists have also argued that racial prejudice serves certain personality functions among White individuals. Given this approach, these negative attitudes would predispose people to discriminate against and/or to reject policies that might benefit communities of color.

Realizing this fact, Charles Pierce, a Black psychiatrist, was disturbed by the daily microaggressions he saw on television. In 1969, he helped create Sesame Street, a show for preschoolers with "the most racially diverse cast that public television has ever seen" and the most successful children's show of all time (Harrington 2019).

Racist Ideology

Eduardo Bonilla-Silva takes a somewhat different approach by arguing that negative racial views are part of a **racial ideology** used to explain and justify racial oppression (2003, 2). This ideology, which he calls *color-blind racism,* consists of four frames (i.e., "set paths for interpreting information"). The *minimization frame* (racism is no longer important) and the *cultural racism frame* (cultural explanations of inequality, e.g., blaming the victim) are consistent with the various approaches to the new prejudice. He also discusses the *naturalization frame,* the belief that "birds of a feather flock together" because of common interests and values. Finally, he discusses the *abstract liberalism frame,* which makes use of the themes of equal opportunity, individualism, and free choice. This last frame, according to Bonilla-Silva, ignores the reality that all races do not have the same access to equal opportunity and free choice. This ideology

> explains contemporary racial inequality as the outcome of nonracial dynamics. Whereas Jim Crow racism [in the South before the 1960s] explained blacks' social standing as the result of their biological and moral inferiority, color-blind racism avoids such facile arguments. Instead, whites rationalize minorities' contemporary status as the product of market dynamics, naturally occurring phenomena, and blacks' imputed cultural limitations. For instance, whites can attribute Latinos' high poverty rate to a relaxed work ethic ("the Hispanics are mañana, mañana, mañana—tomorrow, tomorrow, tomorrow") or residential segregation as the result of natural tendencies among groups ("Do a cat and a dog mix?").

In other words, Bonilla-Silva argues color-blind racial ideology is not the *cause* of racial inequality but the *result* or justification of existing inequality (see also Feagin 2010).

Trump and his supporters, however, created an atmosphere in which traditional prejudice reemerged from the shadows and coexists alongside color-blind prejudice. Some argue Trump represented *continuity* in US politics rather than an aberration (Rauch 2020).

But whether traditional/new prejudice remains a useful distinction remains to be seen, even though some race scholars have already weighed in. Bonilla-Silva (2018) argues that Trump's brand of traditional racism, less commonly used by the US public, didn't invalidate the significance and importance of color-blind racism. He points out that Trump himself used the color-blind racism frame when he referred to himself as "the least racist person you've ever encountered" (Fischer 2016).

Discrimination: Individual and Systemic

In spite of what many White Americans might think, discrimination is not a thing of the past. Previously, we defined discrimination as actions that deny equal treatment and access to people perceived as members of some racial category or group. As we showed in the previous section, a large portion of White Americans no longer see racial discrimination as a serious problem. They typically point to the demise of legal segregation in the South and the passage of numerous civil rights laws at the federal, state, and local levels.

Although substantial progress might have been made in the past half century, racial discrimination is still alive and well. Nowhere has this been more evident in the twenty-first century with the Covid-19 pandemic and the explosion of the Black Lives Matter protests in response to police murders of numerous Black citizens.

During times of fear, scarcity, and conflict, tribalism (an us versus them mentality) rears its ugly head. In the United States, that means traditional, explicit prejudice and racism reemerges. Under the threat of Covid-19, Asian Americans have been experiencing increased racism and xenophobia. In 2021, for example, near Atlanta, Georgia, a White gunman drove to three massage parlors and killed eight victims, six of whom were women of Asian descent. While the motive is inconclusive, this act of violence appears to reflect an intersection of misogyny and White Supremacy (Anti-Defamation League 2021).

Trump set the tone by continually referring to the novel coronavirus as the "Chinese virus." University of California–Los Angeles (UCLA) basketball player Natalie Chou, who is Chinese American, spoke out about the harassment she experienced since the virus was associated with China. In another report, Shyong (2020) found that Asian American restaurants were experiencing slowdowns, possibly avoided because of the association of coronavirus with China. The most extreme form of Covid-19 racism is the reported case of White supremacist groups encouraging their members to spread the virus to cops and Jewish people (Steinbuch 2020).

The Black Lives Matter movement, which emerged after the 2012 fatal shooting of Trayvon Martin, calls attention to both Black mass incarceration and extrajudicial killings by the police and vigilantes. The Floyd murder provides the opportunity to show how a social issue can be understood at different levels by using the discrimination dichotomy we discussed in Chapter 2. If you recall, four Minneapolis police officers stopped Floyd on May 25, 2020, after he allegedly tried to use a counterfeit $20 bill at a convenience store. After handcuffing Floyd and throwing him to the ground, Officer Derek Chauvin kneeled on Floyd's neck for *more than eight* minutes, even though Floyd said he could not breathe, ultimately killing him. The three other officers did nothing to stop this.

In March 2021, just before Officer Chauvin's trial began, the city of Minneapolis approved a $27 million settlement in the wrongful death lawsuit of George Floyd (Hauck and Yancey-Bragg 2021). Likewise, the city of Louisville reached a $12 million settlement with the family of Breonna Taylor (Griffith 2020). In police use of deadly force cases, civil settlements are more common than criminal prosecution.

Chauvin's actions can be seen as an example of **intentional individual discrimination** in that a White officer killed a Black man. It's difficult to know what motivated Chauvin's actions, but he showed blatant disregard for the life of an unarmed Black man. Various news stories reported that other Minneapolis officers also exhibited anti-Black bias in the weeks preceding and following the killing.

Most White people in the United States, including most police officers, also have implicit bias against Black people. This would be an example of **unintentional individual discrimination.** Those not conscious of their bias can behave in biased ways toward people of color.

Aside from the individual-level explanations, it is also important to understand the Floyd killing from a more systemic level that involves discriminatory laws, policies, and practices on behalf of governments and large institutions. One example of **intentional systemic discrimination** is the Blue Wall of Silence, a tacit agreement among police officers not to reveal their colleagues' wrongdoing. This is an example of how police culture reinforces racism. Police officers are often told to target minority communities for criminal activity and to act more aggressively when they do. Police officers are being increasingly militarized to control communities of color.

A fourth type of discrimination is **unintentional systemic discrimination,** in which laws and policies aren't necessarily intended to discriminate but have that effect. Many states have laws, reinforced by police unions, that make it difficult to convict police officers of wrongdoing. Mass incarceration, the dramatic increase in imprisoning people as a result of the anti-drug laws of the 1990s (supported by then-senator Joe Biden), disproportionately affects Black and Latinx people and Native Americans. The origins of most police departments focus on protecting property and the elite. Assuming these policies were not intentionally directed at people of color, which is debatable, nonetheless they negatively affect people of color, so they are examples of unintentional systemic discrimination.

Let's examine the different types of discrimination in more detail. Intentional individual discrimination can range from racial slurs and graffiti to not hiring or unfairly firing to not renting an apartment or granting a home mortgage to physically assaulting people of color. Even though it is difficult to quantify these microlevel actions, some research has linked everyday acts and exposure to racism to disparate health outcomes for Black people, including a shorter life expectancy (Williams, Lawrence, and Davis 2019).

A current example of unintentional systemic discrimination can be seen in how Covid-19 disproportionately affects the Black, Latinx, and Native American populations (Pilkington 2020). Using data from the Centers for Disease Control (CDC), the authors show that people of color are more likely than White people to be infected with Covid-19 and die from it. The explanation involves multiple factors, including people of color being more likely to have underlying conditions, less likely to have access to medical care, more likely to live in crowded housing, and more likely to be in essential jobs that cause them more exposure to Covid-19. In other words, the structures that developed after several centuries of racist policies have made people of color more vulnerable to the disease.

Microaggression, a type of individual discrimination, refers to the intentional acts motivated by prejudice intending to do physical or psychological harm because of group membership. Gallup asked respondents if they had ever experienced a list of microaggressions: people acted as if they were better than you; people acted as if they thought you were not smart; you were treated with less courtesy/respect than other people; people acted as if they thought you were dishonest;

people acted as if they were afraid of you; you received worse service than other people at restaurants or stores (Lloyd 2020). In each category, Black people were most likely to have experienced it, followed by Latinx people, Asian Americans, and White people. For example, one-quarter of Black people experienced people not thinking they were smart, followed by Latinx people (12 percent), Asian Americans (9 percent), and White people (5 percent).

Sometimes, microaggressions are on public display, as when Governor Ralph Northam of Virginia came under fire in 2019 for being accused of wearing a KKK hoodie, which he denied. Later he reported that he wore blackface to imitate Michael Jackson for a performance.

Hate crimes are also examples of individual discrimination. According to research from the Anti-Defamation League (ADL), a century-old nonprofit organization, 2019 was "the sixth deadliest year on record for domestic extremist–related killings since 1970": forty-two murders, 90 percent by White, right-wing extremists. The organization pointed out that the mass shooting in 2019 at Walmart in El Paso, Texas, was the deadliest attack against the Latinx community in modern times (Anti-Defamation League 2019).

According to Federal Bureau of Investigation (FBI) statistics, 7,120 hate crimes were reported in 2018, 60 percent of which were motivated by race, ethnicity, or ancestry. Of this number, 47 percent were motivated by anti-Black bias, 20 percent by anti-White bias, 13 percent by anti-Latinx bias, 4 percent by anti–American Indian or Alaska Native bias, 3 percent by anti-Asian bias, and 2 percent by anti-Arab bias (Federal Bureau of Investigation 2020).

Most social scientists would agree these figures represent a small fraction of the hate crimes actually committed that year because most victims don't report them and because police departments are inconsistent about reporting them to the FBI. The Southern Poverty Law Center (2004), for example, estimated that the true number of hate crimes is fifteen times higher than the official reports.

Employment discrimination against people of color is even more common, although it is impossible to determine the true number of cases. From 2016 to 2019, more than 109,000 complaints alleging race discrimination in employment were filed with the federal Equal Employment Opportunity Commission (EEOC). Hundreds of thousands more were filed at the state level. The overwhelming majority of these cases were filed by people of color. Proving employment discrimination is extremely difficult, either at the EEOC level or in a court of law. Only 12 percent of the cases were resolved in favor of the plaintiff (Equal Employment Opportunity Commission 2020d).

Two additional studies, however, suggest that employment discrimination is widespread. Pager (2003) sent out fictitious résumés that listed the applicant's race to employers in and around Milwaukee, Wisconsin. Half were from Black people, and half were from White people. Within each racial group, half had criminal records, and the other half did not. Other than race and criminal record, the résumés were comparable. The main variable was whether the fictitious applicant would be invited for an interview.

To no one's surprise, White people with no criminal record were most likely to be called in, and Black people with a record were least likely. The most shocking finding, however, was that whereas 17 percent of the White people *with* criminal records were called for an interview, only 14 percent of the Black people *without* a record were called for an interview. In this study, race was a more important factor than having a criminal record.

Building on that study, Pedulla and Pager (2019) examined race and networking in the job-search process. Although both Black and White job seekers use social networks to apply for job opportunities at similar rates, Black job seekers are less likely than White people to know someone at the company to which they are applying and are less likely to have someone in their network contact the employer on their behalf. They conclude that even networking-based job searches, as compared to submitting a résumé to a call for applications, are less beneficial for Black job seekers compared with their White counterparts.

In a second classic study, Sendhil Mullainathan and Marianne Bertrand sent 5,000 résumés in response to employment advertisements in Boston and Chicago (Associated Press 2003; Glenn 2003). Each employer received four résumés. Half of the résumés showed weak employment histories and job skills, and the other half showed strong employment histories and job skills. In addition, half of the résumés had stereotypical Black names such as Lakisha and Jamal, whereas the other half had more White-sounding names such as Emily and John. Each résumé had a phone number with a voice-mail message by someone of the appropriate race and gender.

Once again, race was a factor in who got a callback. The Kristens and Carries got callbacks 13 percent of the time, whereas the Keishas and Tamikas got callbacks less than 4 percent of the time. Having a strong résumé helped White people more than Black people. Among the White-sounding names, having a strong résumé increased the likelihood of getting a callback by 30 percent compared with the weak résumés. For the Black-sounding names, having a strong résumé increased the callback likelihood by only 9 percent.

Another institution criticized for its systemic discriminatory practices is the criminal justice system. Since the 1980s, when President Ronald Regan declared a "War on Drugs," the US prison population has increased by 279 percent, according to the Sentencing Project (2013), a nonprofit organization that works for fair and effective criminal justice reform. Although Black and Latinx people are not the only populations incarcerated, of course, they are disproportionately affected in terms of number of police encounters, arrests, and convictions to length of sentence. For example, even though White and Black people consume about the same amount of drugs, Black people are more likely than White people to be arrested, convicted, sentenced, and incarcerated for the same offense.

Michelle Alexander (2012), a civil rights attorney and professor, points out that by the first decade of the twenty-first century, more Black people were under the supervision of the criminal justice system than were enslaved in the decade before the Civil War. Because mainstream politicians often have difficulty explicitly reversing civil rights gains, she adds, incarcerating Black people became the new method for legal systemic discrimination. In many states, a person who has a felony record can be disenfranchised, denied employment, and barred from public assistance such as affordable housing. In addition to losing important democratic rights, they are branded a felon, which amounts to a scarlet letter. Because Black people and Latinx people are more likely to have felony records, they are more likely to be negatively affected by these discriminatory policies.

To the extent that using felony records as an instrument of discrimination is intentional, this would be an example of intentional systemic discrimination. If policymakers simply wanted to punish those with felony records, regardless of race, it would be a case of unintentional systemic discrimination.

Although many people believe contemporary discrimination stems from individual attitudes (Neel 2017), the following cases highlight the importance of systemic discrimination. In one of the largest journalistic investigations into real estate sales practices, "differential treatment and possible racial steering" was uncovered in Long Island, New York. One investigator found a real estate agent discouraging a White homebuyer from considering a predominantly Black neighborhood by referring to "gang activity" but encouraging a Black homebuyer to consider the same neighborhood by referring to the residents as the "nicest people" (Freiberg 2019). Because of racial steering, comparable Black neighborhoods are estimated to be about one-fourth the property value of White neighborhoods (Perry 2019).

Native Americans have also been victims of systemic discrimination. In July 2020, the US Supreme Court ruled that more than one-third of eastern Oklahoma was actually part of the Muscogee (Creek) Indian Nation according to an 1833 treaty broken by the US government. Although the ruling concerned who would prosecute alleged criminals, the tribal court or the local and state courts, there are broader implications as well (Healy 2020). Eleven years earlier, Congress approved $1.4 billion to settle claims that Native American lands were illegally sold to non-Indian individuals in the late nineteenth and early twentieth centuries (Southhall 2010).

In a case involving higher education, the Maryland Legislature approved a $580 million dollar settlement for four historically Black colleges and universities (HBCUs). This was a thirteen-year-old lawsuit that alleged racial discrimination by means of duplicating course offerings across the Maryland state universities, when each institution is supposed to fulfil a different mission (Harriot 2020).

Readers might wonder why there is so much talk about fines in these race discrimination cases and no talk of jail sentences. That's because employment discrimination is a violation of civil law, not criminal law. Employers can't go to jail for refusing to hire or promote someone because of his or her race, but they can be sued.

A high-profile case that comes to mind—although not a clear-cut case of racial discrimination—is that of Colin Kaepernick, the National Football League (NFL) quarterback who kneeled during the national anthem in 2016 to protest police brutality and racial injustice. Although he has tried out for multiple teams, he hasn't been re-signed. Although the cause of his rejection cannot be proven, it is apparent that his unemployment had everything to do with his racial politics. In 2018, Kaepernick and his teammate Eric Reid filed grievances against the NFL. After months of negotiations, the two parties reached a settlement in the collusion lawsuit. Little is known about the case because the settlement was subject to a confidentiality agreement. Since then, the NFL has rescinded its decision to punish athletes for kneeling.

* * *

Although many readers might believe racial prejudice and discrimination are no longer problems in the twenty-first century, the empirical data presented in this chapter show that people of color still lack respect and equality of opportunity in the United States. This was true before Trump was elected in 2016, and it has gotten worse with the dual pandemics of Covid and White extremism. The Biden administration seems more interested in confronting racial inequality. Although civil rights laws have not eliminated discrimination and hateful violence, they have made them easier to prosecute.

5

Immigration:
Borders and Bridges

"We are a nation of immigrants." How many times have
you heard the lines from poet Emma Lazarus inscribed on the Statue of
Liberty: "Give me your tired, your poor, your huddled masses, yearning
to breathe free"? These stanzas underscore the reality that most people
come to the United States looking for a better opportunity and trying to
escape poverty or persecution.

Most of us think of immigration to this country beginning with the
British settlement of Jamestown, Virginia, in 1607. However, of course,
Native Americans are estimated to have migrated to North America
around 15,000 years ago. Spanish explorers and conquistadors tried to
colonize Florida in the 1500s, founding the oldest city in United States,
St. Augustine, preceding Jamestown by fifty years (Feuerherd 2017).

Most historians date the arrival of the first Africans in mainland
North America to 1619. Imagine the Lazarus words written on an African
American Statue of Liberty, showing her breaking the chains of bondage.

Despite White mythology, we have a history of anti-immigrant attitudes and policies (xenophobia) that dates back to the nation's founding
in the late eighteenth century. This hostility toward foreigners ebbed
and flowed before and since. During the colonial period, over half of
European immigrants were indentured servants (PBS, 2003). The 1790
Naturalization Act grants citizenship to "any Alien being a free white
person" who had lived in the country for two years; immigrants of color
were excluded, as were enslaved human beings. This would change in
the 1860s with the passage of the Fourteenth Amendment, granting
freedmen and women along with those born in the United States a right
to citizenship (but not yet the right to vote, for women).

The use of Chinese labor for the development of the Western railroad system was met by resistance from European Americans who

thought their jobs were being taken. The Chinese Exclusion Act of 1882 barred most immigrants from that country.

Even White European immigrants have a history of stigmatization. The first major wave of European migrants occurred in the 1820s. These immigrants came from Northern and Western Europe, especially Germany and Ireland. In the 1880s the second wave of immigrants arrived, mostly from Southern and Eastern Europe. These Polish, Italian, and Jewish immigrants, like the Irish before them, were seen as racially inferior to native-born Whites in the late nineteenth and early twentieth centuries because they were thought culturally different from the other European immigrants.

Migration declined drastically in the 1920s because the National Origins Act of 1924 placed strict quotas on immigrants, favoring those from Northern and Western Europe. Japanese Americans, regardless of their citizenship or immigration status, were forced into "internment" camps during World War II. These and other anti-immigrant actions are now viewed by most as stains on US history.

During the past fifty years, there has been increasing concern with illegal immigration from Mexico and Central America, with immigrants from the Middle East after the bombing of the World Trade Center in 2001 and the attacks on 9/11, with the changing racial composition of immigrant groups, and with admitting refugees from war-torn and poverty-stricken countries around the world. All this preceded the 2016 election of President Donald Trump, although he raised xenophobia to new levels.

We have added this new chapter to the third edition of this book because immigration has become such a controversial issue, especially since 2016. Although we could have discussed immigration in the previous chapter, on racism, we decided not to because Chapter 4 deals with the twin concepts of race and ethnicity. This chapter deals mainly with the issue of nationality, though race is also involved. We feel that in this moment and time, the issue of nationality and immigration is posing its own significant social and political challenges and vision for the country for twenty-first century reformations. As we mentioned in Chapter 4, the US Census Bureau predicts that by 2050, White people in the United States will become a numerical minority, largely because of immigration.

Terminology

The term **immigrants** refers to people moving from one country to another to settle in the latter. The term *alien*, used in some legal documents in the United States, has taken on a more pejorative meaning because it also refers to creatures from outer space. Demographers who study immigration sometimes refer to immigrants as *foreign born.*

Most immigrants are in the United States legally; that is, they have whatever documents are needed to enter the country for work, family reunions, as refugees, or as political asylum seekers. When immigrants here temporarily apply for and are granted full citizenship, they are known as naturalized citizens. They have the same rights as all other citizens, except for the right to be vice president or president of the United States.

Some immigrants, as many as 11 million, do not have the proper documents and are here illegally. A variety of terms is applied to this group: illegal aliens/immigrants, undocumented immigrants, unauthorized immigrants, and others. In the not-too-distant past, those who crossed the Rio Grande River into the United States from Mexico were called *wetbacks,* although this pejorative term is not widely used today. We will use the term **undocumented immigrants** to refer to those people who moved to the United States and are here without the necessary legal documents.

Several other terms are also important. **Refugees** are people forced to leave their country to escape war, persecution, or natural disasters. Many legal definitions are narrower, focusing mainly on political and religious persecution. Refugees in the United States may request **political asylum,** meaning government protection because they left their countries as political refugees. All those granted political asylum are refugees, but not all refugees are granted political asylum.

Finally, the dictionary definition of **xenophobia** is the fear and/or hatred of foreigners or anything that seems foreign. In a related term, *Merriam Webster's* defines **nationalism** as a sense of national consciousness, exalting one nation above all others and placing primary emphasis on promotion of its culture and interests as opposed to those of other nations or supranational groups. Trump's "Make America Great Again" slogan was an example of nationalism. His anti-immigrant comments and policies against immigrants were examples of xenophobia.

US nationalism is linked to race, and Whiteness specifically, because many citizens hold that the founding documents such as the Declaration of Independence, the Constitution, and the Bill of Rights were written for and by White people. Today's xenophobia is also often racialized because criticism is leveled against migrants of color coming from Mexico and Central America. But there is also economic nationalism: "Bring back our jobs!" being an example.

Descriptive Statistics

During the presidential campaign of 2016, Trump referred to undocumented immigrants (pejoratively called "illegal aliens") as rapists, drug smugglers, criminals, and terrorists. He promised to build a wall along the 1,500-mile border with Mexico, paid for by Mexico, and to ban all Muslim immigrants. His attempt to fan the flames of xenophobia and racism was a major factor in his winning the election. Most of the claims and policies he implemented during his presidency were based on inaccurate and distorted beliefs about who immigrants are and how they behave.

Rhetoric that focuses on racial animus has been used by Republicans since Richard Nixon employed it in the 1970s. The "Make America Great Again" slogan was first introduced by Ronald Reagan in the 1980s. Historian Sarah Churchwell (2018) explains in an interview with the *Smithsonian Magazine* that the "America First" slogan, although complicated in US history "stopped being a presidential slogan [by the 1930s], and it began to be claimed by extremist, far-right groups who were self-styled American Fascist groups, like the German American Bund and the Klan." In the 1970s, Nixon revived rhetoric that focused on racial animus and called it the "Southern Strategy," because it was intended to help him win White votes.

After Trump's inauguration, he failed to get the money to build his wall, but he did succeed in blocking immigration from some Muslim-majority countries though an executive order often referred to as "the Muslim ban." In an attempt to slow immigration along the US-Mexico border, the Trump administration detained children and separated them from their families. Because of their fear of Immigration and Customs Enforcement (ICE) and deportation, many immigrants flocked to "sanctuary cities" (cities in which the police would not turn immigrants over to ICE) for safety.

For international students enrolled at universities, ICE issued a temporary modification to the Student and Exchange Visitor Program (SEVP) that stated international students risked "immigration consequences" if they didn't enroll in at least one in-person class and that they couldn't take a full course of study online despite the pandemic. The same requirement was not imposed on US students. This decision was quickly rescinded after protest and court challenges from Harvard University and the Massachusetts Institute of Technology.

According to 2017 data analyzed by the Pew Research Center (Connor and Budiman 2019; Kohut 2019), 44 million people in the United States were foreign born, accounting for 12.6 percent of the population.

This referred to people who came to the United States many decades ago as well as new arrivals. Back in 1890, 14.8 percent of people in this nation were foreign born, the highest on record. The percentage of foreign-born people fell to a low of 4.7 percent in 1970 and then began climbing again to the present day.

There has been a dramatic change in immigrants' region of origin since 1960. As the data in Table 5.1 show, in 1960, two-thirds of immigrants came from Europe, with only 9 percent from Latin America and the Caribbean and another 3 percent from Asia. By 2013, slightly more than half of the foreign born came from Latin America and the Caribbean and more than one-fourth from Asia. The European percentage had plunged to 13 percent. The once predominantly White immigrants to the United States have been replaced by immigrants of color.

Slightly fewer than one-quarter of these immigrants were estimated to be undocumented in 2017 (see Table 5.2), about 10.5 million people. The number of undocumented immigrants had increased between 1990 and 2007 and then declined. The number of undocumented immigrants from Mexico, South America, Europe, and Canada is declining, whereas the number from Central America and Asia is increasing.

The number and percentage of undocumented immigrants in the labor force is increasing, as is their time spent in the United States. Although it is tempting for purposes of comparison with the native-born population to lump all immigrants into one workforce pool, the diversity within the immigrant population is important. For example, Table 5.3 shows that the median household income for immigrants in 2016 is about $5,000 less than for the native-born workers ($53,200 and

Table 5.1   Region of Origin of Foreign-Born US Residents, 1960 and 2013 (percent)

Region of Origin	1960	2013
Latin America/Caribbean	9	52
Asia	3	27
Europe	67	13
Africa	< 1	4
Other regions	21	5
Total	100	100

Source: Kohut 2019.
Note: In 1960, 9 percent of the foreign born were from Latin America/Caribbean region; in 2013, that had increased to 52 percent.

Table 5.2   Characteristics of Undocumented Immigrants in the United States, 1990–2017

Characteristic	1990	1995	2007	2017
Number (thousands)	3,500	—	12,200	10,500
Percentage of all immigrants	—	—	—	23
Region of origin declining (thousands)				
Mexico	—	—	6,950	4,950
South America	—	—	900	775
Europe/Canada	—	—	650	500
Region of origin increasing (thousands)				
Central America	—	—	1,500	1,900
Asia	—	—	1,300	1,450
In labor force (thousands)	—	3,600	—	7,600
Percentage of labor force	—	2.7	—	4.6
Average time in United States (years)	—	7.1	—	15.1

Sources: Passel and Cohn 2019; Radford and Krogstad 2019.

$58,000, respectively). However, disaggregating the data by country of origin, we see a wide range of household incomes, from $41,500 for Mexican Americans to $78,000 for Asian Americans. This corresponds to differences in educational attainment, with only 6 percent of Mexican American immigrants having a BA or more compared with 52 percent of Asian American immigrants.

Two-thirds of all immigrants aged sixteen or older are in the labor force, about the same percentage as native-born workers. An even higher percentage of undocumented immigrants are in the labor force: 72 percent. Legal immigrants account for 13 percent of the labor force, whereas undocumented immigrants account for 5 percent.

Immigrants are overrepresented in several industries, including agriculture (29 percent of all agricultural workers), construction (25 percent), food services (23 percent), personal services (22 percent), leisure/hospitality (20 percent), and manufacturing (19 percent). Most recent immigrants work in the lower-paid, non-unionized sectors of these industries (Radford and Noe-Bustamante 2019).

Finally, many immigrants come to the United States to earn money to send to their families back in their countries of origin. The amount of this remittance is staggering. More than $148 *billion* was sent from the United States to other countries in 2017 (Pew Research Center 2019). The top five recipient countries were Mexico ($30 billion), China ($16 billion), India ($12 billion), the Philippines ($11.billion), and Vietnam

Table 5.3 Educational Attainment and Median Household Income in 2016 by Nativity and Region of Birth

Nativity and Region of Birth	Education (percent distribution)					Median Household Income
	No High School Degree	High School Degree Only	Some College/ Two-Year Degree	Bachelor's Degree or Higher	Total	
US born	9	28	31	32	100	$58,000
Foreign born	27	22	19	30	100	$53,200
Mexico	56	25	13	6	100	$41,500
South/East Asia	15	15	17	52	100	$78,000
Europe/Canada	12	22	24	43	100	$65,000
Caribbean	24	31	25	20	100	$44,000
Central America	48	26	16	9	100	$43,000
South America	15	24	25	32	100	$56,000
Middle East	14	20	20	47	100	$53,000
Sub-Saharan Africa	13	20	28	40	100	$52,000
Other	15	25	27	34	100	$81,950

Source: Radford and Noe-Bustamante 2019.
Note: 9 percent of US-born people and 27 percent of foreign-born people did not complete high school.

($8 billion). Other countries in the top ten were Guatemala, Nigeria, El Salvador, the Dominican Republic, and Honduras.

These data clearly show that immigrants, both documented and undocumented, come to the United States to work to support their families here and in their countries of origin. In addition, immigrants are a diverse group in terms of income, education, and country of origin.

Attitudes and Ideology

Trump criticized immigrants during the 2016 presidential campaign when he said, "When Mexico sends its people, they're not sending their best. . . . They're sending people that have lots of problems, and they're bringing those problems with us. They're bringing drugs. They're bringing crime. They're rapists. And some, I assume, are good people."

A qualitative study of immigrant youth found that Latinx youth experienced negative emotions when statements like these were made by Trump (Despres, Cliff, 2020). Given these comments, along with the Trump administration's zero-tolerance immigration policies, it's surprising that attitudes toward immigrants in the general population were relatively positive, according to public opinion polls.

The Pew Research Center asked a national sample whether immigrants "strengthen the country because of their hard work and talents" or whether they "weaken the country by taking jobs, housing, and healthcare" (Jones 2019). In 2019, 62 percent of the respondents believed that immigrants strengthened the country, whereas only 28 percent selected the "weaken" response. This was a significant change from 1994, when the figures were reversed: 63 percent said immigrants burdened the United States, and only 31 percent said they strengthened it.

The results, however, differed dramatically when the respondents' political party was considered. In 1994, Democrats and Republicans had similar responses in terms of beliefs about immigrants strengthening the country, 30 percent and 32 percent, respectively. In 2019, 83 percent of Democrats said immigrants strengthened the country, compared with only 38 percent of Republicans. Since 2016 there seemed to be a decline in the percentage of Republicans selecting the strengthening response, perhaps in reaction to the Trump's anti-immigrant rhetoric.

Age was also a factor in this response, with millennials (born between 1981–1996) being the most likely to indicate the strengthening response (75 percent) and the "silent generation" (born before 1946) being the least likely (44 percent). Again, there appeared to be a decline in all age groups in terms of selecting the strengthening response since 2016.

The Pew survey also asked people to select between two options: "America's openness to people from all over the world is essential to who we are as a nation" or "If America is too open to people from all over the world, we risk losing our identity as a nation." Of the respondents, 62 percent selected the "openness" option, and 33 percent selected the "losing identity" option. In response to another question, 69 percent expressed sympathy toward undocumented workers, whereas 29 percent said they were not sympathetic. The same difference in political affiliation was found in all of the questions, with Republicans selecting the more anti-immigrant responses (Brockway and Doherty 2019).

In a different kind of question, the Pew survey asked respondents about their *knowledge* about immigration. For example, they asked whether most immigrants in the United States were here legally or illegally (Pew Research Center 2018b). Most respondents *overestimated* the percentage of undocumented immigrants. Of the sample, 42 percent said most immigrants were undocumented, and 47 percent said most immigrants were here legally. Pew's estimates were that only one-quarter of immigrants are here without legal papers. It is not unusual for White people to overestimate the size of subordinate racial and ethnic groups.

Once again, political party makes a difference. Almost half (47 percent) of Republicans said most immigrants are undocumented, compared with more than one-third (36 percent) of Democrats. Whites are the most likely to say most immigrants are here legally (48 percent), followed by Blacks (43 percent) and Latinxs (33 percent). It's ironic that Latinx people are most likely to get the question wrong, even though they are the most likely to be immigrants.

Some standard criticisms of immigrants, especially of undocumented immigrants, preceded Trump and his supporters. One is that undocumented immigrants bring crime to the United States, even though the conservative CATO Institute and FactCheck.org review of countless studies have shown that crime rates among undocumented immigrants are the same or lower than those of the native-born population (Farley 2018; Nowrasteh 2019).

The Pew survey also asked if undocumented immigrants were "more likely" or "no more likely" to commit crimes than US citizens. Of Democrats, 80 percent selected the correct response (i.e., no more likely to commit crime), compared with only 46 percent of Republicans. Younger adults and those with more education got the correct answer more often than older people and those with less education (Pew Research Center 2018b).

The Pew Research Center then compared the answers on the crime question to the answers on the question of whether there are more legal than undocumented immigrants. Both questions addressed knowledge, not attitudes. Among those who knew that most immigrants are here legally, more than three-fourths also said that the undocumented were no more likely to commit crimes than US citizens; that is, they got both questions right. Among those who got the first question wrong, only 53 percent got the crime question right. This trend was true for members of both political parties.

A second standard accusation is that immigrants take jobs from native-born people. Recall that more than three-quarters of respondents in 2019 said that *undocumented* immigrants mostly fill jobs US citizens don't want. Almost two-thirds said the same about *legal* immigrants. Although there were sharp differences between Republicans and Democrats, even most Republicans said that immigrants take jobs native-born people don't want (Cohen 2019; Krogstad, Lopez, and Passel 2020; Yaffe-Bellany 2019).

Another controversial topic concerns interacting with immigrants who don't know English. Three-quarters of respondents in 2019 said they came into contact with non-English speakers "often" or "sometimes." Of those who came into contact, almost three-quarters said they weren't bothered by the lack of English, whereas just more than one-fourth said they were bothered. These are more tolerant responses than when the question was asked in 1993. In 2019, even most Republicans (59 percent) said they weren't bothered by non-English speakers, compared with 85 percent of Democrats (Pew Research Center 2018b).

These data suggest that Trump's anti-immigrant rhetoric appealed to a large minority of Republicans and a smaller minority of Democrats. We believe Trump used anti-immigrant rhetoric to exacerbate and play on racial tensions, although his supporters would probably disagree. As the data show, the overall direction of attitudes toward immigrants seemed to be getting more tolerant. And assuming these responses were not just socially desirable answers, we might see these attitudes translate into more positive policies in several years, after Trump was voted out of office.

Finally, it is important to understand the causes of immigration. How many times have you heard the statement, "We can't take care of the whole world. Let them solve their own problems"? The reality is that US foreign policy has helped to create problems in other countries, which causes immigration. When the Vietnam War ended in 1975, for example, thousands of Vietnamese who supported the US side flocked to the United States as refugees (Sassen 1989; Lappe 2019).

In 2018 and 2019, tens of thousands of Hondurans, Guatemalans, and Salvadorans fled their countries because of poverty and violence. The United States has had a long history of economic and political interventions in Central America, usually on the side of rich landowners and the political elite. US-owned agribusinesses have driven workers off the land and increased unemployment. M-13, the violent gang Trump often talked about, was actually formed in Los Angeles and taken back to Central America when gang members were deported.

In short, the flow of immigrants to the United States won't be stopped until conditions in the countries we exploit improve. The United States helped to cause the problems, and we should be part of the solution.

Discrimination

The discussion of discrimination against immigrants is complex. On the one hand, many employers actively discriminate against immigrants in hiring, promotion, and pay. In 2019 alone, the Equal Employment Opportunity Commission (EEOC) received almost 12,000 complaints of what they call "national-origin" discrimination (Equal Employment Opportunity Commission 2020b). Unfortunately, the Federal Bureau of Investigation (FBI) doesn't have a separate national-origin category for tabulating hate crimes.

On the other hand, some industries including personal services, food services, and hospitality actively recruit immigrants, both legal and undocumented, because they want people who will work for low pay and are less likely to complain about harsh working conditions out of fear of deportation. Although this is not discrimination in the traditional sense, it is part of a structure of exploitation that benefits employers. It's also significant that low wages are often blamed on the immigrants rather than the employers. There's little outrage in public opinion against employers who pay janitors, dishwashers, and farmworkers such low wages to increase their profits.

Prior to the 2016 election, both Democratic and Republican administrations passed legislation that restricted immigration. In 1996 because of the growing concern over undocumented immigrants in the country, President Bill Clinton signed the Illegal Immigration Reform and Immigrant Responsibility Act. After the September 11, 2001, terrorist attacks by Osama Bin Laden on the Twin Towers in New York City, President George W. Bush signed into law the PATRIOT Act. This law was supposed to improve the capacity and ability of the government to surveil, detain, and deter terrorists (i.e., Muslims) within the United States, which also resulted in the surveillance of US citizens. Many critics and social scientists argued that the PATRIOT Act amounted to racial profiling.

The administration of Barack Obama began deporting immigrants in large numbers, and he was known by critics as the "deporter in chief." On a more positive note, Obama adopted Deferred Action for Childhood Arrival (DACA) by executive order and supported legislation for "dreamers," children of undocumented immigrants raised in the United States, to have temporary citizenship and a path toward permanent citizenship.

The Trump administration was more explicit in its attempt to reduce and control immigration. Taking a zero-tolerance position, the White House website articulated the administration's immigration policy in this way: "To restore the rule of law and secure our border, President Trump is committed to constructing a border wall and ensuring the swift removal of unlawful entrants. To protect American workers, the President supports ending chain migration [i.e., family reunification], eliminating the Visa Lottery, and moving the country to a merit-based entry system. These reforms will advance the safety and prosperity of all Americans" (White House 2020).

In pursuit of these goals, Trump made an end-run around Congress to appropriate money to begin building a wall, banned immigration from a number of predominantly Muslim countries, made it more difficult for immigrants to claim political asylum, separated children of asylum seekers from their families, reduced the number of refugees that could be admitted, and increased deportations. Some of these policies were upheld by the courts, and some were not (Ballotpedia 2020; Denvir 2020; Ibe 2020).

Trump also tried to end the DACA program by executive order. Many of the "dreamers" came to the United States when they were young and know little if anything about their countries of origin. The US Supreme Court upheld DACA in 2020.

Trump also instituted a "wealth test" for prospective immigrants to prove that they would not have to rely on government assistance after they arrived; that is, they would not become "public charges." When asked about the Statue of Liberty quote about the tired, poor, and huddled masses, the acting head of ICE said: "Give me your tired and your poor who can stand on their own two feet and who will not become a public charge." We would argue that these are all examples of intentional systemic discrimination because they are policies and practices that intentionally targeted, disadvantaged, and harmed immigrants.

During the first few weeks of his administration, President Joe Biden issued a number of executive orders intended to overturn many of Trump's immigration policies. He called for a hundred-day moratorium on deportations, a sixty-day pause on building the border wall, an increase in the number of refugees that would be admitted, an end to the ban on immigration from certain predominantly Muslim countries, a pledge to preserve the DACA program, the elimination of the "public charge" rule, a speed-up of the naturalization process, and an attempt at family reunification (Libowsky and Oehlke 2021).

However, there are limits on what Biden can do through executive orders. For example, a federal judge blocked the deportation moratorium. There are also complexities in the wordings of some of the executive orders, some policy changes will take time, and other policies have to be approved by Congress. In early 2021, the Biden immigration policy was still a work in progress.

6

Men and Women: Why Feminism Still Matters

Gender conflicts are different from the class and race conflicts we discussed in previous chapters. People of different classes and races often live separate lives and often don't have direct interactions with each other—and if they do have contact, it is often in impersonal ways. Men and women, in contrast, often live together in families and have intimate contact with each other. Most children know both male and female peers as well as adult relatives. Despite this more personal contact, gender conflict has some of the same structural issues as do race and class conflict: **occupational sex segregation, discrimination,** and unequal pay.

In the past two decades, several well-publicized books and articles have argued that male supremacy has substantially diminished. In 2000, Lionel Tiger published *The Decline of Males: The First Look at an Unexpected New World for Men and Women.* Nine years later, the cover story of the October 2009 issue of *Time* magazine was "The State of the American Woman." The subhead of the lead articles stated: "What unites men and women matters more than what divides them as old gender battles fade away" (Gibbs 2009, 25). A decade later, Andrew Yarrow (2018) published *Man Out: Men on the Sidelines of American Life.*

Is male supremacy really on the way out? We think not. As this book was being completed, for example, the *Wall Street Journal* carried a patronizing op-ed that began: "Madame First Lady—Mrs. Biden—Jill—kiddo: a bit of advice. . . . Any chance you might drop the 'Dr.' before your name?" The author, Joseph Epstein (2020), was objecting to the fact that Biden had only a PhD and was not a medical doctor. In addition to insulting the millions of PhD holders around the world, it's difficult to imagine Epstein using this same condescending tone addressing a man.

Terminology

Although people including social scientists often use the terms *sex* and *gender* interchangeably, they are really quite different. **Sex** refers to the physical and biological differences between the categories of male and female. This includes hormones, reproductive organs, body shape, and other physiological characteristics. **Gender** refers to the behavior and identity presentation that is culturally defined as appropriate and inappropriate for males and females. Gender, therefore, is largely socially constructed, whereas sex has *some* basis in physical reality.

Although this distinction seems simple enough, the reality is considerably more complex. The ability to bear and breastfeed a child, for example, is clearly related to sex differences. Most women can do it, and men can't. But what of the fact that in most societies, including our own, women tend to do most of the child-care work, both at home and in the paid labor force? Most social scientists would argue that this has to do with gender, not with sex. Physically, men can care for children and feed them out of bottles, either with formula or with expressed breast milk. Culturally, however, this is often defined as women's work.

Of course, sex (i.e., physiological) differences are not always clearly defined. A small minority of the population is **intersexed,** in that they have physical attributes of both males and females. At birth, it is sometimes difficult to tell if an intersex baby is male or female because the genitalia are ambiguous. For years, pediatricians had suggested that surgery be performed on babies so that they could be assigned to one sex or the other. Is someone with both a penis and a vagina a male or female? What happens when hormones are inconsistent with chromosomes? In our society, we think we have to know which of the two sexes this individual *really* belongs to.

Anne Fausto-Sterling (1993, 2000) has done some fascinating work on this topic. In a well-known 1993 article, she argued that there are really five sexes, not just two. "True hermaphrodites," who have one testis and one ovary, she called *herms.* Female pseudohermaphrodites, who have ovaries and some aspect of male genitalia but who do not have testis, she called *ferms.* Male pseudohermaphrodites, who have testes and some aspects of female genitalia but who don't have ovaries, she calls *merms.* Rather than trying to force the herms, ferms, and merms into the categories of male and female, Fausto-Sterling argues to leave them separate. In a subsequent article, Fausto-Sterling (2000) rejects her own five-sexes argument and says that sex should not be seen as a simple continuum: "Sex and gender are best conceptualized as points in a multidimensional space. . . . The medical and scientific communities have yet to adopt a language that is capable of describing such diversity" (107).

Transgender people, for example, feel that their gender identity doesn't match their physiological body. These are physiological men who feel female or physiological women who feel male. Others might identify more as gender fluid or nonbinary because they don't accept the either/or binary of masculine and feminine. They prefer using the pronouns they, them, and theirs.

One of our female students who identifies as a **lesbian** has a female partner who is transgender. Although the partner always dressed in male-like clothing, at one point the partner decided to live as a male by taking a male name and insisting that everyone use the masculine pronoun to refer to him. After a few months, the partner returned to the female name. Eventually, she began the complex transition process that will end in her becoming a female-to-male **transsexual**.

Although the overwhelming majority of people in 2014 identified with the sex-appropriate definitions of masculinity and femininity, a small proportion did not. More importantly, millennials were more likely to identify as "nonconforming" or "equally masculine and feminine" than gen Xers or baby boomers (Johfre and Saperstein 2019). This suggests that gender roles might be relaxing somewhat.

When transgender people take hormones, begin to live as the opposite sex, and have sex-change operations, they are transsexuals. This raises some really confounding questions. Is a male-to-female transsexual a woman or a man? Should one refer to a transsexual as he or she? Which bathroom should she or he use? If a female-to-male transsexual has sexual relations with the man he used to be married to, is this a heterosexual, or homosexual, relationship? As we said earlier, the male/female dichotomy is not as simple as it seems (Boylan 2003). We will discuss transgender people further in Chapter 7.

Gender is even more fluid than sex. First, gender varies from culture to culture. Men, for example, tend to be much more emotionally and physically expressive in many Latinx cultures than White men in the United States. Gender also varies in a single culture over time; for instance, men in our country are much more involved with their children now than they were fifty years ago. Gender also varies within a culture: working mothers have always been more prevalent among working-class and Black women than among middle-class and White women. Gender is also situational. Men hugging each other on the athletic field is not viewed in the same light as that action on a street corner.

Some cultures have more than two genders. In many Native American cultures, the *berdache* is a biological male who assumes the feminine gender. S/he dresses and acts like a woman and is a highly respected member of the community seen as having special spiritual powers. Young men have to participate in a special ceremony to assume the berdache status.

In traditional Albanian culture, a woman can become a "sworn virgin" and assume the role of a man. This would occur when the males in the extended family have died or been killed in war, leaving no one to assume property ownership and to care for the rest of the women. The sworn virgin dresses and acts like a man and is recognized as such by the rest of the community, in part because of the sacrifice she has made (Bilefsky 2008).

As Michael Kimmel writes,

> [Our gender] identities are a fluid assemblage of the meanings and behaviors that we construct from the values, images, and prescriptions we find in the world around us. Our gender identities are both voluntary—we choose to become who we are—and coerced—we are pressured, forced, sanctioned, and often physically beaten into submission to some rules. We neither make up the rules as we go along nor do we glide perfectly and effortlessly into preassigned roles. (2004, 194)

We will discuss gender diversity in more detail in Chapter 7.

Understanding gender relations involves more than just culture. It also involves power and hierarchy. Most social scientists who write about gender would define **patriarchy** as a hierarchical system that promotes male supremacy. This refers to a set of institutions organized in a way that benefits the majority of men over the majority of women in the economy, the political system, the family, and so on. Of course, not all men benefit from patriarchy in the same way, and not all women are hurt in the same way. In fact, a small group of wealthy white men are at the top of the patriarchy, and they have power over all women and most men. This is known as **intersectionality,** or the ways race, class, and gender intersect to produce disparate outcomes.

Many men reject the concept of patriarchy by saying that they don't *feel* powerful. Working-class and poor men have little power as a result of their *class* position, and men of color have little power because of their *race*. However, most of these men, along with White middle-class men, do exert power over women in their families and communities.

Domestic violence and rape are usually male-initiated behavior in all communities. The concept of patriarchy is not an all-or-nothing concept. Different men benefit in different ways.

Finally, we come to the concept of **sexism**. Like the concept of racism, discussed in Chapter 4, the term *sexism* has been used in a variety of ways since the 1960s. Some see sexism as an ideological support for patriarchy. This refers to a set of cultural beliefs and personal attitudes that support male control of major social institutions. According to this view, believing that men should be the head of the household or that women should not supervise men on the job would be considered sexist. Later in the chapter, we will discuss the way social psychologists measure sexist beliefs.

Though others agree, they would extend *sexism* to include both attitudes and behaviors that hurt women. According to this argument, those who refuse to hire women as managers or those who commit violence against women are exhibiting sexist behavior. It's not just the attitudes that are the problem, it's also the behavior.

Still others use *sexism* synonymously with patriarchy to describe a gender-based system of oppression that includes ideology and attitudes as well as behavior and institutional organization. In this case laws and religious practices that discriminate against women would be considered sexist. The important point here is that most writers in the diversity field agree on a system that oppresses women, and part of that system consists of ideology and attitudes. The disagreement is over what labels to use.

In this book, we use the more inclusive term *sexism* to mean a system of oppression based on gender. This includes prejudice and discrimination against women as well as ideologies and policies that keep women second-class citizens. Since only women are oppressed because of their gender, only men and male-dominated institutions can be sexist, according to this definition. Women, of course, can be prejudiced against men and, in some limited cases, have the power to discriminate against men. As much as we might dislike these behaviors, they are not sexist because women as a group do not have the power over men as a group in the oppressive system. Marilyn Frye (1983) argued that though men can (and should) be unhappy because they are not allowed to express their feelings, this is not the same as being oppressed.

Finally, we come to the concept of **feminism,** often associated with what came to be known as the women's liberation movement. Although most young women believe in equal pay for equal work, the need for more women in traditionally male jobs, and the need for men and women to share in child care and housework, many would not describe themselves as feminists. What does feminism mean, and why is it so threatening to so many?

More than twenty years ago, bell hooks wrote, "A central problem within feminist discourse has been our inability to either arrive at a consensus of opinion about what feminism is or accept definition(s) that could serve as points of unification" (hooks 2000, 238). This statement is still true today because there are many different types of feminism. Barbara Price and Natalie Sokoloff (2004, 2–3), for example, describe five approaches to feminism:

- Liberal feminism, the most mainstream of the perspectives, stresses the importance of equality of women with men within the existing political and economic structures in society. From this perspective, the most common cause of gender inequality is identified as cultural attitudes with regard to gender role socialization. . . .
- Radical feminism identifies male dominance and control as the cause of gender inequality and argues that these must be eliminated from all social institutions. Men's control of women's sexuality and the norm of heterosexuality are identified as the core of women's oppression. . . .
- Marxist feminism views women's oppression as a function of class relations in a capitalist society. . . . Women are twice burdened in this analysis; they are oppressed economically in low-wage jobs in the labor market and they are oppressed by their unpaid family responsibilities centered around reproductive labor (childbearing, child care, husband care, and housework). . . .
- Socialist feminists combine the Marxist and radical feminist perspectives and identify as the causes of gender inequality and women's oppression both patriarchy and capitalism in public as well as private spheres of life. . . .
- Multicultural feminists . . . introduce the concept of "intersectionalities" to understand the interlocking sites of oppression; they examine how the categories of race, class, gender, and sexuality in intersecting systems of domination rely on each other to function. (See also Lorber 1998.)

Ecofeminists, not discussed by Price and Sokoloff, argue that a patriarchal society will exploit its resources without regard to long-term consequences as a direct result of the attitudes fostered in a patriarchal/hierarchical society. Ecofeminists often draw parallels between the treatment of the environment and the treatment of women.

These diverse viewpoints can be frustrating for those who want a short answer to the apparently simple question: What do feminists believe? Fortunately, Margaret Anderson (2003, 9) tries to identify some of the issues common to all forms of feminism:

> Feminism begins with the premise that women's and men's positions in society are the result of social, not natural or biological factors. . . . Feminists generally see social institutions and social attitudes as the basis for women's position in society. Because in sexist societies these institutions have created structured inequities between women and men, feminists believe in transforming institutions to generate liberating social changes on behalf of women; thus, feminism takes women's interests and perspectives seriously, believing that women are not inferior to men. Feminism is a way of both thinking and acting; in fact, the union of action and thought is central to feminist programs for social change. Although feminists do not believe that women should be like men, they do believe that women's experiences, concerns, and ideas are as valuable as those of men and should be treated with equal seriousness and respect. As a result, feminism makes women's interests central in movement for social change.

This view of feminism is quite different from the popular stereotype of bra-burning, man-hating lesbians many people wrongly associated with feminism. Although many lesbians are feminists, the overwhelming number of feminists are not lesbians. Although some feminists hate men, most do not. The bra-burning stereotype stems from a 1968 protest of the Miss America pageant in Atlantic City, New Jersey. Some of the two hundred protesters threw bras and high heels into a "freedom trash can" to oppose the sexual objectification of women; they never burned them (Albert and Albert 1984).

So, what is the "true" definition of feminism? Our own inclination is to go with Anderson's general comments cited above and to read about the different types of feminism in Ollenberger and Moore (1998), Lorber (1998), or Renzetti and Curran (1999). For those who absolutely need a formal definition, here's a short, snappy one provided by bell hooks (2000, 240): feminism is "a movement to end sexist oppression."

Feminist as a self-identity fell out of favor in the late twentieth century even though an increasing number of women behaved like feminists. In 2020, in contrast, 61 percent of women and 40 percent of men said feminism describes them very well or somewhat well (Barroso 2020b).

Descriptive Statistics

In discussing gender in the United States, it is important to understand that the majority of women work in the paid labor force. We use the phrase "work in the paid labor force" to underscore the importance of work that women perform in the home as well; they just don't get paid.

According to the most recent data in Table 6.1, 58.9 percent of women aged twenty or older worked in the paid labor force in 2019, compared with 71.6 percent of similarly aged men. Almost three-quarters of women with children under eighteen worked in the paid labor force, including two-thirds of women with children under six. The stay-at-home housewife/mom is becoming a role of the past.

There has been a sea change in the labor force participation rates of women since the 1950s. Table 6.1 shows that in 1948, only 31.8 percent of all women worked in the paid labor force. In other words, the labor force participation rate for women almost doubled between 1948 and 2000. There has been a slight decline since then. This increasing labor force participation rate applies to single women, married women, and women with young children.

Table 6.1   Labor Force Participation Rates of People Aged Twenty and Older, 1948–2019, by Race/Ethnicity and Sex (percent)

	Total Population		White		Black		Latinx	
Year	Male	Female	Male	Female	Male	Female	Male	Female
1948	88.6	31.8	—	—	—	—	—	—
1960	86.6	37.6	—	—	—	—	—	—
1970	82.6	43.3	82.8	42.2	78.4[a]	51.6[a]	85.9[a]	41.3[a]
1980	79.4	51.3	79.8	50.6	75.1	55.6	84.9	48.5
1990	78.2	58.0	78.5	57.6	75.0	60.6	84.7	54.8
2000	76.7	60.6	77.1	59.9	72.8	65.4	85.3	59.3
2009	74.8	59.2	75.3	60.4	69.6	63.4	83.2	59.2
2019	71.6	58.9	71.8	57.9	68.1	61.4	80.2	60.4

Source: US Bureau of Labor Statistics 2020e.
Notes: a. 1973 data. As the table indicates, in 2019, 71.6 percent of males and 58.9 percent of females were in the labor force.

In comparison, men are *less* likely to be in the labor force now than in 1948. Although men have always been more likely than women to work in the paid labor force, the gap has been steadily declining.

These same trends are true when White, Black, and Latinx people are compared. The labor force participation rates of White, Black, and Latinx women have increased dramatically since 1970, when data gathering for these groups began. The rates for White and Black men have declined. Latinx men, who have the highest participation rates of any of the race/gender groups, have been employed at a stable rate.

The 2020 recession resulting from the Covid-19 pandemic caused a disproportionately large number of women to drop out of the labor force entirely (Alon et al. 2020; Gupta 2020). Between August and September, 1.1 million people dropped out of the labor force. Of these, more than 800,000 (almost three-quarters) were women. Of these women, 358,000 were Black and Latinx.

During most recessions, men's unemployment rates go up faster than women's. The 2020 recession was different. Although both men's and women's unemployment increased, women's unemployment increased faster.

Men and women also have different types of jobs. Table 6.2 shows the gender composition of the labor force at different skill levels. At low-skilled jobs such as truck driving, grounds maintenance, and miscellaneous labor, workers are more than 75 percent male, whereas nurses aides, psychiatric and home-health-care aides, personal-care aides, and maids and house cleaners are more than 75 percent female. At high skill levels, computer software engineers, construction managers, and miscellaneous computer workers are more than 75 percent male, whereas elementary and middle school teachers, registered nurses, and counselors are more than 75 percent female. This differential distribution of men and women in the labor force is called *occupational sex segregation*.

These data clearly show occupational sex segregation is alive and well in the twenty-first century. Even more sobering is the fact that these data are *improvements* over segregation in the past. One common way to measure occupational sex segregation is through the Index of Dissimilarity, which ranges between 100 and 0. An index value of 100 means that all jobs are either totally male or totally female. A value of 0 means that all jobs have equal numbers of males and females. Ariane Hegewisch and her colleagues (2010) show that the Index of Dissimilarity declined from about 68 in 1970 to 50 in 2002, a substantial

Table 6.2   The Three Largest Occupations for Broad Skill Level and Gender Composition, 2019

Skill Level of Job	Gender Composition of Occupation		
	Male-Dominated (25% or less female)	Mixed (25.1–74.9% percent female)	Female-Dominated (75% or more female)
Low-skilled	Truck drivers and driver/sales workers; grounds maintenance workers; miscellaneous laborers	Janitors and building cleaners; customer service representatives; retail sales workers	Nursing, psychiatric, and home-health aides; personal-care aides; maids and housekeeping cleaners
Medium-skilled	Construction laborers; security guards and gaming security officers; carpenters	First-line retail supervisors and managers; miscellaneous managers; cashiers	Secretaries and administrative assistants; bookkeeping, accounting, and auditing clerks; receptionists
High-skilled	Computer software developers; construction managers, miscellaneous computer workers	Accountants and auditors; lawyers; postsecondary teachers	Elementary and middle school teachers; registered nurses; counselors

Source: US Bureau of Labor Statistics 2020f; adapted from Hegewisch et al. 2010.

decline in segregation. The 2009 figure was 51, which shows that previous progress had all but ceased. There is still a long way to go.

Educational attainment has also shown substantial changes. As Table 6.3 illustrates, in 1940 only about one-fourth of the US population aged twenty-five or older had graduated from high school, and less than 5 percent had graduated from college. In that same year, women were somewhat more likely than men to graduate from high school but less likely than men to graduate from college.

By 2018, things had changed dramatically. In the United States, 90 percent of the population had graduated from high school, and 35 percent had graduated from college. High school graduation rates for men and women have been equal since 1970. More importantly, the male/female gap in college graduation diminished substantially. In 1940, men were 1.45 times more likely than women to graduate from college. By 2018, that gap had not only narrowed but had reversed to 0.98: more women than men are graduating from college.

Despite these developments, men and women in the United States do not get the same type of education. In 2016, for example, women

Table 6.3   Males and Females Aged Twenty-Five Years and Older Who Completed High School and College, 1940–2018

Year	Completed Four Years of High School or More			Completed Four Years of College or More		
	Males (%)	Females (%)	M/F Ratio[a]	Males (%)	Females (%)	M/F Ratio[a]
1940	22.7	26.3	0.86	5.5	3.8	1.45
1950	32.6	36.0	0.90	7.3	5.2	1.40
1960	39.5	42.5	0.93	9.7	5.8	1.67
1970	55.0	55.4	0.99	14.1	8.2	1.72
1980	69.2	68.1	1.02	20.9	13.6	1.54
1990	77.7	77.5	1.00	24.4	18.4	1.33
2000	84.2	84.0	1.00	27.8	23.6	1.18
2009	86.2	87.1	0.98	30.1	29.1	1.03
2018	89.4	90.2	0.99	34.6	35.3	0.98

Source: Snyder, deBray, and Dillow 2020.

Note: a. Male rate divided by the female rate; for example, in 2018, 89.4 percent of males aged twenty-five and older and 90.2 percent of females aged twenty-five and older had graduated from high school or more. The high school graduation rate of males was 99 percent of the rate of females.

earned 81 percent of the bachelor's degrees in education and 70 percent of the degrees in English and literature but only 27 percent of the degrees in engineering and 15 percent of the degrees in computer science and information systems (Snyder, de Brey, and Dillow 2020). Needless to say, engineers and computer professionals make a lot more money than teachers. Although women earned more PhDs than men in the United States since 2002, the same disciplinary differences occur.

These differences in fields of study and occupational distribution certainly have implications for gender differences in income. Table 6.4 shows median incomes for year-round, full-time, male and female workers between 1960 and 2019. Seasonal and part-time workers, most of whom are women, are excluded from these data. In 1960, women earned only 61 percent of what men earned. By 2019 the gap had narrowed so that women made 82 percent of what men made—still a substantial gap. Most of this progress occurred since 1980 and was the result of the declining wages of men. At this rate, women would not achieve wage parity for at least 30 years!

Table 6.4   Median Income of Year-Round Full-Time Workers Aged Fifteen and Older, by Sex

Year	Male	Female	F/M Ratio[a]
1960	$5,358	$3,257	0.61
1970	8,966	5,323	0.59
1980	18,612	11,197	0.60
1990	27,678	19,822	0.72
2000	37,252	27,462	0.74
2009	49,164	37,234	0.76
2019	60,876	50,129	0.82

Source: US Census Bureau 2020b.
Note: a. Female income divided by male income; for example, in 2009, the female median income was 76 percent of the male income.

It is also important to disaggregate these data by race/ethnicity. In Table 4.7 in Chapter 4, the data for race/gender groups were presented from 1967 to 2019 and comparisons were made between races *within* a single sex; that is, the incomes of Black men were compared with the incomes of White men. We can compare the incomes of the two sexes within a given race using the same raw data. Table 6.5 compares the incomes of White women with the incomes of White men.

By reading down each column, we can see that for White, Black, and Latinx people, the income gap between men and women has closed somewhat. In 1967, White women made only 58 percent of the income of White men. By 2018, White women made 78 percent of the income of White men. The male/female gap among Whites was still substantial, but it had closed some. The same general patterns exist for male/female income differences among Black and Latinx people. However, the data for Asian Americans show fluctuations between 1990 and 2018, although the income gap in 2018 was similar to that in 1990.

Because statistical data can be somewhat sterile, another way to view the income inequality between men and women is using the concept of the "Equal Pay Day," or the date on the following year that the average woman has to work year-round, full-time to earn the same annual income as the average man earns the previous year. Using the 2019 income data, for example, the average woman would have to work until March 31, 2020, to earn the same as the average man would earn by December 31, 2019. Equal Pay Days for Asian American, Black, Native American, and Latinx women were February 11, August 13, October 1, and October 29, respectively (Equal Pay Day 2020; Leisenring 2020).

Table 6.5   Median Income of Year-Round Full-Time Female Workers Compared with Male Workers, 1967–2018, by Race/Ethnicity (as percentage)

Year	White	Black	Latinx	Asian American
1967	58	67	—	—
1970	59	70	67	—
1980	59	79	71	—
1990	69	85	82	80
2000	73	83	87	75
2009	77	82	88	83
2018	78	88	87	81

Source: Calculated from data in Table 4.7 in Chapter 4.
Note: For example, in 2018, Black women who worked year-round full-time made 88 percent of the income that comparable Black men made.

Next, we control for education. In Table 4.12 in Chapter 4, we presented the incomes of year-round, full-time workers by race/ethnicity, sex, and education and then compared racial/ethnic differences in income. Using these same data, we can compare gender differences in income in Table 6.6. In all comparisons but one, women have lower incomes than comparable men.

For example, non-Latinx White women with a bachelor's degree earn only 74 percent of the income of comparable men. The comparable

Table 6.6   Women's Income Compared with Men's Income for Year-Round Full-Time Workers in 2018, by Education and Race/Ethnicity (as percentage)

Education	White	Black	Asian American	Latinx
Some high school	64	77	75	74
High school graduate	72	78	75	75
Some college	72	79	82	81
Associate degree	72	73	77	79
Bachelor's degree	74	98	76	88
Master's degree	67	83	79	69
PhD	83	111	83	—
Professional degree	72	—	81	—

Source: US Census Bureau 2020b.
Note: Data calculated using median incomes from Table 4.12. For example, Black women with a bachelor's degree earn 98 percent of what Black men with a bachelor's degree earn.

figures for women of color with bachelor's degrees are as follows: Black women, 98 percent; Asian American women, 76 percent; and Latinx women, 88 percent. At each level of education, the gender gap for people of color is generally lower than it is for non-Latinx Whites.

Unfortunately, the gender gap does not decrease as the level of education increases. Some of the income differences between men and women are a result of the sex-segregated labor force, in which women are overrepresented in lower-paying jobs. What would happen if we compared male and female incomes in the same occupations? Fortunately, a report by the Institute for Women's Policy Research (IWPR) allows us to do this (see Table 6.7).

IWPR looked at the largest occupations for both male and female full-time workers in 2019 (Institute for Women's Policy Research 2020). Looking at the last column in Table 6.7, we see that four of the five largest occupations for women were more than three-quarters female. In contrast, three of the five largest occupations for men were less than 20 percent female. Men and women still don't work in the same jobs.

Table 6.7 also shows that for both male and female occupations, men tend to have higher weekly incomes than women do. For drivers/sales workers and truck drivers, the largest male-dominated occupation, women's weekly earnings were slightly more than three-quarters the income of men. Out of the more than 120 occupations IWPR studied, only 5 showed women's incomes as more then men's.

The sex-segregated labor force also has implications during the Covid-19 pandemic. One out of three jobs held by women have been deemed essential, compared with only one out of four jobs held by men. For example, three-quarters of social workers and health-care workers are women as well as half of essential retail workers. This is especially true for women of color (Robertson and Gebeloff 2020).

Women are underrepresented in leadership roles as well. In the 117th Congress, elected in 2020, only 27 percent of the two houses were female: 24 percent of the Senate and 27 percent of the House of Representatives. The House had the highest percentage of women in US history (Blazina and DeSilver 2021; Center for American Women and Politics 2019).

The Center for the Study of Women in Television and Film looked at women's representation in film and television (Lauzen 2019a, 2019b). The data in Table 6.8 tell two stories. In the 2019 films, men are more likely than women to be represented as protagonists and major

Table 6.7   The Gender Wage Gap in the Five Largest Occupations for Men and Women in 2019 (full-time workers only)

Occupation/Gender	Median Weekly Earnings		Women's Earnings as a Percentage of Men's Earnings	Share of Women Workers in Occupation
	Women	Men		
Women's Occupations				
Elementary, middle school teachers	$1,042	$1,161	89.8	79.8
Registered nurses	$1,217	$1,256	96.9	87.9
Secretaries, administrative assistants	$763	$795	96.0	93.4
Managers, other	$1,317	$1,725	76.3	40.3
Nursing, psychiatric, home-health aides	$556	$588	94.6	87.5
Men's Occupations				
Drivers/sales workers, truck drivers	$660	$861	76.7	5.8
Managers, other	$1,317	$1,725	76.3	40.3
Laborers and freight, stock and material movers, handlers	$567	$657	86.3	20.5
Construction laborers	—	$724	—	2.9
Software developers, applications and system software	$1,718	$1,920	89.5	19.5
All full-time workers	$821	$1,007	81.5	44.7

Source: Institute for Women's Policy Research 2020.
Note: Female teachers made $1,042 a week, and males made $1,161. Female teacher earnings were 89.9 percent of male teacher earnings, and 79.8 percent of teachers were female.

characters and have speaking roles. Second, the male-female gap is smaller in 2019 than in 2002.

In a second study of broadcast, cable, and streaming television in 2018–2019, a similar pattern emerged when it came to female major characters and speaking roles. In addition, only 31 percent of the behind-the-scenes jobs and only 25 percent of program creators were women.

Even Barbie dolls have been moving away from the impossibly thin, White, blond look since the 2000s; there are now dolls with a variety of

Table 6.8   Male and Female Characters in Selected Roles in Top-Grossing Films, 2002 and 2019 (percent)

Year	Protagonist[a]		Major Character[b]		Speaking Role[c]	
	Male	Female	Male	Female	Male	Female
2002	—	16	73	27	72	28
2019	43	40	63	37	66	34

Source: Lauzen 2019a.
Notes: a. Data do not add to 100 percent because some films had an ensemble of protagonists, or characters from whose perspective the story is told.
b. Appeared in more than one scene and are instrumental to the narrative of the story.
c. Speaking at least one line.

skin tones, hair textures, and shapes. They even sell Barbies in wheelchairs. According to Mattel, a curvier Black Barbie with an Afro was one of the top-selling Barbies in 2019 (Cramer 2020).

Despite some genuine progress, there is a long way to go to achieve economic parity for men and women.

Attitudes and Ideology

Unlike the longer tradition of research into racial prejudice, social scientists only began to systematically study prejudice toward women since the 1970s. Although public opinion pollsters and feminist social scientists have discussed negative stereotypes and attitudes toward women for decades, this has largely been done outside of the discourse of the social psychology of prejudice.

In 2017, for example, the Pew Research Center (Parker, Horowitz, and Stepler 2017a) asked a sample of US adults the following open-ended question: "What traits or characteristics do you think people in our society value most for men/women?" Respondents could list up to three traits for each sex.

The results in Table 6.9 show dramatic differences for what is valued for men and women. The top two desirable traits for men were honesty/morality (33 percent) and professional/financial success (23 percent). The top two traits for women were physical attractiveness (35 percent) and empathy/nurturing/kindness (30 percent). As you read down both lists, you can see how gender-stereotyped male traits such as ambition/leadership are twice as likely to be mentioned for males (19 percent) than for females (9 percent). Conversely, gender-

Table 6.9   Respondents Who Say Society Values a Trait in Men or
Women, 2017 (percent)

Values Most for Men		Values Most for Women	
Honesty/morality	33	Physical attractiveness	35
Professional/financial success	23	Empathy/nurturing/kindness	30
Ambition/leadership	19	Intelligence	22
Strength/toughness	19	Honesty/morality	14
Hard work/good work ethic	18	Ambition/leadership	9
Physical attractiveness	11	Hard work/good work ethic	9
Empathy/nurturing/kindness	11	Professional/financial success	8
Loyalty/dependability	9	Loyalty/dependability	7
Intelligence	8	Competence/ability	7

Source: Parker, Horowitz, and Stepler 2017a.
Note: For example, 33 percent said honesty/morality was an important trait for men,
but only 14 percent said it was an important trait for women. Columns will not add up
to 100 percent.

stereotyped female traits such as physical attractiveness are three
times more likely to be mentioned for females (35 percent) than for
males (11 percent).

These findings should be seen in the light of how gender stereotypes have been changing. Eagly and her colleagues (2019) studied how
these stereotype lists have changed by combining the results of sixteen
different national polls between 1946 and 2018. The poll questions
asked whether men or women were *better* at a variety of different traits.

Respondents were more likely to say that women are better at
empathy/nurturing/kindness than men in 2018 than they were in the
1940s. In terms of ambition and courage, men were ranked higher on
this dimension than women in the 1940s and in 2018, but there was an
increase in those who said the two genders were equal in ambition and
courage. When it came to intelligence, the male advantage in the 1940s
was replaced by an increasing number of people who saw men and
women as equally intelligent. Unfortunately, this study did not look at
the ratings of physical attractiveness or some of the other categories
mentioned in Table 6.9. Gender stereotypes can change over time.

The 2020 presidential campaign provided examples of how some
gender stereotypes still prevail. During the Democratic presidential primary, Kamala Harris and other women candidates were criticized for
being too ambitious. After the vice-presidential debate, Harris was
described by critics as "unlikeable." "It's something of a tightrope:

Stereotypically feminine behavior can lead voters to see women as more likable but less of a leader, while stereotypical masculine behavior can make voters see them as more of a leader but less likable" (Astor 2020). Harris was also criticized for being Black by being referred to as "Aunt Jemima" by one Southern politician and as "angry," "mean," "aggressive," and "disrespectful" by former president Trump.

Trump and President Joe Biden present two different images of masculinity (Bennett 2020; Faludi 2020). "Macho Man" was the song played at most of Trump's rallies. He bragged about his accomplishments (regardless of whether they were true), he was verbally aggressive toward critics, he not only refused to wear a mask during the Covid-19 pandemic but made fun of Biden for wearing one, and he boasted about "dominating" the virus although most US citizens disapproved of how he handled the pandemic.

Biden, in contrast, was seen as a fatherly or grandfatherly figure, a protector of his family and his country. He would get us through the pandemic with a combination of strength, compassion, and empathy. Unity was also a major theme. Every now and then, hints of a strongman image would emerge, such as when he'd challenge opponents to a pushup contest. Although Trump and Biden expressed different forms of masculinity, both were part of mainstream culture.

It is also important to know how people view the position of women in today's United States. The Pew Research Center also asked whether men or women have it easier these days (Horowitz, Parker, and Stepler 2017). Table 6.10 shows that although the majority of men and women say there is no difference these days, 41 percent of women but only 28 percent of men say that men have it easier. Younger people are more likely than older people to say men have it easier. In addition, almost half of those identifying as Democrats say men have it easier compared with less than one-fifth of Republicans.

Another Pew study asked how far the country has come in equal rights for women (Horowitz, Parker, and Stepler 2017). In Table 6.11, more than half of all adults said that the country didn't go far enough, a third said it has gone the right amount, and a tenth said it had gone too far. Men were less likely than women (49 percent versus 64 percent) to say the country hasn't gone far enough and more likely (12 percent versus 8 percent) to say it had gone too far. Republicans were more than four times as likely as Democrats (18 percent versus 4 percent to say the country has gone too far, whereas Democrats are more than twice as likely as Republicans (69 percent versus 26 percent) to say that the country hasn't gone far enough.

Table 6.10 Attitudes About Whether Men or Women Have It Easier, 2020 (percent)

	Men Have It Easier	No Difference	Women Have It Easier	Total
All adults	35	56	9	100
Men	28	58	14	100
Women	41	54	5	100
18–36	52	45	3	100
37–52	37	58	5	100
53–71	37	57	5	100
72–89	31	61	8	100
Republicans	19	68	12	100
Democrats	49	45	6	100

Sources: Horowitz, Parker, and Stepler 2017.
Note: For example, 28 percent of men and 41 percent of women say men have it easier.

Those with more education were more likely than those with less education to say that the country hadn't gone far enough. Self-identification as a feminist was a substantial determinant on attitudes. In Table 6.11, Republican feminists (of both sexes) were twice as likely as Republican nonfeminists to say that the country hasn't gone far enough. The gap between Democratic feminists and nonfeminists was smaller but in the same direction.

The Pew survey also asked whether differences between men and women are because of biology (i.e., essentialism) or society (i.e., social construction). "Most women who see gender differences in the way people express their feelings, excel at work, and approach parenting believe those differences are mostly based on social expectations. Men who see differences in these areas tend to believe biology is the driver" (Horowitz, Parker, and Stepler 2017b).

Scarborough, Sin, and Risman (2019) look at how attitudes toward women in society changed between 1977 and 2016 by studying 27,000 respondents in the General Social Survey. "Traditionals" believed men should be dominant in both politics and family life, whereas "egalitarians" believed men and women should be equal in both spheres. "Ambivalents" believed men should be dominant in one sphere and there should be equality in the other.

In 1977, 59 percent of the respondents were traditionalists, 22 percent were egalitarians, and 19 percent were ambivalents. In 2016, the

Table 6.11   **How Far the United States Has Gone in Terms of Women Having Equal Rights, 2020 (percent)**

	Didn't Go Far Enough	Is About Right	Went Too Far
All adults	57	32	10
Men	49	37	12
Women	64	27	8
High school or less[a]	41	46	11
Some college[a]	53	37	10
BA+[a]	58	31	10
Republicans	33	48	17
Nonfeminists	25	—	—
Feminists	49	—	—
Democrats	69	26	4
Nonfeminists	60	—	—
Feminists	85	—	—

Sources: Horowitz, Parker, and Stepler 2017; Horowitz and Igielnik 2020; Minkin 2020.
Note: a. 2017 data.

data had changed dramatically. Only 7 percent were traditionalists, 69 percent were egalitarians, and 24 percent were ambivalents.

Younger people, women, Blacks, and the better educated were the most likely to be egalitarians. Older people, men, Whites, and the less educated were the most likely to be traditionalists.

Because there is a variety of ways in which prejudice toward women is expressed, psychologists have developed different ways to measure it. Consider the following statements:

"Sons in a family should be given more encouragement to go to college than daughters."

"Women should worry less about their rights and more about becoming good wives and mothers."

Agreeing with these statements indicates a type of traditional anti-woman prejudice (Spence, Helmreich, and Stapp 1973).

As a result of the changing attitudes toward women, it became less fashionable in the late twentieth and early twenty-first centuries to express these beliefs. However, that didn't mean antiwoman prejudice had disappeared. Consider the following statements:

"Women often miss out on good paying jobs because of sexual discrimination."

"It is easy to understand the anger of women's groups in the United States."

"Government and news media have been showing more concern about the treatment of women than is warranted by women's actual experience."

A prejudiced person would disagree with the first two items and agree with the third. These items are considered examples of modern antiwoman prejudice because "they support the maintenance of the status quo of gender inequality" (Swim and Campbell 2001, 221).

Unfortunately, the Trump era brought the reemergence of the more traditional prejudice, and it is often difficult to distinguish between the two. The important point to take away from this discussion is that prejudice toward women is a complex phenomenon. A person can be prejudiced even if he or she doesn't endorse traditional gender stereotypes and even if he or she believes a man is not complete without a woman. These beliefs also reinforce the inequality associated with patriarchy.

Discrimination

Although recent US public opinion polls show that two-thirds of respondents believe discrimination against women is still a problem, these views are not consistently held among all sectors of the population. Horowitz and Igielnik (2020) asked a national sample of adults to select which of these options is a greater problem: people *see* gender discrimination where it really *doesn't* exist, or people *don't* see gender discrimination where it really *does* exist. Whereas 85 percent of Democrats chose the second option, only 46 percent of Republicans did. Within each political orientation, women were more likely to see discrimination as a problem than men were.

The evidence shows discrimination is still a serious problem. The income data presented earlier in this chapter clearly shows women earn substantially less than men, even with the same education and in similar occupations. However, though these findings should raise suspicions, they do not *prove* discrimination exists. The pay gap could be a result of sex differences in amount of time out of the labor force, level of education, subspecialization within a given job, occupational sex segregation, and so on. In large-scale studies, when these factors are considered, the male/female income gap generally declines but is still substantial (General Accounting Office 2003; Weinberg 2004). At least some of this unexplained income gap is certainly the result of discrimination. Whether one examines discrimination at the individual, institutional, or structural level, the evidence clearly shows discrimination is alive and well.

A national survey in early 2017 asked men and women whether they had experienced different types of gender-based discrimination (National Public Radio, Robert Wood Johnson Foundation, and Harvard T. H. Chan School of Public Health 2017). In several cases in Table 6.12, men and women experienced about equal rates of discrimination in applying for jobs and considering moving because of housing discrimination. In other cases, women were more than twice as likely as men to say they experienced discrimination in sexist language, while at a doctors' office or health clinic, in pay/promotion, as sexual harassment/threats, as violence, and in seeking housing. Of the respondents, 37 percent of women said they experienced sexual harassment, but the survey did not provide any data for men.

A second national survey shortly after the 2016 presidential election asked women whether they had experienced a range of sexist events (Perryundem 2017). The responses, showing the percentage of women who experienced these events "at least once in a while," were shocking. Of the respondents, 76 percent had heard sexist language, 71 percent had felt unsafe as a woman, 68 percent reported feeling they were treated with less respect because of their sex, 58 percent felt judged as a sexual object, and 54 percent said they had been touched by a man in an inappropriate way without their consent.

One of the fascinating findings showed that married men tended to underestimate the number of times married women experienced sexist events. In terms of inappropriate touching, for example, 49 percent of married women said they had been inappropriately touched, but only 30 percent of married men believed their wives had been inappropriately touched.

The workplace is another common place in which to experience discrimination. In 2019 the Equal Employment Opportunity Commission (EEOC) resolved 26,647 complaints of employment-related sex bias discrimination (Equal Employment Opportunity Commission 2020c). Of these complaints, 84 percent were dismissed because of insufficient evidence or for technical reasons. The remaining 16 percent of cases were decided in favor of the complainant, but if the employer refused to accept the EEOC decision, the complainant would have to sue the employer in court. It's difficult to prove sex discrimination in employment.

The EEOC dismissal data hasn't improved much. Twenty-two years earlier, 88 percent of cases were dismissed, slightly higher than the

Table 6.12   Women's and Men's Experiences of Discrimination, 2017

Types of Discrimination	Women (%)	Men (%)	Women/Men Ratio
Applying for jobs	18	18	1.0
Equal pay and promotion	41	18	2.3
Seeking housing	16	10	1.6
Considered moving due to discrimination	14	15	0.9
At doctor or health clinic	18	8	2.3
Sexual harassment	37	—	—
Violence	21	16	1.3
Nonsexual harassment or threats	29	13	2.2
Slurs	18	7	2.6

Source: National Public Radio, Robert Wood Johnson Foundation, and Harvard T. H. Chan School of Public Health 2017.

Note: For example, 18 percent of women and 7 percent of men said they experienced gender-related slurs. Women are 2.6 times more likely to have experienced slurs than are men.

2019 figure. The dismissal rate fell to 75 percent in 2007 and then began to increase again.

Social psychologists have also conducted audit studies in which subjects are asked to evaluate the résumés or work experiences of anonymous people. The résumés and work experiences would be the same except that one had a female name and the other had a male name. Men are generally given higher ratings than women, even with the same résumé (see Swim and Campbell 2001 for a review). It is likely this bias toward males also spills into the workplace.

More recent audit studies also indicate employment discrimination by gender. Although there are fewer gender-related audit studies than race-related audit studies, Pedulla (2019) summarizes some findings in his report:

1. Women who are parents received fewer callbacks for job applications than childless women, while men who are fathers are not penalized;
2. Upper-class men applying for legal jobs received four times more callbacks than upper-class women;
3. Men with a history of part-time employment were penalized compared to men with full-time employment histories, while women with part-time histories were not penalized. Part-time

employment was expected for women but was a sign of lack of commitment to employment by men.

4. Women were discriminated against when applying for male-dominated working-class jobs, while men were discriminated against when applying for female-dominated jobs of all categories.

Despite all of the laws on the books, there are still many examples of intentional systemic sex discrimination. Although women began to enter government-run military academies in the mid-1970s, they were barred from certain occupations in various military branches. Women serving in front-line military units and in special forces (e.g., the Green Berets and Navy Seals) was particularly controversial. The first woman wasn't accepted as a Green Beret until July 2020 (Gibbons-Neff 2020). This was an example of intentional systemic discrimination because women didn't have a chance to even try out for these positions. Because the all-volunteer armed forces were having difficulty getting enough qualified men to fill the necessary positions, all occupations are now open to women, according to the "Fact Sheet: Women in Service Review (WISR) Implementation" on the US Department of Defense website (2020).

Although the armed forces should be commended for eliminating this form of sex discrimination, they are not off the hook. Sexual harassment in the armed forces is still a major problem. According to the Defense Department, 6,676 reports of sexual assault were made by servicemembers along with 932 complaints of sexual harassment in 2018. Even these numbers are probably conservative estimates. In an anonymous survey, an estimated 12,927 female and 7,546 male servicemembers had experienced sexual assault (mostly by men) within the previous year.

Intentional gender discrimination has also been found in police departments throughout the United States. The National Institute of Justice (2019) outlines continuing problems in police culture, recruitment, retention, and promotion. Women constitute less than 13 percent of all police officers. Similar problems occur in fire departments, where only 7 percent of firefighters were women in 2017.

Organized religion provides numerous examples of intentional systemic discrimination. The Catholic Church bars women from being priests. Orthodox Jewish synagogues prohibit women rabbis, although other Jewish denominations ordain women rabbis. Most forms of Islam have male-only imams. It would be possible to write an entire book on institutional discrimination in religion, but these are some prominent examples.

Professional sports also provide examples of intentional systemic discrimination. In March 2019, the 2015 World Cup–winning US women's soccer team sued the US Soccer Federation for discriminating against them in terms of pay. They also alleged that women soccer players had inferior training and travel considerations as well as unequal support and development for their games. The women's team has won multiple World Cup championships in recent years, whereas the men's team usually has difficulty even qualifying for the quarter finals (Svokos 2019). In December 2020, the women's team won an out-of-court settlement for equality in working conditions. The pay issue is still an open question (Peterson and Blum. 2020).

This is not just an issue in the United States. According to the Global Sports Salaries Survey 2017, soccer star Lionel Messi made $84 million, whereas the combined salaries of all 1,693 women soccer players in the seven top leagues combined made only $42.6 million, or just more than $25,000 each per year.

Pay inequity also exists in professional tennis. Although the four major tournaments (the Australian Open, French Open, US Open, and Wimbledon) finally have equal purses for men and women, more than 70 percent of the 200 top-ranked male tennis players earned higher annual incomes than their female counterparts (Levitt 2018).

In general, the United States does not rank at the top of all countries when it comes to gender equality. The Organization for Economic Development and Cooperation (OEDC) has developed a Social Institutions and Gender Index that ranks nations on a variety of criteria. The index ranks the United States 26th out of 120 countries. This mediocre ranking was the result of a lack of paid maternity leave, an uneven application of laws protecting women in the workplace, an ongoing gender pay gap, the existence of states that permit child marriage, and the persistence of unconscious gender bias that results in underrepresentation of women in public and political office (Bach 2018). Switzerland was ranked as the least discriminatory country.

Walmart, the largest US retailer, has a long history of sex-related lawsuits filed against them. In 2010, Walmart paid $11.7 million to settle charges that it refused to hire women in order-filling positions in its London, Kentucky, distribution center (Equal Employment Opportunity Commission 2010).

However, a much larger suit was filed against Walmart in 2001 alleging a variety of types of sex discrimination in employment. Betty Dukes, a longtime employee, filed suit for the retail giant's failing to advance women employees. At the time, 67 percent of the hourly sales employees were women, compared with only 14 percent of its managers. In 2004, a lower court agreed that the case could proceed as a class action suit representing 1.5 million women workers (Covert 2019).

Unfortunately, in 2011, the US Supreme Court ruled that the 1.5 million employees did not have enough in common to be considered a class. The women decided to group themselves into smaller classes, but the court made this impossible. The justices ruled in a separate case that once a class is rejected, each person could only sue individually. Some are doing just that.

In 2017, Walmart reported that women are 60 percent of its labor force. Women represented 70 percent of sales workers, 43 percent of store managers, and less than one-third of the senior executives. This is an improvement from 2001, even though women are still underrepresented in managerial positions (Covert 2019).

Much of the sex-segregated labor force described in Table 6.2 can be attributed to unintentional systemic discrimination. Many male-dominated occupations have entrance standards and/or performance standards that tend to favor men. To the extent that golf and squash are important networking activities for corporate executives, women are again disadvantaged when they don't play these sports. The camaraderie/male bonding atmosphere so prevalent among police officers and firefighters also disadvantages women. These standards might not have arisen to harm women, but they have that effect. Once again, it is important to realize that structural discrimination might well exist *in addition to* more intentional individual and institutional discrimination.

The structure of work has changed so that long hours (often sixty or more per week) required in many upscale law firms and corporations make it impossible for dual career couples to have anything approaching a normal family life. After they have children, one of the parents has to be available when child-care arrangements break down. Because women tend to take more responsibility for children than men, these long hours have a disproportionate impact on them (Miller 2019). The Covid pandemic certainly proved this. A study of women scientists shows that they spend twice as much time as their male counterparts doing household chores (Laster 2010).

In another subtle example, Linda Babcock and Sara Laschever (2003) report that although new male and female hires are offered similar starting salaries, males tend to feel more entitled to negotiate, so they obtain better starting salaries than women. Employers, wanting to pay *all* employees as little as possible, regardless of sex, simply accept this state of affairs. This is structural discrimination because women get unequal pay for equal work.

The world of education also has a great deal of structural discrimination. Competitive and individualistic pedagogical techniques in math and science classes throughout the educational system favor males over females because of differential socialization practices. There is growing evidence that women and girls learn better in more cooperative settings. The lack of female role models among the faculty in many disciplines also hurts women.

In higher education, the relatively small number of women faculty results in greater demands on their time for advising students and participation in committee work. This, in turn, reduces the amount of time women faculty have to spend on research, important for promotion and tenure decisions.

In the studies of women's underrepresentation in film and television discussed earlier in the chapter, we can see examples of subtle discrimination. In films with at least one woman director or writer, the percentage of women protagonists, major characters, and speaking roles was higher than if there was no women director or writer. A similar pattern was found in television programming.

The film study also provided data showing that males and females were not portrayed in the same social roles. Male characters were more likely than females to be portrayed in work-related roles, whereas they were less likely than females to be shown in personal life–related roles. In addition, men were three times more likely than women to be portrayed as leaders (Lauzen 2019a, 2019b).

Another demonstration of the complexity of gender discrimination concerns playwrights of Broadway theater productions. According to researcher Emily Glassberg Sands, plays written by men and women are produced at about the same overall rate (Cohen 2009). The fact that more plays produced on Broadway are written by men than women can be explained by the greater number of male playwrights (no discrimination). Plays that featured women characters, however, were less likely to be produced than plays with male characters (discrimination).

Glassberg Sands sent out identical scripts to artistic directors and literary managers, except half had a female author and half had a male author. The author's gender did not influence the way in which male directors and managers evaluated the plays (no discrimination). Female directors and managers, however, favored the male authors over the female authors (discrimination). Glassberg Sands next studied 329 plays produced on Broadway in the previous ten years. She found that although plays written by women were more profitable than those written by men, they didn't have longer runs on Broadway (discrimination). This indicates that patterns of discrimination are not always clear-cut.

One of the disappointing and disturbing developments about gender inequality is the backlash against programs intended to eliminate gender gaps. For example, many universities have developed special programs and scholarships intended to increase the percentage of women in science, technology, engineering, and math (STEM). Many conservative groups oppose these programs, saying they discriminate against men (Watanabe 2019).

* * *

Although the articles in *Time* magazine and the *Atlantic* mentioned earlier in the chapter might disagree, we have shown that women are still a subordinate group in the United States. In spite of some modest progress, women still have lower incomes and are occupationally segregated into lower-paying jobs than men. Women have less representation in Congress, and a woman has yet to crack the glass ceiling of the presidency, though she is getting closer! In addition, women are the targets of prejudice and intentional discrimination. Many attitudinal and institutional changes must still be made in order to achieve true gender equality.

7

Sexual Orientation and Gender Diversity

People have been having sexual and romantic relations with same-sex partners for centuries. The Bible and the Koran discuss this fact, although critically. Homosexual liaisons were seen as normal and acceptable behavior among the ancient Greeks. Throughout most of history, same-sex relations were usually viewed as a *behavior* in which some people participated rather than as a separate *status* or identity. In some societies homosexual behavior was condemned; in others it was not.

It wasn't until the second half of the nineteenth century that homosexuality began to be discussed in a way that defined one's sense of being; that is, one *is* a homosexual if one engages in homosexual behavior (Baird 2001; Katz 1995). In fact, the noun forms of *homosexual* and *heterosexual* were popularized in the 1890s and probably weren't even used in the English language prior to the 1860s.

The American Psychiatric Association's *Diagnostic and Statistical Manual of Mental Disorders* classified homosexuality as a mental illness until 1973. After a divisive vote of the association members and protests by gay activists, homosexuality was removed from its list of mental illnesses.

Terminology

Like the concepts surrounding class, race, and gender that we discussed in earlier chapters, there is often disagreement about the terminology surrounding **sexual orientation**, which is determined by those to whom we are attracted sexually and emotionally. This is preferred to the term *sexual preference* because the latter suggests that there is a choice about whether we are attracted to people of the same or opposite sex (or both).

Today, there is still a debate about why some people are LGBTQ and some are not.

Heterosexual refers to individuals sexually and emotionally attracted to people of the opposite sex. **Homosexual** refers to individuals sexually and emotionally attracted to people of the same sex. Homosexual males are often called **gay** men, and homosexual females are often called **lesbian** women. However, *gay* is also used as an umbrella term to refer to all homosexuals, and the term **straight** refers to heterosexuals. **Bisexual** refers to individuals sexually and emotionally attracted to both same- and opposite-sex partners.

Separate from but related to sexual orientation is gender diversity. In the previous chapter, we defined **transgender** people as those whose gender identity doesn't match their physiological sex. They can be gay, lesbian, bisexual, or straight in terms of their sexual orientation because gender and sexual identities are distinct (yet related) statuses. **Cisgender** refers to people whose gender identity matches their physiological sex; that is, they would be seen as "normal" by the general population. "Cis" is the Latin prefix for "on the same side" and is used as the opposite of transgender (Ipsos 2020).

Another gender diversity term is **gender nonconforming/gender nonbinary/genderqueer**. These interchangeable terms refer to people whose gender expression does not fully conform to sex-linked gender expectations. These individuals might not identify with any gender and wish to use the pronouns "they," "them," and theirs" rather than "he" and "his" or "she" and "hers." In some circles, when you introduce yourself or create a name tag, you are asked to include your preferred pronouns.

All of these different categories of people are part of the general discussion of sexual orientation and gender diversity. In fact, it is common to refer to nonheterosexual and noncisgender people as the **LGBTQ** population—lesbians, gays, bisexuals, transgender people, and queer people—because they are all sexual and gender minorities who differ from mainstream heterosexual, cisgender people. Some argue that other letters could be added to this acronym, including a second "Q" (questioning), a second "T" (transsexual), a "2" (twospirited), an "I" (intersexed), and two "As" (asexual and ally). Sometimes LGBTQ+ is used, with the plus representing the full range of nonheterosexual and noncisgender sexual and gender identities.

In the Thirteenth Annual LGBTQ Community Survey, seven out of ten respondents said either LGBT or LGBTQ was the favorable term (Community Marketing Inc. 2019). For the purposes of this book, we use LGBTQ. When we are solely discussing sexual orientation and thus not talking about transgender people per se, we use LGB.

The term **queer** in also an umbrella term for LGBTQ people—one deemed much more inclusive than "gay people." Originally a term of approbation, LGBTQ people have turned it around and adopted it as a term of pride. This is similar to the way some Black people refer to each other as "nigga," though with far less disagreement among community members.

LGBTQ people might or might not acknowledge their sexual orientation to themselves and others. A person **in the closet** has not revealed one's LGBTQ status to others. The process of **coming out** means an individual has revealed their LGBTQ identity to others. Coming out is usually a process rather than a discrete event because individuals might acknowledge their LGBTQ status to a close friend before telling other acquaintances or their families. Because of the common assumption that every person is cisgender and heterosexual, LGBTQ people are faced with the often-painful decision of whether to come out each time they meet new people.

The categories of homosexual, heterosexual, and bisexual might seem to be straightforward, but there are substantial difficulties in determining who is in which category. Although the concepts are all defined in terms of to whom one is attracted, attraction is not the same thing as actually having sex with that person. **Sexual behavior** refers to whom we have sex with. This raises some important questions. Is it necessary to have a sexual relationship with a same-sex partner to be categorized as homosexual or identify as gay or lesbian? Is *attraction* to a same-sex partner sufficient to warrant the label homosexual or bisexual? For example, can a male carpenter who is attracted to his male coworker but who remains celibate be called gay, or would he have to engage in sex with his coworker to earn the gay label?

Another conceptual problem is about the timing and frequency of same-sex sexual behaviors. In the islands of Melanesia, for example, part of the rite of passage for boys is to have fellatio with older men. Eating another man's sperm is seen as a way to gain masculinity and bond with their male ancestors. After the initiation, most men are exclusively heterosexual until they have to initiate younger men (Heyl 2003). We might describe this as a kind of transitional, culturally approved homosexuality, though the Melanesians would simply see it as normal ritual behavior—not sexual activity.

In our own society, is a forty-five-year-old man gay, straight, or bisexual if his only same-sex sexual experience was an experimental one-night stand with another boy when both were teenagers? Is a thirty-five-year-old woman married to a man considered a lesbian if she had a six-month relationship with another cis woman when she was twenty-five? What about a fifty-year-old man who first came out in his late forties? Can we use the same label to describe these different behaviors?

More than sixty years ago, Alfred Kinsey and his colleagues (1948, 1953) documented the variety of sexual experiences by rating people according to the following scale:

0. exclusively heterosexual; no homosexual experiences
1. predominantly heterosexual; only incidental homosexual experiences
2. predominantly heterosexual; more than incidental homosexual experiences
3. equally heterosexual and homosexual
4. predominantly homosexual; more than incidental heterosexual experiences
5. predominantly homosexual; only incidental heterosexual experiences
6. exclusively homosexual; no heterosexual experiences

Where on this scale must someone fall to be classified as homosexual or bisexual or heterosexual? As we have seen in previous chapters, the answer to this question is philosophical and cultural, not scientific. The concept of sexual orientation, like the concepts of class, race, and gender, is socially constructed.

Another way to express the complexity and fluidity of sexual orientation can be seen in the Klein Sexual Orientation Grid (see Table 7.1). Along the left side of the table are seven different elements that make up an individual's sexuality. Along the top are columns asking about these elements in the past and present and what the person's ideal is. A person can put one of the Kinsey numbers (0–6) in each box and then average all of the boxes to come up with a sexual orientation score. In terms of sexual attraction, for example, a person might put a 3 in the past, a 6 in the present, and a 6 in ideal. This would average out to a score of 5 for sexual attraction. Although this is a lengthy exercise, it illustrates that sexual orientation is not a simple concept (Meem, Gibson, and Alexander 2010).

The answer, however, is important in determining the prevalence of homosexuality in the general population. According to Kinsey and his colleagues, for example, about 6 percent of adult men and 3 percent of

Table 7.1   Klein's Sexual Orientation Grid (on a scale of 0 to 6)

Variable	Past	Present	Ideal
Sexual attraction			
Sexual behavior			
Sexual fantasies			
Emotional preference			
Social preference			
Self-identification			
Straight/gay lifestyle			

Source: Meem, Gibson, and Alexander 2010.

adult women were exclusively homosexual (a 6 on Kinsey's scale) in the late 1940s. Under a broader definition (4–6 on that scale), 10 percent of men were exclusively or predominantly homosexual. Which figure should be used?

Lee Ellis (1996) takes a similar approach in trying to determine the prevalence of homosexuality in the United States some forty years after Kinsey. Using the broad criterion of ever having a same-sex fantasy or sexual desire, 25–30 percent of men and 10–20 percent of women would be defined as LGB. According to the more restrictive criterion of ever having a same-sex erotic experience to the point of orgasm, 5–10 percent of the men and 1–3 percent of the women would be categorized as LGB. Using the strictest criterion, having more or less exclusive erotic preference for one's own sex (or gender), only 1–4 percent of the men and less than 1 percent of the women would qualify. Ellis also argues that these same patterns can be found in studies in other countries. Men's rates are always substantially higher than women's.

So far, we have discussed whom people are attracted to and have sex with. There is yet another issue to contend with. **Sexual identification** is what people call themselves with regard to their sexual orientation. When Gallup asked whether they identify themselves as LGBT, 5.6 percent of the adult population answered affirmatively (Jones, 2021). Yet, sexual identity does not always correspond to sexual behavior. For example, the 2010 National Survey of Sexual Health and Behavior found that 11 percent of adults reported having same-sex sexual experiences, but the majority identify themselves as heterosexual (Herbenick et al. 2010).

Many men who are attracted to and/or have sexual relations with other men do not define themselves as gay or bisexual. For example, many male prisoners have sex with other male prisoners but identify as straight and even return to leading exclusively heterosexual lives upon release. Only the "penetrated" men tend to be defined by other inmates as gay, in part because of the absence of potential female partners. Also some men who have public heterosexual relationships with women and multiple secret relationships with other men insist on defining themselves as straight rather than gay or bisexual (King 2004). Although such men are said to be "on the down low" in Black communities, men of all races and ethnicities lead these secret lives to avoid the stigma associated with homosexuality. Researchers find that men are more likely to report having same-sex behavior than experiencing same-sex attraction (Rupp and Taylor 2010). Yet, among women, a 1992 national survey found that less than 2 percent of women identified as lesbian or bisexual, whereas more than 8 percent reported experiencing same-sex desire or engaging in same-sex behavior.

It is extremely difficult to answer what seem to be simple questions: Who is LGBTQ? How many people are LGBTQ? The answers always have to be qualified by another question: What do you mean by LGBTQ? There is no "objective" answer because labels and identities are socially constructed. Despite this, we do have some estimates of how many people participate in different kinds of sexual behaviors and identify as LGBTQ.

What difference does it make if one's sexual behavior is labeled gay or straight? For one, it is common for members of the dominant group to overestimate the size of the subordinate groups. Gallup (2019) found that more than half of adults believed that at least 20 percent of the population is gay or lesbian. Such overestimation exaggerates the fears of dominant group members about losing their dominant status in society.

There are several other concepts important to understanding sexual orientation and gender diversity. **Heteronormativity** is the worldview that promotes heterosexuality and the gender binary as the normal or default pattern of behavior. Everyone wrongly assumes that everyone else is a heterosexual, cisgender man or woman unless told differently. As we noted earlier, this requires many LGBTQ people to continually come out to others—coming out is a lifelong process.

Homophobia refers to fear and hatred against those who love and sexually desire people of the same sex. This refers to an anti-LGB set of attitudes and an ideology that are major problems in the United States. Similarly, **transphobia** refers to fear and hatred against transgender people and gender nonconformity more generally. Homophobia and transphobia can lead to hate crimes and other forms of discrimination against LGBTQ people by cisgender, heterosexual people. These attitudes and behaviors can make coming out as LGBTQ a risky (or even deadly) decision.

Heterosexism, in contrast, refers to a system of oppression against LGB people, whereas **cissexism** is a system of oppression against transgender and nonbinary individuals. Prejudice and ideology are one part of oppression, but there is more. Heterosexuals have certain privileges that LGB people don't, such as being able to have a picture of one's partner on one's desk at work without being hassled or fired, or being able to hold hands with one's partner in public without having to worry about verbal or physical harassment. Similarly, trans and nonbinary people are denied privileges afforded to cisgender people, such as not having to worry about being refused service at a bakery because of one's gender identity or being able to serve in the military. There also are discriminatory laws that don't protect LGBTQ civil rights. Hate crimes and violence are also part of heterosexism. We will further explore these issues in the following sections.

Descriptive Statistics

In previous chapters, we provided statistics on income, employment, and education collected by various agencies of the federal government. These data all show substantial inequalities between the dominant and subordinate groups.

For a variety of reasons, it is impossible to obtain comparable data for sexual orientation and gender diversity. First, the federal government doesn't collect data on sexual orientation. Even if it did, many closeted LGBTQ people would not acknowledge their sexual or gender identities on the census forms. Finally, most of the fine books on LGBTQ populations don't address the issue of large-scale differences in employment, occupation, income, and education by sexual orientation and gender identity.

As we said earlier, 5.6 percent of adults in the United States identified as LGBT in 2020. A previous Gallup poll asked the same question four years earlier but provided more background information (Newport 2018a). The data in Table 7.2 show that 4.5 percent of adults identified as LGBTQ in 2017, compared with 3.5 percent in 2012. This would amount to more than 11 million adults across the country. Women and people of color are more likely to identify as LGBTQ people than men

Table 7.2   US Adults Identifying as LGBTQ by Gender, Race/Ethnicity, Income, and Educational Attainment, 2012 and 2017 (percent)

	2012	2017	Change
Identify as LGBTQ	3.5	4.5	+1.0
Gender			
Man	3.4	3.9	+0.5
Woman	3.5	5.1	+1.6
Race/Ethnicity			
White non-Latinx	3.2	4.0	+0.8
Black non-Latinx	4.4	5.0	+0.6
Latinx	4.3	6.1	+1.8
Asian American	3.5	4.9	+1.4
Household income			
Less than $36,000	4.7	6.2	+1.5
$36,000–$89,999	3.1	4.7	+1.6
$90,000 and above	3.0	3.9	+0.9
Education			
High school graduate or less	3.5	4.5	+1.0
Some college	3.8	4.7	+0.9
College graduate	2.9	4.4	+1.5
Postgraduate	3.3	4.3	+1.0

Source: Newport 2018a.

Note: In 2012, 3.5 percent of adults identified as LGBTQ and 4.5 percent in 2017. In this six-year period, the percentage of adults identifying as LGBTQ increased by 1 percentage point.

and non-Latinx Whites. In terms of household income, those with low household income are the most likely to identify as LGBTQ, but educational attainment does not appear to affect LGBTQ identity. Women, Latinx, and Asian American adults; those with lower income; and college graduates had the fastest rate of increases in LGBTQ identification from 2012 to 2017.

Andrew Flores and colleagues (2016) asked a national sample if they identified specifically as transgender. Just under 0.6 percent, about 1.4 million people, said yes. Young people were more likely than older people to identify as transgender.

In terms of the number of same-sex couples, the US Census Bureau estimated that there were 358,390 in 2000 and 646,464 in 2010. This represents an 80 percent increase in same-sex couples during this ten-year period (Compton and Baumle 2018; Moore and Stambolis-Ruhstorfer 2013). Gallup puts the number of same-sex couples at 1.3 million in 2020, including 750,000 same-sex marriages (Jones 2021b). Compton and Baumle (2018) also provide data, summarized in Table 7.3, compar-

Table 7.3   Characteristics of Same-Sex and Different-Sex Couples, 2008

	Same Sex	Different Sex
Number of families	564,743	61,341,135
Average age (years)	46.2	48.5
Both partners college degree	30.6 percent	20.1 percent
Both partners employed	63.5 percent	52.5 percent
Household income	$107,300	$92,400
Homeowner	72.8 percent	79.1 percent
Interracial couple	11.2 percent	6.5 percent
Raising children	20.5 percent	43.2 percent

Source: Compton and Baumle 2018.
Note: Both partners had college degrees in 30.6 percent of same-sex couples and 20.1 percent of different-sex couples.

ing same-sex and different-sex couples based on the 2008 American Community Survey. Compared with different-sex couples, same-sex couples are slightly younger, more educated, more likely to have both partners employed, and more likely to have higher incomes, yet slightly less likely to be homeowners. In addition, same-sex couples are more likely to be interracial and less likely to be raising children than different-sex couples. In light of systemic gender gaps in wages, it is unsurprising that female same- and different-sex couples have lower incomes than their male counterparts. Also, White same-sex couples have higher incomes than Black and interracial couples (Dang and Frazier 2004).

In a partial update of married couples only, the American Community Survey (2020) found that same-sex couples were more likely than different-sex couples to be in the labor force (85 percent versus 80 percent) and to have worked in the past year (86 percent versus 82 percent). Same-sex couples were also more likely to have higher unemployment rates (2.9 percent versus 2.2 percent). White unemployment rates were lower than those of people of color in both types of couples.

The top ten occupations for people part of same-sex couples are first-line supervisors of retail sales workers, truck drivers, retail salespeople, secretaries and administrative assistants, elementary and middle school teachers, nurses, miscellaneous managers, cashiers, customer service representatives, and nursing/home health aides. There was a familiar gender division of labor in the occupations held by same-sex couples. Gay men made up 66 percent of the designers who had same-sex partners; the remaining 34 percent of designers were lesbians. Of the respondents, 61 percent of the auto mechanics, 60 percent of the truck drivers, and 57 percent of the janitors were gay men. Lesbians, in comparison, were 72 percent of the child-care workers, 68 percent of the counselors, 62 percent of the accountants, and 53 percent of the waitresses (gaydemographics.org). Remember, the base upon which these percentages were calculated is people in a particular occupation who were also members of a same-sex couple only; that means single individuals and those not out of the closet are not included in these statistics.

Badgett (2000) and Allegreto and Arthur (2001) have completed complex analyses of 1990 census data and several other large-scale studies to assess sexual orientation differences in income. After statistically controlling for factors such as education, occupation, and age, these researchers found that the incomes of gay, male unmarried partners were *lower* than the incomes of heterosexual, married men. Lesbian incomes, however, were the *same* as the incomes of heterosexual, married women. Looking at *household* income, gay, male, unmarried partnered households earned the same or less than heterosexual, male, married couples. Lesbian unmarried couples earned less than heterosexual married couples. Badgett (2000) concludes that contrary to the stereotype of wealthy LGB people, "lesbians, gays and bisexuals are spread throughout the range of household income distribution" (24).

Finally, we have more recent data showing that low-income LGBTQ people have higher rates than low-income non-LGBTQ people of receiving government benefits such as SNAP, Medicaid, public housing assistance, and unemployment benefits. Table 7.4 shows that this is true after controlling for gender orientation and gender for each type of benefit. In addition, LGBTQ people of color and LGBTQ people with disabilities are more likely to receive benefits than LGBTQ White and LGBTQ nondisabled people.

Prejudice and Attitudes

Unlike the paucity of data about LGBTQ people in the labor force, there is an abundance of data on heterosexuals' attitudes and how they have changed over time toward LGBTQ people. However, the interpretation of these data is a "glass half empty or glass half full" dilemma. During the past twenty to thirty years, attitudes have been moving in the direction of more tolerance, but a great deal of homophobia and transphobia still exists.

National polls show that the US population is much more accepting of LGBTQ people now than it was in the late 1970s and 1980s

Table 7.4   **LGBTQ and Non-LGBTQ People Receiving Selected Government Benefits, 2017 (percent)**

	SNAP (food stamps)	Medicaid	Public Housing Assistance	Unemployment
Total sample				
Non-LGBTQ	9.7	12.9	2.5	4.2
LGBTQ	22.7	20.9	6.3	6.3
Gender orientation				
Cisgender	10.5	13.4	2.7	4.3
Transgender	20.0	21.4	14.3	14.3
Women				
Non-LGBTQ	9.7	15.9	3.8	4.4
LGBTQ	26.1	21.7	7.4	7.2
Men				
Non-LGBTQ	9.6	9.7	1.0	4.1
LGBTQ	18.3	19.7	5.1	5.1
LGBTQ race				
White	19.2	18.8	3.8	6.3
People of color	28.0	24.0	12.5	6.3
LGBTQ disability status				
Nondisabled	16.0	11.8	2.2	5.4
Disabled	41.2	44.4	17.6	8.8

Source: Rooney, Whittington, and Durso 2018.
Note: For example, 9.7 percent of non-LGBTQ people receive SNAP (food stamps), and 22.7 percent of LGBTQ people receive SNAP (food stamps).

(Gallup 2019). Table 7.5 shows that overwhelming majorities of the population in 2019 believed same-sex relations between consenting adults should be legal (73 percent) and legally recognized (63 percent). Also, they believed gays and lesbians should have equal job rights (93 percent), be hired in a number of jobs including the military (95 percent), and be able to adopt children (75 percent). The improvement in these views over time has been dramatic.

Gao (2015) also asked a sample of adults how they would react if their child were gay or lesbian and, as with the previous data, there was a dramatic shift in a positive direction. The percent saying that they would *not* be upset jumped from only 9 percent in 1985 to 57 percent in 2015, a sixfold increase. This is all good news.

Other data, however, show more mixed results. Gallup (2019) also asked several questions about attitudes toward transgender people, specifically. On the one hand, a large majority (71 percent) said that transgender women and men should be allowed to openly serve in the military. On the other hand, only 41 percent said that bathroom use

**Table 7.5   Respondents Who Agree That LGBTQ
People Should Have Rights**

Selected Rights	Percentage of Respondents		
	In Selected Years	In 2019	Percentage Change
Gay or lesbian relations between consenting adults should be legal	32 (1987)	73	+41
Marriages between same-sex couples should be legal	27 (1997)	63	+36
Gays and lesbians should be allowed to adopt children	14 (1977)	75	+61
Gays and lesbians should have equal rights in terms of job opportunities	56 (1977)	93	+43
Gays and lesbians should be hired as:			
Members of armed forces	51 (1977)	95	+44
Doctors	44 (1977)	91	+47
Clergy	36 (1977)	72	+36
Elementary school teachers	27 (1977)	81	+54
High school teachers	47 (1989)	83	+36
President's cabinet	54 (1992)	88	+34

Source: Gallup 2019; Saad 2007.
Note: For example, the percentage of adults saying that gay or lesbian relations between consenting adults should be legal jumped from 32 percent in 1987 to 73 percent in 2019, an increase of 41 percentage points.

should be based on gender identity, whereas 51 percent said it should be based on sex at birth regardless of how one identifies.

Despite no federal civil rights laws protecting LGBTQ people from discrimination prior to 2020, more than half (53 percent) of the 2019 sample said no new laws were needed. Previous research has shown that respondents are sharply divided when it comes to dealing with their own children. Earlier samples were sharply divided about whether they would hire an LGBTQ babysitter (45 percent no; 43 percent yes) or permit their child to read a book that features a same-sex couple (45 percent no; 44 percent yes). In terms of political power, 32 percent felt that LGBTQ people had too much, 32 percent said that they had the right amount, and only 20 percent said that they had too little. More than half of those surveyed said the media gave too much coverage to LGBTQ issues (Bowman 2004; Pew Research Center 2010; Pinkus and Richardson 2004).

When these data are disaggregated to see how demographic factors affect attitudes, there are some consistent findings. Men, older people, fundamentalist Christians (those who interpret the Bible literally), frequent church attendees, Black people, those with no college education, and political conservatives are less positive toward LGBTQ people than are women, younger people, White people, Catholics, Jews, infrequent church attendees, college graduates, and political liberals (D'Arcy 2005; Pew Research Center 2010).

The aforementioned dramatic increases in positive views toward LGBTQ people might not be all they seem. As we just noted, certain populations remain relatively intolerant toward LGBTQ people and issues. Also, there is the issue of social desirability; culturally, it is less acceptable to express strong anti-LGBTQ attitudes today than it was several decades ago. Perhaps more concerning is that some positive views come with conditions set by the heterosexual cisgender dominant society.

In one study, Doan, Loehr, and Miller (2014) found that a nationally representative sample was more positive about LGBTQ people having formal rights (e.g., family leave, hospital visitation, inheritance rights, and insurance benefits) than informal rights (e.g., telling others, holding hands in public, kissing on the cheek in public, and French kissing in public). In this study, the right to marry was the least popular formal right the sample wanted for gays and lesbians. The study was done prior to the 2015 Supreme Court decision upholding same-sex marriage. These findings suggest great support for LGBTQ people's equal status under the law—as long as same-sex intimacy remains, in a sense, closeted.

Several other studies also point to limitations and qualifications some cisgender heterosexuals put on LGBTQ rights. Sumerau, Grollman, and Cragun (2017), for example, interviewed twenty heterosexual Christian women who said they supported same-sex marriage legalization. The researchers found that these women qualified their acceptance in several different ways. First, there was always a "but" that went along with their views of equality. One respondent, for example said, "I have no problems with gay people personally . . . but I also know it's something God is not okay with" (72). Another said "[Lesbians and gays] are born that way—they can't help it, and it is sad" (73). Others objected to LGBTQ activism, saying "That's you, go ahead, but don't make such a big deal about it and draw so much attention because that causes more people not to agree with them" (74). Then, of course, there is the "Hate the sin, love the sinner" argument. All of these Christian women who said they *supported* same-sex marriage qualified their attitudes in significant ways, such as that LGBTQ people should not challenge homophobia and transphobia or call into question anti-LGBTQ religious beliefs.

In a related article, Sumerau and Grollman (2018) asked thirty-five college students about their views toward transgender-inclusive bathroom access. The authors found that most of the interviewees responded in ways that obscured the oppression transgender people face. First, the respondents argued that "more awareness and education" of the general population was all that was needed, thus overlooking the ways in which transphobia is perpetuated by laws and social institutions. Second, interviewees criticized the "social disorder" that trans activism presumably caused. Finally, they minimized or outright denied the pervasive discrimination and harassment transgender people face. For example, one respondent said, "What they're saying is not fair to others; I mean, they want to use any bathroom they want to, but other people in that bathroom have no say. I did not sign up for that" (333).

Although these are only small samples of college students, they suggest that some of the increasingly positive attitudes toward LGBTQ people might be overstated and are much more nuanced than tolerance versus intolerance. According to the authors, "It may be useful to return to calls to investigate the differences in 'what people say' versus 'what people do.' To this end, investigating processes whereby people obscure oppression may become a powerful tool for understanding practices that maintain the persistence of social inequality and possibilities for social change" (Sumerau and Grollman 2018, 335).

As in our discussions of race and gender, there are different ways anti-LGBTQ prejudice can be expressed. Consider the following statements:

"Homosexual relations are always wrong."

"Pro-gay books should be removed from the public library."

These statements represent traditional anti-LGBTQ prejudice and are less likely to be expressed now than they were fifty years ago.

What about these three statements?

"Many gay men use their sexual orientation so that they can obtain special privileges."

"Lesbians should stop shoving their lifestyle down other people's throats."

"If gay men want to be treated like everyone else, then they need to stop making such a fuss about their sexuality/culture."

These three statements represent a more modern form of anti-LGBTQ prejudice that focuses on the belief that LGBTQ people make illegitimate and unnecessary demands, that discrimination against LGBTQ people is a thing of the past, and that LGBTQ people exaggerate the importance of their sexual orientation and gender diversity (Morrison and Morrison 2002).

There are no hard-and-fast lines between traditional and modern LGBTQ prejudices (Lottes and Grollman 2010). We are concerned that both might have increased during Donald Trump's administration.

Before leaving this section on attitudes, we wanted to mention a recent study on attitudes specifically about gender diversity. Oscar Yuan (2020), president of Ipsos, asked a national sample whether they agreed or disagreed with the following question: "A person is either a man or a woman and not anything in between." Almost half agreed and over one-fourth disagreed. This would indicate that most adults still had fairly rigid definitions of the man/woman dichotomy. Looking at only the LGBTQ adults in the sample, almost two-thirds disagreed, showing a more fluid sense of gender.

Yuan also asked the following agree/disagree question: "There is a spectrum of gender identities." Of the respondents, 40 percent of the men and 50 percent of the women agreed that there is a gender spectrum, whereas only 23 percent of the men and 19 percent of the women disagreed. This would suggest a more open attitude toward gender. Unfortunately, no comparative data are presented for either question to know which way attitudes are headed.

Discrimination

Given the strong incentives for many LGBTQ people to remain in the closet as well as the lack of systematic data collection, it is difficult to be precise about the amount of discrimination based on sexual orientation and gender identity that takes place. Verbal harassment is probably too frequent to even count. Among middle and high school students, for example, terms like *fag* and *dyke* are commonly used to tease and harass heterosexual classmates who are not members of the "in crowd," especially boys deemed too feminine (Pascoe 2011). Known LGBTQ classmates also are the targets of verbal harassment and bullying.

Verbal harassment is the most common form of **intentional individual discrimination** against LGBTQ people. A national survey by the Gay, Lesbian, and Straight Education Network showed that 82 percent of LGBTQ students aged thirteen to twenty reported being verbally harassed at school during the previous year because of their sexual orientation or gender identity (Gay, Lesbian, and Straight Education Network 2012).

Physical violence is also common. The same survey showed that 38 percent had been physically harassed (e.g., shoved), and 18 percent had been physically assaulted. Although these data showed improvement over previous years, 64 percent of LGBTQ students said that they felt unsafe at school—an *increase* from previous years (also see Gerstenfeld 2004; Potok 2010).

Since the federal government began collecting data on hate crimes in 1991, more than 30,000 anti-LGBTQ hate crimes have been reported to the police. In 2019 alone, 1,195 sexual-orientation-based hate crimes were reported along with 198 hate crimes based on gender identity and expression. Taken together, this accounted for one-fifth of all reported hate crimes that year (Federal Bureau of Investigation 2020).

Everyone agrees that this is only the tip of the iceberg because most hate crimes, regardless of type of victim, are not reported to the police. Studies have shown that anti-LGBTQ victimization follows predictable patterns—men are victimized more than women and people of color more than Whites. Threats and physical violence are more common than property crime. The perpetrators of anti-LGBTQ hate crimes are most likely to be young, lone, cisgender men.

Until 2009, the federal government was not able to prosecute perpetrators of anti-LGBTQ hate crimes because they were not included in federal hate crimes bills passed by Congress. After years of protest by LGBTQ groups and pushback by politicians, the Matthew Shepard and James Byrd Jr. Hate Crimes Prevention Act of 2009 finally permitted federal prosecutors to bring charges on the basis of both sexual orientation and gender identity. This was the first time these two categories were included in the US Code. Forty-three states now include sexual orientation in their hate crime legislation, although only twelve also include gender identity (Federal Bureau of Investigation 2020; Human Rights Campaign 2009).

Prior to 2020, LGBTQ people were not protected by federal civil rights laws preventing employment discrimination. Consequently, data on anti-LGBTQ discrimination are not available from the Equal Employment Opportunity Commission (EEOC). Twenty-eight states had no laws protecting LGBTQ people from discrimination in employment, education, housing, and public accommodations on the basis of sexual orientation and gender identity. This meant that more than 4 million people lacked protection against discrimination (Williams Institute 2019).

Transgender people—particularly those who are racial and ethnic minorities—were particularly vulnerable to employment discrimination (Black Futures Lab 2019). A 2015 survey showed that more than one in three Black transgender workers reported discrimination in hiring, promotion, and firing because of their gender identity. Also, in 2019, 40 percent of Black transgender men reported that "people act as if they are afraid of you" almost every day. Less than one-quarter of Black transgender women, cisgender men, and gender nonbinary people reported the same phenomenon. Only 10 percent of Black cisgender women report that people act afraid of them (Black Futures Lab 2019).

The subtitle of a *Bloomberg Business Week* article states, "Gays are making huge strides everywhere but in the executive suite" (Edwards 2003, 64). An audit of sexual orientation discrimination in hiring found that fictitious gay male job candidates were 40 percent less likely to be called back for an interview for over 1,700 job postings by private employers (Tilcsik 2011). The homophobic discrimination was most pervasive in jobs that emphasized worker traits deemed stereotypically masculine. Lesbian and bisexual women face a similar disadvantage in applying for jobs (Mishel 2016).

These workplace experiences are compounded by transphobic discrimination and violence that occurs in public spaces. In 2019, one in five Black transgender women reported being sexually harassed and threatened almost daily, and another 45 percent said it happened to them at least once a week. The comparable figure for Black cisgender people was 19 percent. Over the past few years, there have been record numbers of murders of transgender people, overwhelmingly Black transgender women.

Employment discrimination policies changed in 2020 when the Supreme Court issued a landmark decision saying that LGBTQ people were included in Title VII of the civil rights act. The 7-2 *Bostock v. Clayton County, Georgia,* decision said sexual orientation and gender identity discrimination are included under Title VII's prohibition against sex discrimination. This is a major legal victory for LGBTQ people, although its impact remains to be seen.

A month later, for example, the Supreme Court issued two decisions that upheld religious institutions' right to discriminate. In *Our Lady of Guadalupe v. Morrissey-Berru,* the Court ruled that religious schools can fire teachers for being LGBTQ if employing them violates the school's religious principles. In *Little Sisters of the Poor v. Pennsylvania et al.,* the Court said religious institutions don't have to provide contraception for their employees if it violates religious principles. To paraphrase an old cliché, "The Supreme Court giveth, the Supreme Court taketh away."

In February 2021, the US House of Representatives passed the Equality Act that prohibits "discrimination based on sex, sexual orientation and gender identity in areas including public accommodations and facilities, education, federal funding, employment, housing, credit and the jury system (Newport 2021). Although the public seems to favor such a bill, its fate remained uncertain in the US Senate.

When it comes to systemic discrimination against LGBTQ people, the situation in the United States is still problematic. The military, for example, has a sordid history. Prior to 1991, the military simply excluded openly LGBTQ people and those in the military suspected to be LGBTQ were dishonorably discharged. The Bill Clinton administration, in a compromise, "liberalized" this policy in 1994 by instituting the "Don't Ask, Don't Tell" rule. No one was supposed to ask whether a servicemember was LGBTQ. This meant that LGBTQ women and men could serve if they were discreet (i.e., not publicly out) about their sexual orientation. Nevertheless, Defense Department data show that more than 14,000 LGBTQ people were discharged from the military between 1993 and 2010 (Mascaro and Oliphant 2010). Black LGBTQ people were disproportionately discharged. The Palm Center puts the figures considerably higher (Jordan 2010).

LGBTQ servicemembers were unlikely to file harassment suits because doing so would require them to come out, which would in turn lead to their dishonorable discharge. They had no meaningful protection from discrimination other than remaining in the closet.

In addition to civil rights concerns, this institutionalized anti-LGBTQ discrimination hurt the military itself. During the first half of 2005, the various branches of the military failed to meet their recruitment quotas, in part because of the war in Iraq. At the same time, at least twenty Arab-speaking LGBTQ soldiers were discharged. The Government Accounting Office (GAO) reported that it cost more than $200 million to recruit and train new soldiers to replace the LGBTQ individuals discharged (Files 2005). More than twenty countries permit LGB people to serve in their military (Palm Center 2009).

In early 2010, President Barack Obama appointed a high-level commission to determine *how* the Don't Ask, Don't Tell policy could be efficiently repealed. Congress passed a law officially repealing Don't Ask, Don't Tell during the lame-duck session late in 2010. LGBTQ people were finally permitted to serve in the military. The Trump administration, however, again banned transgender people from enlisting and serving in 2018 but President Joe Biden overturned the Trump ban.

Federal agencies have also engaged in other types of systemic discrimination against LGBTQ people. For example, during the George W. Bush administration in 2005, there was a major controversy over the PBS-funded program *Postcards from Buster*. Buster is an animated character who interacts with live people on the show for preschoolers that is supposed to promote diversity. During a program on maple syrup, a girl introduces Buster to her two mothers. This was too much for then-secretary of education Margaret Spellings, who dissociated the department from supporting the show. She also suggested the producers return any federal money used to make the program. As a result of the controversy, only 18 of the 349 PBS affiliates aired the program (Zurawik 2005).

Another federal agency objected to the title of a workshop, "Suicide Prevention Among Gays, Lesbians, Bisexuals, and Transgendered [*sic*] Individuals." The workshop was to be part of a conference sponsored by the Suicide Prevention Resource Center in 2005. Organizers were informed that the head of the Substance Abuse and Mental Health Service Administration would not attend the conference unless the reference to LGBTQ individuals was removed from the workshop's title. The workshop was renamed "Suicide Prevention in Vulnerable Populations," but the term sexual orientation couldn't even be included in the workshop description (Vandenburgh 2005).

Laws against same-sex marriage and civil unions were also examples of systemic discrimination. At the federal level, during the Clinton administration, the Defense of Marriage Act of 1996 defined marriage as between a man and a woman, thus making same-sex partners ineligible for a wide range of federal benefits from taxes to Social Security. In February 2011, both President Obama and Attorney General Eric Holder announced that the Justice Department would no longer enforce the law.

The majority of states also prohibited same-sex marriages at the time. In 2010, only five states and the District of Columbia permitted same-sex marriages, and two others recognized same-sex marriages performed in other states.

For more than a decade, conservatives had promoted an amendment to the US Constitution that would have banned same-sex marriages. This would have been the first time a constitutional amendment would have *limited* rather than expand the rights of an entire group of people.

The marriage controversy even filtered down to school textbooks. Two major publishers—Holt, Rinehart, and Winston and McGraw-Hill—had used terms such as "married partners" and "when two people marry." Several members of the Texas Board of Education ruled that because of this wording, the books could not be used in Texas, the nation's second-largest buyer of school textbooks; the wording was contrary to a state law banning gay civil unions and marriage. After the publishers agreed to use phrases such as "husband and wife" and "when a man and a woman marry," the board approved the books for use in Texas (Associated Press 2004).

The US Supreme Court issued a landmark ruling in 2015 upholding the right of same-sex couples to marry. The 5–4 decision in *Obergefell v. Hodges* struck down laws in fourteen states that prohibited gay marriage. The ruling was based on the equal protection clause of the fourteenth amendment to the Constitution.

Systemic discrimination can also be seen in organized religion. The Jewish and Christian versions of the Bible and the Koran denounce homosexuality as a sin, although these texts are open to interpretation. According to the Human Rights Campaign (HRC) in 2019, some religions are generally hostile to LGBTQ people, including the Roman Catholic Church, Orthodox Judaism, the Church of Jesus Christ of the Latter-Day Saints, the African Methodist Episcopal Church, the Church of the Nazarene, the Orthodox Church, the Pentecostal Church, the Presbyterian Church in America, the Seventh-Day Adventist Church, the Southern Baptist Convention, and the United Methodist Church. Their religious ideologies are one major cause of homophobia and transphobia. For example, a lesbian teacher at a Catholic school in Miami was fired immediately after marrying her girlfriend in February 2018. The archdiocese said that she had violated her contract, which required her to abide by Catholic teachings (Caron 2018). Unfortunately, the *Our Lady of Guadalupe* Supreme Court decision in 2020 upheld the right of a religious school to do this.

Other religions are more accepting of LGBTQ people, including the Disciples of Christ, the Episcopal Church, the Evangelical Lutheran Church, the Metropolitan Community Church, the Presbyterian Church USA, the Religious Society of Friends, the United Church of Christ, and three branches of Judaism (Human Rights Campaign 2019).

There are, however, divisions within some religious denominations. The Alliance of Baptists, for example, is more welcoming to LGBTQ people than the American Baptist Churches USA and the Southern Baptist Convention. Conservative, Reconstruction, and Reform Judaism are more welcoming than Orthodox Judaism. Within many anti-LGBTQ religions, groups have attempted to liberalize their policies. For example, a group of 100 Modern Orthodox rabbis, educators, and mental health professionals issued a letter saying that homosexuals should be welcomed into the religion even though their sexual behaviors are still not seen as acceptable (Baird 2001; D'Arcy 2005; *Feminist News* 2010). Recall, as we discussed earlier, that this reflects a form of conditional acceptance in which the dominant group sets the terms upon which they are willing to accept LGBTQ people. For some religious denominations, acceptance is granted if LGB people do not "act" on their same-sex desires.

The Kansas-based Westboro Baptist Church, led by the late Fred Phelps, is one of the most homophobic churches in the country. Phelps and his followers picketed the funerals of soldiers killed in Iraq and Afghanistan. They believe the soldiers' deaths were God's way of punishing the United States for being too tolerant of LGBTQ people. The noisy picketers carried signs like "God hates fags" and "Thank God for dead soldiers." In March 2011, the US Supreme Court said their picketing was a form of free speech protected by the Constitution and, therefore, allowed this behavior to continue (Marso 2011)—and it does, even after Phelps's death in 2014.

According to the church website (godhatesfags.com), homosexuality "is so insidious by its nature, and those who commit such things so abominable by their nature, that it serves as the litmus test for a society. . . . If you enable, support, condone, legislate for, or attempt to legitimize that sin, you should be ashamed. It was your ilk who brought destruction on Sodom, and it will be your ilk who fuels God's wrath to the point that there will be no remedy." Westboro Baptist Church members also believe God sent the novel coronavirus pandemic (Covid-19) to earth to punish its people for their sins. Homosexuality is only one of them.

According to Newport (2021), much of the opposition to the Equality Act comes from religious groups who fear that the act would prevent anti-LGBTQ discrimination on religious grounds. In other words, some religious groups want to continue discriminating.

Along with the continuing high incidence of anti-LGBTQ intentional individual and **intentional systemic discrimination, unintentional systemic discrimination** (i.e., neutral policies that have negative impacts on LGBTQ people) is also important. One example of anti-LGBTQ unintentional systemic discrimination would be elementary school assignments asking children to draw pictures of their families. In this seemingly innocuous assignment, teachers expect children to draw a man and a woman. The children of LGBTQ parents, however, are put in the position of "outing" their families to the entire class and bringing harassment onto themselves. Unless the teacher is sensitive to these issues, this could cause real problems for both the children and their families (Hofmann 2005).

Of course, there is still a great deal of intentional discrimination in the field of education. In one example of an outrageously insensitive teacher, a Louisiana elementary school student was punished for telling a classmate that his own mother was a lesbian. When one child asked Marcus McLaurin about his mother and father, Marcus replied that he has two mothers. During the brief discussion, Marcus said that his mothers were gay, meaning "gay is when a girl likes another girl" (Stepp 2003, C10). The teacher overheard the conversation and criticized Marcus for using a bad word. The teacher then filled out an official "behavior report," writing, in part, "This kind of discussion is not acceptable in my room. I feel that parents should explain things of this nature to their own children in their own way" (Stepp 2003, C10).

Before leaving the topic of anti-LGBTQ discrimination, it's important to acknowledge that there is some progress in trying to combat intentional individual and systemic forms of discrimination. In 2003, the US Supreme Court overturned the antisodomy laws in Texas that had outlawed oral and anal sex. The *Lawrence v. Texas* decision also invalidated antisodomy laws in fourteen other states. The 2010 repeal of Don't Ask, Don't Tell and 2015 US Supreme Court decision that same-sex marriage is constitutionally protected are major civil rights milestones. The 2020 Supreme Court *Bostock* decision gave LGBTQ people some protection from employment discrimination in nonreligious institutions.

Increasing numbers of large companies have adopted important LGBTQ-friendly policies. In 2020, for example, 93 percent of Fortune 500 corporations had explicit policies banning discrimination based on sexual orientation, compared with 88 percent in 2008. Of these companies, 91 percent had policies opposed to gender-identity-based discrimination in 2020, compared with only 35 percent in 2008. And 53 percent provided same-sex partner benefits in 2020 (Human Rights Campaign 2020). Since 1996, the HRC has issued an annual list of the best and worst companies for LGBTQ employees. Since 2002, the HRC has rated corporations on their Corporate Equity Index (CEI) based on nondiscrimination policies for LGBTQ people, equitable benefits for LGBTQ people and their families, and supporting an inclusive culture and corporate responsibility. In 2020, 214 of the Fortune 500 companies received the highest rating of 100 percent. This is a dramatic increase from previous years.

One caveat. Walmart Inc. was one of the corporations that received a 100 percent rating from HRC despite their relatively low pay and the many complaints and lawsuits alleging gender and race discrimination. Perhaps Walmart treats all workers badly regardless of their sexual orientation and identity.

The number of open LGBTQ people serving at the top of the federal government has also increased. Pete Buttigieg, the first openly gay cabinet member, was appointed secretary of transportation in 2021. In addition, a record eleven openly LGBTQ people serve in the 117th Congress.

LGBTQ representation on television is also improving, according to an annual survey of TV networks conducted by the Gay and Lesbian Alliance Against Defamation (Gay and Lesbian Alliance Against Defamation 2020). In terms of primetime original programming (not including reruns), the networks devote more time to LGBTQ issues, have more LGBTQ characters, and have more race and gender diversity than ever before. In 2020, 8.8 percent of the regular characters appearing on scripted primetime programing were LGBTQ people. (Unfortunately, there was insufficient data to provide statistics for cable TV and streaming services.)

Scholarships.com (2021) list nineteen organizations that grant scholarships directed to LGBTQ individuals. The Pride Foundation, eQuality, and the League Foundation are some examples (also see Kahn 2004).

In contrast, there is growing evidence that hostility against LGBTQ people intensified during the Trump administration. The number of anti-LGBTQ hate groups increased from forty-nine groups in 2018 to seventy in 2019, according to the Southern Poverty Law Center (Moreau 2020). Trump also opposed the Equality Act, which would extend federal nondiscrimination protections to LGBTQ people, and banned transgender people from serving in the military. In addition, the former administration prevented transgender people from (1) entering single-sex homeless shelters not consistent with their biology and (2) using gender-appropriate bathrooms in schools. It also eased rules protecting transgender people against discrimination by hospitals, doctors, and health insurance companies (Cameron 2020). Early in 2021, Biden overturned the ban on transsexuals serving in the military.

The Trump administration also backed defendants sued for anti-LGBTQ discrimination. A Christian baker who refused to bake a cake for a gay wedding was affirmed by the US Supreme Court in 2019. In another case that has yet to be decided, a Detroit funeral home director fired a transgender woman undergoing transition. The Trump administration filed court briefs favoring both defendants. Hopefully, the Biden administration will not support these suits.

* * *

There's no doubt that things are much better for the LGBTQ community today than they were several decades ago. Increasing numbers of people in the dominant cisgender straight community are becoming allies to LGBTQ people or at least have a "live-and-let-live" philosophy. Despite this progress, the United States still has a long way to go to eliminate discrimination based on sexual orientation and gender diversity. How much the Trump administration turned back the clock and whether Biden can reset it remains to be seen.

8

Disability: How Society Handicaps People

One of the newer groups included in diversity studies is "people with disabilities." Of course, such individuals have been present throughout human history, but the sense of group consciousness among people with disabilities is relatively new.

People with physical and mental disabilities have been stigmatized and discriminated against for centuries. Having a physical impairment has often been seen as a religious punishment or as a sign of evil in a wide variety of religions, including Christianity and Judaism. People with disabilities have been kept behind closed doors in the home or placed in asylums or other institutions to be kept out of sight. In the nineteenth and early twentieth centuries, eugenicists and social Darwinists promoted forced sterilization so that people with disabilities could not have children that would "weaken" the gene pool. This practice was upheld by the US Supreme Court in 1927. During World War II, Nazi Germany took this one step further by murdering tens of thousands of people with physical and mental disabilities in Europe, along with millions of Jews, LGBTQ people, communists, and people of Romani descent (pejoratively referred to as "gypsies").

Terminology

Like other subordinate groups we discuss in this book, the perception of people with disabilities is socially constructed, and there has been considerable debate over terminology. Pejorative words such as *cripple, abnormal,* and *invalid* are no longer considered appropriate to describe people with physical disabilities. Likewise, terms such as *idiot* and *retarded* are no longer used to describe those with mental disabilities.

In 2010, for example, President Barack Obama signed a law that replaced *mental retardation* with *intellectual disability* in the US Code (West 2010). Most people who are activists or writers in the field of disability studies also eschew terms such as *handicapped, physically/mentally challenged,* and *special,* preferring *people with disabilities.* Those without disabilities would be called *nondisabled.*

There is not, however, agreement about the definition of *disability.* Many contemporary writers, who use the social model of disability, differentiate between *impairment* and *disability.* According to this view, **impairment** refers to *physical or mental limitations* such as the inability to see, hear, walk, or read. This is an individual-level term. **Disability**, in comparison, is a *social exclusion* or "a disadvantage or restriction of activity caused by a contemporary social organization which takes little or no account of people who have physical impairments and thus excludes them from participation in the mainstream of social activities" (Shakespeare 2006, 198).

This is an important distinction to understand. Not being able to walk, for example, is a physical impairment. Not being able to access a building because there is no wheelchair ramp is a disability. Similarly, not being able to see is an impairment, but not being able to read a book because it is not available in braille or on audiotape is a disability. This impairment/disability distinction has certain similarities to the sex (physical/biological) and gender (cultural) distinction we discussed in Chapter 6.

The Americans with Disabilities Act (1990), however, equates disability and impairment. According to this landmark piece of legislation,

> The term "disability" means, with respect to an individual—
>   (a) a physical or mental impairment that substantially limits one or more of the major life activities of such individual;
>   (b) a record of such impairment; or
>   (c) being regarded as having such an impairment.

This, of course, is an individualistic medical and legal definition. There are certain medical categories people either fit or don't fit. In addition, if one is legally declared disabled, certain payments, accommodations, and treatment options become available. If one is designated as "learning disabled," for example, he or she must be allowed to take more time to complete an exam.

The federal government uses diverse definitions of disability. The American Community Study (ACS) has a relatively narrow definition, whereas the Survey of Income and Program Participation (SIPP) has a much broader definition and differentiates between *severe* and *nonsevere* disabilities. Although both programs are part of the US Census Bureau, they come up with dramatically different estimates of how many disabled people live in the United States. On the one hand, the most recent ACS data for 2018 estimates 40.6 million people with disabilities, or 12.6 percent of the population (US Census Bureau 2018b). On the other hand, the most recent SIPP data estimates 85.3 million people with disabilities, or 27.2 percent of the population (Taylor 2018). Twenty million people are defined as having disabilities by one measure and nondisabled by the other!

In this book, we use the impairment/disability distinction from the social model. Whereas some of these impairments have mainly biological causes (e.g., genetic illnesses, birth defects, hormone imbalances), others have social causes. Some mental impairment results from lead exposure in poor communities, for example. Wars cause the loss of limbs and other traumatic physical and mental injuries. Unsafe working conditions and environmental contamination cause many cancers. These are all preventable impairments that can be reduced by changes in the larger society.

Some contemporary analysts use the term **ableism** to describe the system of oppression based on disability status. Because the nondisabled are politically and economically powerful, they define dominant cultural standards and stigmatize and discriminate against those with disabilities, for example, denying them access to accommodations. According to this view, people with disabilities must redefine themselves as a group with common interests to gain power vis-à-vis the dominant group (i.e., the nondisabled). Their diverse impairments should not keep them apart.

There is some evidence that this might be happening. The National Organization on Disability (NOD)/Harris Poll (2004) reported that in 1986, only 40 percent of people with disabilities said they had a "somewhat strong" or "very strong" sense of common identity with other people with disabilities. By 2004, that figure had jumped to 56 percent. The more severe a person's disability, the stronger sense of common identity he or she was likely to have (see also Darling 2003).

Descriptive Statistics

Estimating the number of people with disabilities is difficult, as we discussed above, because of the different measures used. We use the estimates of SIPP because it provides the most detailed statistics available

(Taylor 2018). When the results of the 2020 Census are released, more accurate figures will be available.

The most common types of impairments are physical in nature (see Table 8.1). Men are somewhat more likely to be disabled than women, 12.8 percent versus 10.9 percent, respectively. Black people have the highest rate of disability (34.9 percent) followed by other/mixed race (33.2 percent), non-Latinx White people (31.5 percent), Latinx people (24.6 percent), and Asian Americans (20.1 percent).

Almost 65 million people have physical disabilities, 33 million have mental disabilities, and 28 million have communication disabilities. And of these, 34 million have disabilities in more than one domain.

Age is a major factor in having a disability. Table 8.2 shows that the older people are, the more likely they are to be disabled. For example,

Table 8.1   Characteristics of People Aged Eighteen and Older with a Disability in the United States, 2014

	People with Disabilities (thousands)	People with Disabilities as Percentage of Category
Total population of people with disabilities[a]	85,300	27.2
Sex		
Males	14,824	12.8
Females	13,542	10.9
Race		
White, non-Latinx	49,108	31.5
Black	10,360	34.9
Latinx	8,996	24.6
Asian American	2,776	20.1
Other race and two or more races	2,299	33.2
Domains of disability[b]		
Physical	64,800	27.8[c]
Mental/intellectual	32,880	13.7[c]
Communication	28,320	11.2[c]
More than one domain	34,080	14.2[c]

Source: Taylor 2018.

Notes: For example, 85 million people have disabilities, accounting for 27.2 percent of the entire population, and 28.3 million people have communication disabilities, accounting for 11.2 percent of the entire population.

a. Refers to all ages.

b. Physical: for example, lifting, walking, standing, sitting, grasping. Mental: for example, learning, dementia, intellectual, mental/emotional. Communication: for example, seeing, hearing, speaking.

c. Percentage of entire population, eighteen and older.

Table 8.2   Rate of Disability by Age Group, 2014

Age Group	Number of Disabled (thousands)	Age Group with Disability (percent)
Less than 18	12,557	17.1
18–64	46,238	23.7
65 and older	26,494	58.5
Total	85,289	—

Source: Taylor 2018.
Note: 12,557,000 people under age eighteen have disabilities; 17.1 percent of all people under age eighteen have disabilities. The percentages in the third column are not additive.

Table 8.3   Highest Grade in School Completed by People Aged Twenty-Five to Sixty-Four, by Disability Status, 2014 (percent)

Highest Grade in School Completed	People with Disabilities	People Without Disabilities
Less than high school graduate	17	9
High school graduate, GED	34	23
Some college, assoc. degree	27	25
College graduate	20	43
Total	100	100

Source: Taylor 2018.
Note: As the table indicates, for example, 20 percent of people with disabilities and 43 percent of people without disabilities graduated from college.

17.1 percent of those under eighteen have disabilities, compared with the 58.5 percent of those aged sixty-five and older.

People with disabilities tend to be less educated than nondisabled people (see Table 8.3). The college graduation rate for people with disabilities is less than half of the rate of nondisabled people, and the rate of not finishing high school is almost double the rate of nondisabled people.

People with disabilities are also disadvantaged in the labor force. As the data at the top of Table 8.4 indicate, one-fifth of people with disabilities participate in the labor force; that is, they are working or looking for work. The participation rate is higher for men than for women. Latinx people, White people, and Asian Americans have higher participation rates than Black people do. Finally, as level of education increases, labor force participation rates also increase. Comparing all

Table 8.4   Labor Force Characteristics of People with and Without Disabilities Aged Sixteen and Older, 2019

Disability Status	Labor Force Participation Rate (%)	Unemployment Rate (%)
All people with disabilities, 16 and older	20.8	7.3
Gender		
Men	24.3	7.4
Women	17.8	7.3
Race		
White	21.0	6.6
Black	17.7	11.8
Asian	20.3	6.7
Latinx	22.4	8.6
Educational attainment		
Less than high school graduate	10.0	9.3
High school graduate, no college	16.7	7.2
Some college, assoc. degree	23.8	7.2
Bachelor's degree or higher	29.6	4.5
All nondisabled, 16 and older	68.7	3.5
Gender		
Male	74.9	3.5
Female	62.9	3.5
Race		
White	68.8	3.1
Black	69.0	5.9
Asian	66.4	2.6
Latinx	70.6	4.2
Educational attainment		
Less than high school graduate	57.2	5.1
High school graduate, no college	66.0	3.5
Some college, assoc. degree	71.6	2.8
Bachelor's degree or higher	77.7	2.0

Source: US Bureau of Labor Statistics 2020g.
Note: For example, 20.8 percent of people with disabilities are in the labor force, compared with 68.7 percent of people without disabilities; 7.3 percent of people with disabilities are unemployed, compared with 3.5 percent of people without disabilities.

these figures with those of nondisabled people (see bottom half of Table 8.4), participation rates of people with disabilities are lower than those for nondisabled people in each category.

The *unemployment* rates in Table 8.4 are *higher* for people with disabilities compared with those for nondisabled people. Remember, the unemployed are defined as those actively looking for work. Before Covid, more than 7 percent of people with disabilities were unemployed, double the rate of nondisabled people (3.5 percent). That higher unemployment rate is true for both sexes, all races, and all educational levels.

Given all these data, it's predictable that people with disabilities have lower incomes than nondisabled people. Table 8.5 shows that the median annual income, including government disability payments, is $23,848 for employed people with disabilities, about $11,000 less than the earnings of employed nondisabled people. The family income of people with disabilities is $27,000 less than that of nondisabled people. In addition, the poverty rate for people with disabilities (24 percent) is almost double the rate for nondisabled people (12.9 percent).

There are also important differences in wealth. The median net worth of households with an adult with disabilities was $43,390, compared with $76,798 for households with nondisabled adults.

As a consequence of the differences in income and wealth, people with disabilities have a smaller financial cushion to use during hard times. When asked if they had adequate financial assets to "support yourself for three months with no earned income or gifts from others," 58 percent of people with disabilities said "no," compared with only 36 percent of nondisabled people (Darling 2003).

Prejudice and Ideology

Discussing prejudice against people with disabilities is more complex than examining other types of prejudice. More than a half century ago, Erving Goffman (1963) wrote about how people with physical deformities were often stigmatized by the rest of society. However, negative attitudes toward people with disabilities have not been conceptualized

Table 8.5   Median Annual Earnings, Family Income, and Poverty Rate, by Disability Status, 2013

Earnings/Poverty Rate	People with Disabilities	People Without Disabilities
Earnings for employed	$23,848	$35,380
Family income	$40,125	$67,348
Poverty rate	20.0%	11.8%
Net worth	$43,390	$76,708

Source: ProsperityNow.Org 2018; Taylor 2018.

Note: Median annual earnings in 2013 was $23,848 for people with disabilities and $35,380 for people without disabilities.

as prejudice until relatively recently. In addition, there are multiple ways to measure attitudes toward people with disabilities. Reviewing literature available on the subject, Richard Antonak and Hanoch Livneh (2000) identified twenty-four different methods of measurement, including prejudice scales, stereotype checklists, and experimental manipulations. More recent studies look at explicit prejudice, implicit prejudice, and warm/cool feelings as measured by a graphic thermometer.

The multiple types of disabilities also present a challenge to investigators. Some studies ask about attitudes toward people with disabilities in general, whereas others inquire about attitudes toward people who are deaf, blind, quadriplegic, and so on. The results can vary depending upon the object of the question. In addition, several scholars talk about a *hierarchy of disabilities* wherein some are viewed more negatively than others. Brigida Hernandez, Christopher Keys, and Fabricio Balcazar (2000), for example, show that employers view intellectual and emotional disabilities more negatively than physical and sensory disabilities. They argue that this hierarchy has been stable over time. In contrast, Mark Deal (2003) reviews a number of studies of students, practitioners, and the general public that show inconsistent hierarchies that change over time.

Most scholars who write about prejudice argue that although negative attitudes toward people with disabilities still exist, after the passage of the Americans with Disabilities Act in 1990, the degree of prejudice that exists now is thought to be much less than existed in the past.

We reviewed three recent studies including one literature review (Wilson and Scior 2014), one small-scale experiment (Kallman 2017), and one large-scale study with more than 300,000 participants (Harder, Keller, and Chopik 2019). Several tentative conclusions can be drawn from these studies.

- As many as one-third of the US population has "moderate to strong" implicit bias toward people with disabilities.
- Men, those with low educations, and those who had no contact with people with disabilities had the highest levels of implicit and explicit bias as well as the coolest feelings on the warm/cold thermometer. Women, those with higher educations, and those who had contact with people with disabilities tended to have the lowest levels of prejudice and the warmest feelings.
- Asian Americans had the highest level of explicit bias and the coolest ratings on the warm/cold thermometer.

- Black people had the highest level of implicit bias but the warmest feelings on the thermometer.
- Over time, explicit bias probably declined, implicit prejudice might have increased, and readings on the thermometer might have gotten warmer.
- Findings in terms of age are inconsistent.

Although explicit prejudice might be declining and feelings on the thermometer might be getting warmer, this might be a result of social desirability pressures that make people want to show themselves as tolerant and nonprejudiced. The possible increasing levels of implicit bias might mean that many people still have feelings of ambivalence, discomfort, and fear toward people with disabilities.

The nature and extent of prejudice against people with disabilities is still a lively topic for researchers. Most scholars usually end their articles with a phrase such as "more empirical research is needed."

Discrimination

Discrimination on the basis of disability was not part of the public discourse until the last third of the twentieth century. Discrimination regularly occurred, of course, but there was no label for it, and it was not usually illegal.

The first major federal law on the topic was Section 504 of the Rehabilitation Act of 1973, which made employment discrimination against people with disabilities by federal contractors illegal. Although President Richard Nixon signed the act, his administration did little to enforce it.

In 1990 Congress passed the Americans with Disability Act, which banned discrimination in employment, public accommodations, commercial facilities, public transportation, and many other areas of life. This was extended to include information technology in 2001. A variety of Supreme Court decisions clarified the meaning of these laws, sometimes expanding them but often restricting their scope.

Although laws are valuable tools to fight discrimination, unequal treatment still exists. The NOD/Harris Poll (2004) asked a national sample of employed individuals with disabilities if they had encountered discrimination on the job because of their disability. Of the respondents, 22 percent said "yes." When asked what kind of discrimination they had encountered, the top three responses were that they were refused a job (31 percent), refused a job interview (27 percent), and denied a workplace accommodation (21 percent).

The Equal Employment Opportunity Commission (EEOC) recorded disability discrimination complaints filed with the organization between 1997 and 2019 (Equal Employment Opportunity Commission 2020a). During this twenty-two-year period, 553,000 complaints were filed with the EEOC, with more than 24,000 filed in 2019 alone. The number of complaints declined between 1997 and 2005, then increased to a peak of 28,000 in 2016, and then declined somewhat. After completing an investigation of each complaint, the EEOC concluded that about one-fifth of the complaints had enough evidence to warrant an administrative penalty or trial.

People with disabilities have also been victims of hate crimes motivated by bias against their disabilities. The Federal Bureau of Investigation (FBI) found that 157 hate crimes were reported to the police in 2019, 49 against people with physical disabilities and 108 against people with mental disabilities (Federal Bureau of Investigation 2020). In 2000, only 36 hate crimes against people with disabilities were reported. As with other hate crimes, this is only the tip of the iceberg (also see US Commission on Civil Rights 2019).

People with disabilities are also more likely to be victims of other serious crimes including rape, sexual assault, robbery, and aggravated assault. The victimization rate for people with disabilities (12.7 per 1,000) is four times higher than the rate for nondisabled people. Women with disabilities were more likely to be victimized than men with disabilities, and people with mental disabilities were more likely to be victimized than those with physical disabilities (Mueller, Forber-Pratt, and Sriken 2019).

Pamela Robert and Sharon Harlan (2006) conducted a study of workers with disabilities employed by an unnamed state government. Most of the workers reported being "marginalized"—that is, being ignored, excluded, or stared at. This treatment made them feel like outsiders in their own workplace. They also reported being "fictionalized," in that other workers saw them in inaccurate ways. The two biggest fictionalizations were being seen as incompetent and helpless. A third large problem was harassment, whereby disabled workers were subjected to jokes, name-calling, insensitive remarks, needling, and sabotage. This created what is legally known as a *hostile work environment*.

The important part of the Robert and Harlan study was that these actions by individual workers (individual discrimination) often were translated into corporate policy (institutional discrimination). Marginalization led to the creation of a "backroom" or "dumping ground" where many disabled workers were placed. In other words, they were physically segregated from nondisabled workers. Fictionalization led workers with disabilities to be placed in lower-level jobs that required fewer skills and provided more limited career ladders.

Robert and Harlan found that harassment was the result of workplace tensions. When employers were told to improve their performance or that layoffs might occur, for example, workers with disabilities became scapegoats. Coworkers resented workers with disabilities receiving accommodations so that they could do their jobs effectively. Supervisors in the Robert and Harlan study often did nothing to change this hostile environment. Because this was a study of a single state government, it would be helpful to undertake additional studies to see if these findings could be generalized.

Discrimination against people with disabilities continues to occur in the United States. Legal decisions about disability discrimination involve employment issues, often in well-known multinational corporations and government agencies.

For example, in 2009 United Parcel Service (UPS) agreed to an out-of-court settlement with a group of deaf drivers. The company had required drivers to meet the national hearing standard for the drivers of vehicles in excess of 10,000 pounds even though the UPS trucks were significantly lighter. UPS agreed to a new hearing protocol and training for employees who couldn't meet the national standards. Drivers' hearing would also be monitored (Disability Rights Advocates 2009).

In another case, Walmart was sued by a prospective employee with cerebral palsy. The company refused to hire the man out of concern that his crutches and wheelchair would be a safety risk to customers. In 2008 Walmart paid the man $300,000 and initiated a supervisor training process at the local store (Diversity Insight 2008).

Other cases concerned issues of accessibility, not employment. In 2009, Walmart agreed to change its policy of banning service animals (e.g., seeing-eye dogs) from entering its stores. The company paid $150,000 to resolve outstanding complaints and an additional $100,000 to help fund a public service campaign (Disability Rights Online News 2009).

Target, one of Walmart's competitors, was named in a class-action suit by the National Federation of the Blind for having an inaccessible website. Blind people can purchase software to vocalize a visual website, but the website must contain the appropriate enabling software. Target initially refused to alter its website but in 2008 agreed to install the necessary software and pay the plaintiffs $6 million—about $3,500 each (Walker 2008).

State government agencies have also been the targets of disability lawsuits. The University of Michigan began a significant expansion of its football stadium but only planned to add a small number of seats for people with disabilities, claiming it was doing "repairs" rather than a "renovation." The Michigan Paralyzed Veterans of America sued and, in 2008, the university agreed to add additional seats and to take other steps to improve accessibility (Disability Rights Online News 2008).

* * *

Scholarship, lawsuits, and political activism around issues of disability are certain to continue in the coming years. Because the US public seems to be more sympathetic toward people with disabilities than with those who occupy other subordinate master statuses, it is likely that prejudice and discrimination will continue to decline, despite the fact that Donald Trump's administration worked to stiffen eligibility requirements to receive disability benefits.

9

Striving for Change:
Activism and Social Movements

How can we achieve greater equality when it comes to issues of class, race, immigration, gender, sexual orientation, and disability? The answer: more of us must participate in social change activities. According to a slogan popularized in the 1960s, "If you are not part of the solution, you are part of the problem."

Beverly Tatum (2003) uses the analogy of a pedestrian conveyor belt at an airport. Being on the conveyor belt gives you an advantage over those walking beside it, whether you are taking steps or standing still. You must get off the belt or stop the belt to get rid of the unfair advantage. Similarly, members of dominant groups must take action to create more equality for subordinate groups. Doing nothing simply perpetuates the privilege of the dominant groups.

In the aftermath of the May 25, 2020, murder of George Floyd, a Black man, by a White police officer in Minneapolis, Black Lives Matter protests exploded across the United States. The *New York Times* looked at four different national polls that covered the period of June 4 to June 22 (Buchanan 2020). During that time, 6 to 10 percent of respondents said they participated in a protest, an equivalent of 15–26 million people.

The website www.countlove.org keeps a running tally of protests around the country. In the seven days of May following Floyd's killing, 1,069 protests occurred, about 152 each day. Another 4,278 protests were held in June, about 142 each day. The biggest single day of protests was June 6, 2020, with 531 separate demonstrations. The number of protests declined in July (1,161), August (941), September (626), October (260), and November (141).

According to a Pew Research Center survey (Parker, Horowitz, and Anderson 2020), people of color were twice as likely as Whites to participate. However, the large number of Whites who participated, more than 5 million, was highly unusual for protests against police brutality. Fred Pincus contributed in a small way by standing on a corner near his home with twenty to thirty socially distanced White senior citizens holding protest signs.

Democrats were five times more likely than Republicans to participate. Eighteen- to twenty-nine-year-olds were the most likely age group to participate. The *New York Times* reported that the income group most likely to protest was people earning $150,000 or more.

These unprecedented protests were largely spontaneous outpourings of anger and were mostly organized at the local level. They continued for many weeks, depending on the local area, so the figures cited above are probably conservative estimates.

Of course, street protests are not the only way to achieve change. The same Pew survey found that more than two-thirds of adults had conversations with family and friends about the Floyd killing, 37 percent of social media users posted or shared content on networking sites, 9 percent contributed money to an organization, and 7 percent contacted a public official to express their opinion, all within the month preceding the survey. Many more concentrated their energy on the 2020 elections.

Even professional athletes were swept into the protests in the summer of 2020. National Basketball Association (NBA) and Women's National Basketball Association (WNBA) players boycotted several playoff games during the summer of 2020 in solidarity with protesters against police violence. Several Major League Baseball (MLB) games and National Hockey League (NHL) games were also postponed. Even the conservative National Football League (NFL) teams got involved, four years after Colin Kaepernick was banned from professional football for kneeling during the national anthem to protest racial injustice.

So, what is to be done? Neither social scientists nor activists agree on the answer to this important question. Throughout this book we have emphasized the need to look at issues from different levels of analysis. This is also true of change.

Action for Social Change

Levels of Action

There are at least three different levels of action with regard to change. The lowest level is to *change yourself.* To the extent that you hold prejudiced attitudes or buy into the dominant ideology, try to ask yourself whether this is what you really want to believe. One of our aims with this book was to make you aware of various forms of oppression and how you, if you are a member of the dominant group, might be perpetuating them. You might have already begun to examine some of your beliefs and to question others. You can also change your behavior if that is warranted. If you sometimes make racist remarks, you don't have to keep doing that. If you are a male who tends to treat women as sex objects, you can change. We hope that none of you participate in hate crimes, but if you do, stop! We all have the ability to change what we believe and how we act.

Although self-change is a good thing, it is not nearly enough. We live in a world with other people who have their own attitudes and behaviors. More important, we exist within a set of social, cultural, and economic institutions that are all part of the oppressions we discuss in this book. True change must go beyond changing oneself.

The other end of the levels-of-action spectrum is *collective social action,* which refers to joining with others to seek institutional change. This could mean becoming active in an informal group or a formal organization committed to change. The action could involve letter writing, lobbying politicians, and voter registration. It could also involve protest marches, demonstrations, and rallies like those following the Floyd murder. Minimally, you could participate in some of these activities. Those more committed would help to organize these activities. This takes more time and effort than self-change activities.

Sometimes collective social action becomes part of a social movement. According to Jo Freeman and Victoria Johnson (1999, 3), a social movement refers to "the mobilization and organization of large numbers of people to pursue a common cause. It is also used for the community of believers that is created by that mobilization." Social movements usually contain many organizations willing to act on the same issue. A single organization that influences only its own members is not usually thought of as a social movement. Whether the Black Lives Matter protests become a permanent social movement remains to be seen.

The goals of collective social actions are (1) to attract new members, (2) to educate those participating for the first time, (3) to bring awareness about social justice issues, and (4) to let decisionmakers know there will be consequences for not doing what the activists advocate. The consequences could include being voted out of office, being faced with political disruptions around the country, being confronted by consumer boycotts, and being forced to spend more funds on security. In some cases, social movements can result in genuine revolutions in which the nature of political and economic power is fundamentally changed. Strong, broad-based social movements are much more likely to result in institutional change than any kind of individual actions. "Research shows that social movements can affect government policy as well as how it is made. And movement influence extends further. Activism often profoundly changes the activists, and through them, the organizations in which they participate, as well as the broader culture" (Meyer 2003, 31).

The most dramatic contemporary example of collective social action is the political upheaval that took place after the Floyd murder in 2020. The Women's March of 2017 is another important example of a large-scale collective action. More than 800,000 flocked to Washington, DC, and another 650,000 demonstrated in Los Angeles. More than 4 million people across the country demonstrated in 650 cities protesting the election of Donald Trump and calling for a wide range of women's rights. The marches consisted of many different groups promoting diverse issues and had a genuine sense of excitement. Although the Women's March 2017, as an organization, still exists, the 2018 marches were much smaller, with 1.6 to 2.5 million participants. The numbers declined to 736,000 in 2019 and even less in 2020 (Kauffman 2018).

Somewhere in the space between individual change and collective social action lies a third approach to change: *the micropolitics of subtle transformation.* According to this approach,

> We are doing important social justice work when we stop someone at a party from telling a racist joke, when we build ways for people to express themselves in classrooms, [and] when we find ways to get institutions to serve the interests of members of groups that have been excluded. These sorts of actions can change social institutions when many people are doing them at the same time. They operate as subtle but persistent internal pressure. (Kaufman 2003, 296–297)

In this way, micropolitics can result in discussions and actions at the individual level as well as lawsuits against individual employers, schools, and local governments. Cynthia Kaufman cautions that simply being nice to people isn't enough: "A kindness that stays within the boundaries of the social structures that continually reproduce themselves doesn't make much of a difference except to the people it touches. But when our small-scale challenges interrupt the reproduction of a system of oppression, then something more is happening" (2003,

298). A frequent slogan at women's rights protests, for example, was "Well-behaved women seldom make history."

If one were interested in promoting LGBTQ rights, for example, the individual change approach would suggest that you understand and try to overcome whatever homophobia you have internalized over the years. The micropolitics approach would suggest that you object to homophobic remarks among your friends and coworkers. The collective social action approach would suggest that you help to organize and attend local and national demonstrations to promote LGBTQ civil rights or to protest violence against gays.

Political Philosophy

Change also depends on one's political and philosophical perspectives about how society is supposed to work. Although people often identify themselves as conservatives, liberals, or radicals, it is becoming more and more difficult to give concise descriptions of these terms (see Chapter 2).

To review, traditional conservatives tend to put their faith in the market forces of capitalism and favor limited government programs and regulations, especially at the federal level. In terms of race and gender discrimination, conservatives now reluctantly acknowledge that the federal government has a limited role to play by punishing individual perpetrators and compensating individual victims.

Traditional liberals are also procapitalist in that they believe in market forces, but they understand that an unrestrained economy can get itself into difficulty. Liberals, therefore, believe some limited regulation of the economy by the federal government is a necessity, as are programs for the dispossessed. They also believe the federal government has a legitimate role in passing laws and programs to improve equal opportunities for women and people of color.

The 2020 economic crisis related to the Covid-19 pandemic illustrates different liberal and conservative approaches. The Trump administration's refusal to initiate a national plan to confront Covid-19 was classic conservatism. The administration left individual states the job of obtaining personal protective equipment (PPE) and Covid-19 tests. It promoted competition among individual corporations to develop tests and vaccines. Trump also favored deregulating industry to getting the economy moving again.

In contrast, liberals and some conservatives pushed for the federal government to take a more active role in fighting Covid-19. They wanted the president to involve more companies in the Defense

Production Act to produce needed materials and to distribute needed goods in a rational way. Liberals insisted on a massive stimulus package that directly helped individual working- and middle-class people. The initial $2.2 billion stimulus package included up to $1,200 to most American adults and a $600 weekly supplement to state-funded unemployment insurance. These supplemental unemployment insurance payments ran out in July 2020, and conservatives were not quick to renew them, saying they were incentives not to work. An additional $908 billion bill was past in December 2020 during the lame duck period after Trump lost the election. A third stimulus bill of $1.9 trillion was passed in March 2021, but not a single Republican voted for it.

The use of facemasks was contentious during 2020 and 2021. Although scientists were almost unanimous that masks protected people from infecting others, many conservatives saw mask-wearing as an infringement on their individual rights. Conservative Georgia governor Brian Kemp refused to issue mandates to wear masks in his state, saying it was an individual decision. In fact, he sued several mayors for mandating masks in their cities. Liberals, in contrast, were more likely to wear masks and practice social distancing during the pandemic as scientists urged.

In contrast to liberals and conservatives, radicals are anticapitalist in that they see a market-oriented economy as part of the problem. They argue that liberals and conservatives simply have different ways of maintaining US capitalism and the race, class, gender, sexual orientation, and disability inequalities that go along with it. They are likely to promote social movements for change.

Radicals, along with some liberals, argue that both the Covid-19 pandemic and the economic chaos then went with it could have been mitigated if there was a single-payer health-care system that the federal government could quickly mobilize to meet the country's needs. The availability of PPE and testing could be more rapidly mobilized if the federal government had more control over health care. Nationalizing manufacturers, at least temporarily, would provide for needed services. Relying on profit-making corporations to develop Covid-19 treatments and vaccines would be less efficient than if the government had more control over the process. Presumably, a more socialist government would be better at providing services for poor and working people. Liberal solutions, radicals say, don't go far enough.

Electoral Politics

In the United States, when most people think of political activism, they probably think of elections. We always vote, and we usually find ourselves voting for the Democratic Party candidate for the simple reason that he or she is the lesser of two evils. There has rarely been a major party candidate we enthusiastically supported.

During the 2008 presidential election, we voted for Barack Obama and were thrilled when he became the first Black US president. Although we believed he was too moderate for what the country needed, he was better than Republican candidate John McCain and former president George W. Bush. When conservatives called Obama "radical" or "socialist," Fred Pincus laughed and thought to himself: "I wish it were true."

In the 2020 presidential election, more than 152 million US citizens cast their votes—about 78 million for Biden and about 74 million for Trump. Most conservatives supported Trump while most radicals and progressive liberals united with more centrist liberals to elect Joe Biden. Defeating Trump was the most important issue. Radicals and progressive liberals will try to push President Biden to pursue progressive issues.

Encouraged by President Trump who erroneously argued that he had really won the election, a White nationalist mob attacked the US Capitol building on January 6, 2021. The last time this happened was when the British stormed Washington in the War of 1812.

Carrying confederate flags and neo-Nazi symbols, these ultra-right conservatives shocked the nation and much of the world. They threatened mainstream conservatives like Vice President Mike Pence and liberals like Speaker of the House Nancy Pelosi and Representative Alexandria Ocasio-Cortez. Although only a handful of people were arrested on January 6, more than 400 people have been subsequently arrested. Legal indictments and court proceedings followed.

The parliamentary systems that exist in European capitalist democracies are a more democratic alternative than our two-party system. Even small parties in Europe have representation in parliament and can make their voices heard on the national stage. In the United States, neither the Green Party on the left nor the Libertarian Party on the right stand much of a chance to have representation in Congress, let alone make it to the White House.

Although this is not the place to debate the efficacy of electoral politics versus other kinds of activism, we don't include mainstream electoral groups in the list of activist organizations in the next section. In some cases, elections can be part of a program of collective social action. The Bernie Sanders presidential campaigns in 2016 and 2020 pushed the Democratic Party to the left even though he didn't become the party's presidential candidate. His supporters have formed several national groups, such as Our Revolution and Indivisible, that continue to promote his ideas.

The Biden campaign was a more typical, top-down political campaign that relied on donations from wealthy and powerful forces. Fundamental social change requires political action that goes above and beyond electoral politics (Zinn 2003).

Single Versus Multiple-Category Approaches

Some individuals and organizations focus on change in single categories—race *or* class *or* gender *or* sexual orientation *or* disability. They might focus on only one of these issues without dealing with any of the others. Women might focus on gender issues exclusively, or Asian Americans might focus only on racial issues. Other groups might focus on more than one category, but they might see one category as the most fundamental and the others being of lesser importance. Marxists, for example, have traditionally viewed class as the main axis of oppression, with race and gender being less important.

Intersectionality theorists, in contrast, argue that all these categories are so interconnected that change in one requires changes in the others. Domestic violence, for example, is often seen mainly as a gender issue, but scholars such as Natalie Sokoloff (2008) argue that class and race are also involved because the highest rate of domestic violence affects poor Black women. Immigrant status also figures in the mix because immigrant women might not report domestic violence to the authorities because they fear deportation and/or ostracism in their own communities. Any attempt to develop anti–domestic violence policy is likely to fail without considering all these factors. Although many of today's collective action organizations do not necessarily see themselves as intersectional, they increasingly understand the need for connecting different categories of oppression.

This multiple-category approach can be confusing if proponents don't accurately connect the dots to explain how one type of oppression is interrelated with another. In addition, this approach can create tensions when not everyone accepts the connection. Many gay males and lesbians, for example, said laws that prevented them from marrying were a civil rights issue, not unlike the laws that discriminated against Blacks people during the Jim Crow era. Many Black people, especially those involved with Christian fundamentalist churches, strongly objected to this attempt to equate the two types of oppression on moral grounds. Other Black leaders, such as the late US representatives John Lewis (D-GA) and Elijah Cummings (D-MD), supported gay marriage as a civil rights issue.

Our experience tells us that many students feel most comfortable with liberal, single-category approaches to individual change and micropolitics. Our own approach is to emphasize radical, multiple-category, collective social action. Because we have found that most students don't know much about the important impact collective social action, especially social movements, has had in the United States, we spend the rest of the chapter discussing this. First, we provide a brief history of social movements dealing with class, race, immigration, gender, sexual orientation, and disability. Then we discuss contemporary collective social action possibilities in the twenty-first century.

The History of Collective Social Action

The United States has had a long history of collective social action in the fight for class, race, and gender equality. Sometimes the action is carried out by individual organizations and their members. Other times the action rises to the level of being a social movement. Unfortunately, many history books do not emphasize the role of collective social action in achieving progressive change.

Before the Civil War

During the first half of the nineteenth century, a strong biracial anti-slavery movement developed. White abolitionists (e.g., William Lloyd Garrison, Elizabeth Cady Stanton, and John Brown) and Black abolitionists (e.g., David Walker, Frederick Douglass, and Martin Delany) traveled the country calling for the end of slavery. Harriet Tubman and others helped thousands of slaves to escape through the Underground Railroad. In addition, more than 200 documented slave revolts occurred, the most famous of which was led by Nat Turner.

There were important contradictions within the abolitionist movement, however. Many abolitionists believed in genuine racial equality. Others believed Black people were inferior to White people but disagreed with slavery as an institution. White and Black women were an important part of the abolitionist movement, but they were also promoting women's rights. In her famous "Ain't I a Woman" speech in 1851, Sojourner Truth made the argument that Black women were also women even though they didn't have the privileges White women had. In the end, male abolitionists decided to put women's rights on the back burner until slavery was abolished by the Thirteenth Amendment in 1865. With the Fifteenth Amendment, adopted in 1870, Black men got the vote but no women did.

The first convention to promote women's rights, including the right to vote, was held in Seneca Falls, New York, in 1848. Elizabeth Cady Stanton and Lucretia Mott were the main organizers. It took seventy-two more years for the suffragist movement to win the right for women to vote; the states finally approved the Nineteenth Amendment to the Constitution in 1920. These seventy-two years are known as the "first wave" of the women's movement.

Civil War to World War I

After the post–Civil War period of Reconstruction came to an end, legal segregation was reimposed in the South in the 1880s and 1890s. The US Supreme Court put its stamp of approval on legal segregation in the *Plessy v. Ferguson* decision in 1896. The Court declared that policies of "separate but equal" (which were actually separate and unequal) were consistent with the US Constitution.

The Black community was politically mobilized to fight for equality in the late nineteenth and early twentieth centuries. W. E. B. Du Bois and Booker T. Washington had a running debate during this period over the issue of Jim Crow (legal) segregation in the South. Washington argued, on the one hand, that blacks should try to make the best of a bad situation by acquiring business skills and technical education but not directly challenging segregation. Du Bois, on the other hand, argued for high-quality, integrated education and an end to segregation. He helped found the Niagara movement in 1909, which evolved into the National Association for the Advancement of Colored People (NAACP). Using the courts, the NAACP led a decades-long struggle against lynching, school segregation, and the lack of voting rights.

Workers began to organize trade unions in the late nineteenth century to combat the growing power of the owners of large corporations, including J. P. Morgan, John D. Rockefeller, Andrew Carnegie, James Mellon, Cornelius Vanderbilt, and Leland Stanford. These men were often referred to as "robber barons." Because workers didn't have the right to organize at that time, they had to fight against the private armies of the robber barons. This was class struggle in its most literal sense—strikes often involved violent actions on both sides. Gradually, some employers were forced to recognize unions, wages in some industries increased, and the length of the workday was reduced somewhat. Also, this movement was crucial to outlawing child labor. Workers did not get the right to collective bargaining until 1935.

The labor movement had a mixed record when it came to dealing with Black and women workers. The American Federation of Labor

(AFL, founded in 1881) consisted mostly of White male skilled workers. At various times, the AFL excluded Black people, women, and immigrants from Mexico, Japan, and China. The more radical Industrial Workers of the World (founded in 1905) included everyone in its "one big union." The Congress of Industrial Organizations (CIO), which formed in 1935, also organized all workers in a single industry. In some industries, Black people and women formed their own unions, including the Brotherhood of Sleeping Car Porters and the International Ladies Garment Workers Union.

Founded in 1901, the American Socialist Party had 100,000 members at the height of its influence. In 1911 there were more than 1,200 elected socialist officials in 340 municipalities. Eugene Debs ran for president of the United States on the Socialist Party ticket five times. In 1912 in the election eventually won by Woodrow Wilson, Debs received 900,000 votes, about 6 percent of the total vote. Although the Socialist Party included some Black people in its membership, it "did not go much out of its way to act on the race question" (Zinn 2003, 347).

World War I to the 1940s
The Communist Party split off from the Socialist Party after World War I and was active during the Great Depression in an attempt to mobilize working people. The Communist Party fought for stronger unions and more government services for the unemployed and fought against evictions when people couldn't afford to pay rent. It also actively recruited Black people and other people of color and campaigned against segregation and lynching. Black author Richard Wright was a member for a period of time, and W. E. B. Du Bois and Paul Robeson were publicly sympathetic to the party.

The Wagner Act, passed in 1935, finally gave workers the right to collective bargaining. The National Labor Relations Board was established to enforce worker rights. However, the act didn't cover domestic workers and agricultural workers, most of whom were women and people of color.

The federal government, including the military, remained segregated even under liberal president Franklin Delano Roosevelt. In 1941, A. Philip Randolph, the head of the Brotherhood of Sleeping Car Porters, threatened to organize a march on Washington, DC, to protest discrimination, especially in defense industries. Faced with the possibility of 100,000 angry Black people in Washington, President Roosevelt signed Executive Order 8822, which created the Equal

Employment Practices Committee and abolished race discrimination in the federal government and in defense industries. During World War II, Black men, who were still treated as second-class citizens, and Japanese Americans, who were interned in US concentration camps, still enlisted in the armed forces. However, they fought in segregated units led by White male officers. After the end of World War II, in 1948, President Harry Truman finally issued Executive Order 9981, which banned racial discrimination in the armed forces.

Brown *Decision to the 1970s*
After many years of political struggle and legal battles, the US Supreme Court outlawed segregation in public education in the 1954 *Brown v. Board of Education* decision. This overturned the "separate but equal" doctrine of *Plessy v. Ferguson*. Although *Brown* established an important legal precedent, many Southern politicians refused to implement it, so the rule of Jim Crow remained throughout much of the South until a powerful grassroots social movement challenged racism.

The modern civil rights movement is usually said to have begun in 1955 with the boycott of public buses in Montgomery, Alabama. Buses then had a movable partition that Black people had to sit behind. When all the seats for White passengers in the front were filled, the driver would move the partition, and Black passengers would have to give their seats to White passengers. Rosa Parks, an NAACP activist, refused to move one day and was arrested. The Black community boycotted the buses for 381 days, at which point a federal court declared the Montgomery law unconstitutional. The Southern Christian Leadership Conference (SCLC) grew out of this boycott, and the young Martin Luther King Jr. came into national prominence.

The civil rights movement was largely based on a combination of Christian faith and the principles of nonviolence articulated by Mahatma Gandhi during the anti-British revolution in India in 1949. Through boycotts, sit-ins, freedom rides, marches, demonstrations, and various other kinds of civil disobedience, King hoped to embarrass the South in front of the rest of the country to promote federal civil rights legislation. Because of Southern intransigence and the growing strength and militancy of the civil rights movement, Presidents Dwight D. Eisenhower and John F. Kennedy were forced to use federal troops to enforce the *Brown* decision on school desegregation throughout the South.

Because civil rights activists were largely integrationists, in that they wanted Black people to be accepted into mainstream society as equals, they tried to project an image of middle-class respectability.

Demonstrators often marched and went to jail dressed in their Sunday best. They were encouraged to be disciplined and nonviolent and to control their anger at the police, who often abused them. White allies, especially liberals, students, and labor union members, were welcomed in civil rights protests and organizations.

The civil rights movement reached its peak in 1963, when more than 250,000 people went to Washington, DC, to demand that Congress and President Kennedy pass a civil rights bill. This was the largest demonstration of its kind at the time. Martin Luther King Jr. gave his famous "I Have a Dream" speech at that event.

By 1960, however, a parallel movement for Black liberation began to develop. Increasing numbers of young Black activists began to articulate the ideology of Black Power. Organizations such as the Student Nonviolent Coordinating Committee (SNCC) and the Congress of Racial Equality (CORE) talked about Black political and economic power as well as cultural pride in their African heritage. Blacks, they demanded, must be accepted and negotiated with as a group and on their own terms. Black Power advocates downgraded nonviolence from a religious principle to a political tactic appropriate in some situations and not in others. White people interested in civil rights were told to do their political work in the White community and in White organizations, not in the Black community. In some cases, the tactics of the Black Power movement conflicted with those of the civil rights movement. Malcolm X, Stokely Carmichael (Kwame Ture), and H. Rap Brown were some of the major Black Power leaders.

It took the assassination of President Kennedy in 1963 to get the Civil Rights Act of 1964 passed by Congress and signed by President Lyndon B. Johnson, a Southern Democrat. The following year, Congress passed the Voting Rights Act. A few days later, the predominantly Black Watts section of Los Angeles exploded in violence. This was the first of many riots and urban insurrections to plague the country for the rest of the decade, especially after the assassination of King in 1968. US cities were literally going up in flames. According to Howard Zinn (2003), in the year 1967 (almost five decades before the Black Lives Matter movement) there were 8 major riots, 33 serious riots, and 125 minor incidents.

The Black Panther Party and the League of Revolutionary Black Workers were both Marxist, anticapitalist organizations. The league did most of its organizing work in the automobile factories of Detroit and other midwestern cities, seeing its enemies as the big three automobile corporations and the United Auto Workers (UAW) union. The Black

Panthers, in comparison, tried to organize poor Black communities in cities outside of the South. Both groups worked in coalition with predominantly White anticapitalist groups.

The civil rights movement inspired Mexican and Filipino migrant farmworkers in California to form the United Farm Workers (UFW) union under the leadership of César Chavez, who was sometimes called the Mexican Martin Luther King, and Dolores Huerta. Because farmworkers were not covered under the National Labor Relations Act, they had to fight to get growers to recognize their union with no help from federal officials. The strike began in the grape fields in 1965 and later spread to the lettuce fields. Not having enough power to confront the growers at the local level, the UFW launched a national grape boycott in 1967, asking ordinary citizens throughout the country not to buy grapes grown in California. After three years, the growers finally gave in and negotiated contracts with the UFW. This organizing campaign would not have been successful without broad-based support for the grape boycott.

The civil rights and Black Power movements spawned several other important social movements in the early 1960s. Students for a Democratic Society (SDS), a predominantly White and middle-class group, fought for student rights and racial and economic equality on and off college campuses. SDS became more Marxist and anticapitalist by the end of the 1960s and was an important force among young people. The Weather Underground split off from SDS and believed it was necessary to engage in armed struggle to achieve change. As students became older and graduated or became young faculty members, many joined the New University Conference (NUC), known as the "adult SDS."

The movement against the war in Vietnam was also a major force in the 1960s, especially after 1964. Because young men were being drafted into the armed forces, the war had a personal effect on many families. In addition to groups such as SDS and NUC, several large coalitions organized major demonstrations each year in Washington, New York, San Francisco, and/or Los Angeles. More than half a million people gathered at some demonstrations to protest the war. Most of the time the demonstrations were peaceful, but other times demonstrators destroyed property symbolically linked to the war (e.g., a recruiting station) or to the capitalist class (e.g., a bank). SDS was one of the main organizers of the militant demonstrations and the resulting police riot at the Democratic National Convention in Chicago in 1968. The antiwar movement had become so strong that national leaders had to consider the potentially militant reaction by demonstrators when they talked about escalating the war in Vietnam.

Government officials were so concerned with the rising level of militancy, especially in the Black community, that the Federal Bureau of Investigation (FBI) launched a counterintelligence program in the late 1960s called COINTELPRO. The FBI spied on activist groups and individuals (including Fred Pincus), tried to disrupt the planning of demonstrations, and worked to discredit movement leaders (e.g., tapping King's phone). Local police departments organized "red squads" that did the same thing on the local level. As a result of violent attacks by the police and political repression by the courts, the Black Panthers were eliminated as an effective organization by the early 1970s.

Black athletes also participated in their own protests. Los Angeles Laker star Elgin Baylor refused to play when he and his Black teammates were denied permission to stay in the team hotel in Cincinnati in 1959. Boston Celtics star Bill Russell and his Black teammates sat out a game in St. Louis after they were refused service in the coffeeshop of the team hotel in 1961.

Muhammad Ali, heavyweight boxing champion, refused to be inducted into the US Army during the Vietnam War in 1966 on religious grounds. He was convicted of draft evasion and stripped of his title. One of his famous quotes was "No Vietnamese ever called me nigger."

Sprinters John Carlos and Tommy Smith raised black-gloved, clenched fists in a Black Power salute on the medal stand during the 1968 Olympic Games. They were immediately sent home and banned from future games. NBA star Kareem Abdul Jabbar boycotted the 1968 Olympics and was harshly criticized for being ungrateful.

The late 1960s also brought the early developments of the second wave of the women's liberation movement. In 1963, the President's Commission on the Status of Women issued a widely publicized report documenting the second-class status of women in and out of the labor force. That same year, Betty Friedan's *The Feminine Mystique* (1963) raised a number of issues, including educated, middle-class women being unhappily confined in isolated nuclear families. In 1964 the word *sex* was inserted into the Civil Rights Act, thereby banning discrimination against working women. The EEOC, however, didn't enforce the sex provision and said that an NAACP-like organization for women was needed.

As a result, the National Organization for Women (NOW) was founded in 1966. A predominantly white, middle-class organization, NOW began to raise issues such as discrimination in job advertisements, child care, financial credit for women, sex-role socialization, reproductive rights, equal pay for equal work, and electing more women to political office. The organization, along with many others, unsuccessfully tried to gain passage of an equal rights amendment to the US Constitution from the 1970s onward. This simple amendment stated, "Equality of rights under the law shall not be denied or abridged by the United States or by any State on account of sex" (Eisler and Hixson 2001, 424). The amendment was passed by Congress in 1972 but fell three states short of ratification.

Women around the country began meeting in small "consciousness-raising groups" to discuss what was going on in their families, work, and political lives. By learning that what appeared to be personal, private problems were also shared by other women, thousands of women grew to understand the nature of patriarchy. One important slogan was "The personal is political." Whereas NOW represented mostly liberal feminists, these smaller groups fed into the radical feminist and socialist feminist wings of the women's movement.

In 1973, male chauvinist tennis player Bobby Riggs bragged that at age fifty-five, he could beat any active woman player. Billie Jean King, a superstar in women's tennis, accepted his challenge and trounced Riggs in a televised match known as the Battle of the Sexes.

The gay liberation movement came to national prominence in 1969 when gay males fought back after police raided the Stonewall Inn, a gay bar in New York's Greenwich Village. However, two early gay rights organizations, the Mattachine Society and the Daughters of Bilitis, had been founded in California in the 1950s. After the Stonewall protest, gay men and lesbians began coming out of the closet in large numbers and demanding their rights in the workplace, schools, and cultural institutions as well as freedom from police harassment (Esterberg 1996).

The disability rights movement became active in the 1970s. Prior to this, a number of organizations had been lobbying on behalf of people with specific disabilities. This resulted in the passage of the Vocational Rehabilitation Act of 1973, a landmark law that prevented discrimination against people with disabilities. Because the regulations to enforce this law were slow in coming, a group called the American Coalition of Citizens with Disabilities organized sit-ins in the offices of the Department of Health, Education, and Welfare in 1977 in San Francisco, Washington, DC, and several other cities. This eventually led to the signing of Section 504 of the Vocational Rehabilitation Act.

Also in the 1970s, centers for independent living began to emerge in Berkeley, California, and other cities. These centers were run by people with disabilities and promoted living in the community rather than in institutions. Mentally ill patients also began to mobilize to protest against the abuses that existed in many institutions around the country.

These movements had an impact on social change. The antiwar movement put restraints on how much military force could be used in Vietnam, and this contributed to the US withdrawal in 1973. The civil rights and Black Power movements, along with the urban rebellions, forced policymakers to think about how to address the issues in inner cities. The women's movement helped to produce a sea change in the relations between men and women as well as changes in the labor market.

One of the slogans that came out of the 1960s was "The people, united, can never be defeated." Although the different social movements were not always united with each other, they show that groups of people, acting together, can achieve meaningful institutional change. This lesson should not be lost in the twenty-first century.

Contemporary Issues and Activism

Because a complete history of social activism in the United States is beyond the scope of this book, we'd like to fast-forward to the first decades of the twenty-first century. Despite the increasingly conservative nature of the political times, there are still a variety of issues of interest to college-age people, and there are a variety of organizations that address these issues. Toward the end of the semester, a handful of students usually ask us that big question: What can I do? In the last part of this chapter, we'd like to answer that question by discussing some of the main activist organizations working on the issues discussed in previous chapters.

We've tried to limit this discussion to national organizations that have regional or local affiliates readers can join and be active in. We have omitted many excellent organizations that exist in only one or two cities. Because of space limitations, we have also omitted organizations that provide excellent educational resources but that do not participate in activism themselves. Finally, most of the organizations have a liberal or radical political orientation. This reflects the reality that most conservatives are just not interested in promoting the rights of workers, people of color, immigrants, women, LGBTQ people, and people with disabilities either through activism or other means.

Workers' Rights

US workers face difficult times in the early twenty-first century. During the four years of the first George W. Bush administration (2000–2004), there was a net loss of more than 1 million jobs from the United States, partly caused by multinational corporations outsourcing some jobs and moving entire factories overseas because of cheaper labor. Computers and other labor-saving devices have also reduced a number of jobs. Benefits and retirement pensions have been reduced, as have government transfer payments. The percentage of workers in labor unions has been declining for several decades, and, as a result, workers have less decision-making power than they did in the past. During the Great Recession (2007–2009), unemployment peaked at 9.6 percent as a result of the contracting economy.

Although the economy began to grow again and the unemployment rate declined to less than 4 percent in 2019, the Covid pandemic changed everything. The economy went into a deep recession, and unemployment shot up to 14.7 percent in April 2020, the worst since the Great Depression of the 1930s. Up to ten million jobs were lost between the winter of 2020 and early 2021. Millions of Americans filed for unemployment insurance.

Some unions are beginning to understand "that organizing and growth are linked to mobilizing outsiders in the new labor markets, including new-economy workers, people of color, women, and immigrant workers" (Ness 2003, 56). The Hotel Employees and Restaurant Employees (HERE) union has been increasingly successful in organizing hotel workers around the country, especially in Las Vegas, Nevada. The Service Employees International Union (SEIU) has successfully organized custodians and other building service workers. The United Needletrades, Industrial, and Textile Employees (UNITE) union has organized industrial laundries. In order to increase their bargaining power, UNITE merged with HERE in 2004 to form UNITE HERE.

SEIU and UNITE HERE have been critical of the AFL-CIO leadership for spending too much time supporting Democratic Party candidates and not enough resources increasing the number of workers in unions. In September 2005, these two unions along with five others broke away from the AFL-CIO and formed another national labor organization called Change to Win.

College students can support workers' rights in several ways. If workers on your campus are trying to organize a union, support them. They could be janitors, clerical workers, or teaching assistants. Join their picket lines and help pressure the administration to recognize the union and increase wages and benefits. Because many campus workers are people of color, immigrants, and women, union struggles involve more than just class issues.

United Students Against Sweatshops (USAS; www.USAS.org) often supports these struggles. It also focuses on increasing funding for higher education and making sure that the licensed equipment sold by universities is not made in sweatshops either here or abroad. The term *sweatshop* usually refers to workplaces with long hours, low pay, and unsafe and/or unhealthy working conditions. With chapters at over 150 college campuses around the country, USAS has gotten many universities to adopt campus codes of conduct that include public disclosure of factory sites, independent monitoring of factory conditions, and guaranteed living wages for workers who produce the licensed equipment (Kelly and Lefkowitz 2003). In 2009, after numerous demonstrations, USAS forced Russell Athletic to rehire 1,200 Honduran workers who had lost their jobs during the course of a union organizing campaign (Greenhouse 2009).

Jobs With Justice (JWJ; www.jwj.org) is a somewhat broader organization that "connect[s] labor, faith-based community, and student organizations to work together on workplace and community social justice campaigns." According to its website, JWJ has coalitions in thirty-seven cities throughout the country. Its Student Labor Action Project is geared specifically to high school and college students.

Another summer experience is the Strategic Corporate Research Summer School at the Cornell University School of Industrial and Labor Relations (www.ilr.cornell.edu/worker-institute/education-training/strategic-corporate-research-summer-school/course-details). Graduate students and advanced undergraduates are exposed to a course emphasizing "understanding and researching corporate ownership structure, corporate finance, and the sources of corporate power." The goal is to provide students research skills that can be helpful during union-organizing drives. The AFL-CIO also has an Organizing Institute (www.aflcio.org/about/programs/organizing-institute) that offers several programs that teach the basic tactics and strategy used by the labor movement.

The Asian-Pacific American Labor Alliance (www.aplanet.org), affiliated with the AFL-CIO, is a membership organization of Asian Pacific Union members. It sponsored the 2003 Immigrant Workers Freedom Ride, which toured the country to raise consciousness about the problems of immigrant workers. The "freedom ride" designation, of course, was taken from the freedom rides of the 1960s, which protested segregated public transportation.

Those interested in the concerns of women in the labor force should check out 9 to 5, National Association of Working Women (www.9to5.org). Founded in 1974, 9 to 5 is committed to improving the position of women in the paid labor force. It lobbies for legislation at the federal, state, and local levels to win family-friendly policies for low-wage women, including welfare reform and equal rights on the job. It also has a Job Survival Hotline to handle individual complaints.

Finally, the Poor People's Campaign: A National Call for Moral Revival (www.poorpeoplescampaign.org) is a national group taking the name of the organization founded by Martin Luther King Jr. shortly before his death in the late 1960s. Its more current incarnation emerged from the Moral Mondays movement, led by the Rev. Dr. William J. Barber in North Carolina. According to the Poor People's Campaign website, "The political and economic systems in the U.S. are plagued by the interlocking injustices of systemic racism, poverty, militarism and a war economy, ecological devastation and a distorted moral narrative of religious nationalism. Somebody's hurting our people. It's gone on far too long, and we won't be silent anymore." The website contains a list of local chapters.

Racial and Ethnic Rights
Many organizations are involved in protecting and enhancing the civil rights of specific racial and ethnic groups. This includes education, voting rights, employment, and government programs providing help for disadvantaged groups. Typically, these groups are politically liberal and tend to focus on a specific race and/or ethnic category, but many recognize the importance of interracial coalitions.

The oldest of the organizations is the 100-year-old NAACP (www.naacp.org). Although it gained a somewhat "stodgy" reputation during the turbulent 1960s and 1970s, the NAACP has begun to recruit more young people in recent years and is one of the most well-known of the civil rights organizations in the Black community. The National Urban League (www.nul.org) is another traditional civil rights organization.

Other racial and ethnic groups also have this type of civil rights organization. UnidosUS Action Network (www.unidosus.org) is the umbrella group for the Latinx community. The Asian American community has the OCA-Asian Pacific Americans Advocates (www.ocanational.org), which advocates for all Asian and Asian-Pacific Americans. American Indians don't have a national organization that individuals can join at the local level; the closest to that would be the National Congress of American Indians (www.ncai.org), a tribal membership organization, and American Indian Movement (www.aimovement.org), founded in 1968.

The civil rights organizations of Arab Americans and Muslims have become especially important since the terrorist attacks of September 11, 2001. They include the American-Arab Anti-Discrimination Committee (www.adc.org) and the Council on American-Islamic Relations (www.cair.com). Jewish Voice for Peace (www.jewishvoiceforpeace.org) also supports Arab and Muslim rights in both the United States and the Middle East.

In addition to these civil rights organizations, other race-related groups go beyond civil rights. Black Lives Matter (BLM) is a loose network of local groups organized to oppose police violence against people of color (www.blacklivesmatter.com). It began after the 2012 killing of Trayvon Martin in Sanford, Florida, by a local White neighborhood watchman who was acquitted of the killing. It grew bigger after a White police officer killed Michael Brown in Ferguson, Missouri, and then the movement exploded after a White Minneapolis police officer killed George Floyd by kneeling on his neck for almost nine minutes. BLM protests have also called for reforming the entire criminal justice system and taking some funds from police departments and putting them into anticrime projects in local communities.

Critical Resistance (www.criticalresistance.org), a left-leaning group, focuses on prison reform because of the disproportionate numbers of Black and Latinx people incarcerated. According to its website, "Critical Resistance seeks to build an international movement to end the Prison Industrial Complex by challenging the belief that caging and controlling people makes us safe. . . . As such, our work is part of global struggles against inequality and powerlessness." The Inside Out Prison Exchange Program (www.insideoutcenter.org) brings undergraduates into prisons to take for-credit college classes with prisoners.

The Anti-Defamation League (www.adl.org) is a more mainstream group that does excellent work monitoring a broad range of White nationalist hate groups such as the Aryan Nation, the Proud Boys, the Boogaloo Boys, and the various formations of the Ku Klux Klan. In addition to being explicitly racist, these predominantly White hate groups promote a vicious form of anti-Semitism. The Southern Poverty Law Center (www.splcenter.org) also monitors hate groups.

Color of Change (www.colorofchange.org) is an internet-based group that deals with a variety of issues affecting people of color. Although there are no local chapters, it is possible to sign petitions and contact powerbrokers about a wide variety of issues described on their website.

Finally, Showing Up for Racial Justice (www.showingupforracialjustice.org) is a predominantly White organization that promotes racial justice. Its website describes SURJ as "a national network of groups and individuals working to undermine white supremacy and to work for racial justice. Through community organizing, mobilizing, and education, SURJ moves white people to act as part of a multi-racial majority for justice with passion and accountability." SURJ has 200 local chapters around the country.

Immigrant Rights

The National Network for Immigrant and Refugee Rights (www.nnirr .org) handles issues regarding immigrants of all races. Although it does not appear to have local chapters, NNIRR does enable online activism.

The Fair Immigration and Reform movement (www.fairimmigration .org), the Immigration Advocates Network (www.immigrationadvocates network.org), and the National Partnership for New Americans (www .partnershipfornewamericans.org) are national coalitions of local groups promoting immigrant rights. Local participating groups can be found on their websites.

United We Dream (www.unitedwedream.org) is a youth-led immigrant advocacy group. Its website says it has more than 100 participating groups across twenty-eight states.

Gender Rights

There are a wide variety of national women's organizations with local chapters. The largest is the National Organization for Women (NOW; www.now.org). NOW claims chapters in most states and Washington, DC. The organization is involved in a large variety of issues, including economic justice, the ERA, LGBTQ rights, racial justice, reproductive rights, and ending violence against women. Their political action committee (PAC) works to elect more women to public office. Their Campus Action Network is specifically geared to college students.

The Feminist Majority (www.feminist.org) is another multi-issue organization, and it has an affiliated student organization called Feminist Campus (www.feministcampus.org). The Feminist Majority Foundation also publishes *Ms.* magazine.

Women's March (www.womensmarch.com) is an organization and coalition that sponsored the huge January 21, 2017, march to protest the inauguration of Donald Trump. As we have discussed earlier, millions of people have been mobilized to come to single-day marches. The many local affiliates can be found on their website.

Several women's organizations focus primarily on reproductive rights. Planned Parenthood (www.plannedparenthood.org) is primarily a service provider where women can get birth control counseling, gynecological exams, and abortions. NARAL Pro-Choice America (www .naral.org) fights for reproductive rights in terms of national and state legislation and court decisions. SisterSong.net focuses on reproductive rights for women of color. The pro-choice March for Women's Lives brought a million people to Washington to demand reproductive rights for women in 2004.

The Women of Color Network (www.womenofcolornetwork.org) is a national coalition of organizations and individuals that opposes violence against women and families in communities of color. INCITE! Women of Color Against Violence (www.incite-national.org), one of the member organizations of the network, works against all forms of violence against women. As stated on its website, the organization's goal is to "advance a national movement to nurture the health and well-being of communities of color."

The MeToo movement (metoo.org) was founded in 2006 by Tarana Burke to oppose sexual harassment and assault. The group went viral when women accused celebrities in the entertainment field of a range of sexual improprieties.

The National Organization for Men Against Sexism (www.nomas .org) is also dedicated to stopping violence against women and to promoting gender equality. A Call to Men (www.acalltomen.org) also opposes violence against women and calls for new forms of masculinity.

Finally, there are a number of women's organizations whose mission is to achieve peace and justice around the world and in the United States. The Women's International League for Peace and Freedom (www.wilpf.org) was founded in 1915 by Jane Addams of Hull House fame. Women's Actions for New Directions (www.wand.org) was founded in 1982 as Women's Action for Nuclear Disarmament. Women in Black (www.womeninblack.org) is an international organization founded in 1988 by Israeli women who called for a just peace between Israelis and Palestinians. Women in Black still focuses on the Middle East but is now also involved in other international issues. Code Pink: Women for Peace (www.codepink.org) was founded in 2002 as part of the movement against the war in Iraq. All of these organizations have participated in the demonstrations around a wide variety of issues.

LGBTQ Rights

As we discussed in Chapter 7, a lot of work remains to be done to achieve equality for the LGBTQ population. There are civil rights and legal issues with regard to employment, housing, education, and health care. In addition, acquired immunodeficiency syndrome (AIDS) prevention and treatment is a major issue, especially for gay men and for heterosexual women of color. In April 2000, 500,000 people attended the Millennium March for Equality in Washington, DC.

There are two national civil rights organizations with local chapters for the LGBTQ community. The Human Rights Campaign (HRC; www.hrc.org) website describes it as "a bipartisan organization that works to advance equality based on sexual orientation and gender expression and identity, to ensure that gay, lesbian, bisexual and transgender Americans can be open, honest and safe at home, at work and in the community." The HRC lobbies Congress, provides campaign support for gay-friendly candidates, and conducts public education campaigns. It has recently established Partnerships for Equality, which provides funds to state advocacy organizations to promote gay-friendly legislation.

The National Gay and Lesbian Task Force (NGLTF; www.thetaskforce.org) has a similar mission with a somewhat more activist orientation. According to its website, "We're building a social justice movement that unites ideas with action. We organize activists. We train leaders. We equip organizers. We mobilize voters. We build coalitions. We teach-and-learn from today's vibrant GLBT youth movement. We're proud of our commitment to the linkages between oppressions based on race, class, gender, and sexual orientation." The NGLTF also has a think tank (the Policy Institute), tracks state legislation, and promotes local organizing through the Federation of Statewide Lesbian, Gay, Bisexual, and Transgender Political Organizations. Soulforce (www.soulforce.org) is another gay activist organization that focuses on overcoming the homophobia often found in fundamentalist Christian churches. Southerners on New Ground (www.southernersonnewground.org) organizes LGBTQ people in the South.

The main national activist organization with local chapters that deals with AIDS is ACT UP (www.actupny.com). ACT UP is really a loose network of groups that began in New York City and had spread to a dozen other cities. In 2020 ACT UP existed mainly in New York, Boston, and Rhode Island. Historically, its main focus has been around the issue of human immunodeficiency virus (HIV) and AIDS. Tactically, ACT UP has been more militant than most other groups in that it advocates direct action and civil disobedience to get its point across. Members have disrupted professional conferences and political meetings. Civil disobedience manuals are offered on the ACT UP website. In one of its early actions in 1993, ACT UP members dumped the ashes of friends and loved ones who died of AIDS on the steps of the California capitol to protest cuts in health-care spending (Shepard 2003). A twentieth-anniversary march in 2006 ended at Wall Street in New York with the group adorning the ears of the famous bull with condoms.

According to ACT UP activist Vito Russo, "After we kick the shit out of this disease, I intend to be able to kick the shit out of this system, so that this never happens again" (Shepard 2003, 153). Russo was referring to the fact that "fighting the AIDS pandemic [means] fighting institutional racism, sexism [and] the class system as well as homophobia" (Shepard 2003, 153).

Straight people who want to be supportive of LGBTQ friends and relatives can join Parents, Families, and Friends of Lesbians and Gays (PFLAG; www.pflag.org). With more than 500 affiliates throughout the country, PFLAG engages in a number of activities, including "education, to enlighten an ill-informed public; and advocacy, to end discrimination and to secure equal civil rights." It also provides opportunities to "dialogue" about a variety of issues around sexual orientation. The Gay, Lesbian, and Straight Education Network (www.glsen.org) focuses on safety in the schools for gay students.

Happily, Freedom to Marry (www.freedomtomarry.org) was able to disband after the Supreme Court legalized same-sex marriage in 2015. Log Cabin Republicans (www.logcabin.org) is a conservative organization that calls for the Republican Party to be more inclusive when it comes to LGBTQ issues. Its website was strongly supportive of Trump.

Disability Rights

Although many national organizations promote the rights of people with disabilities, most represent a single type of disability (e.g., blindness or a particular illness) and tend to use conventional methods of lobbying, education, service, or advocacy.

ADAPT (www.adapt.org) is one of the few groups that has local chapters that participate in direct action. Its April 2010 action, "Defending Our Freedom," featured five days of marching, lobbying, and online protests in Washington, DC. Its members demanded that President Obama fully implement the American with Disabilities Act as well as other legislation. They encouraged people with disabilities to file complaints of discrimination with the Office of Civil Rights of the US Department of Justice, and they encouraged members to learn from each other about local successes and failures to fight state budget cuts.

More recently, ADAPT has been promoting the Disability Integration Act, which would enable people with disabilities to live independently

rather than in nursing homes and other institutions. The Arc (www
.thearc.org) promotes the civil rights of people with intellectual and
developmental disabilities, and Active Minds (www.activeminds.org)
does the same for young people with mental health issues.

Peace and Justice

A number of organizations focus on war and militarism. The current
focus is on the US wars against Afghanistan, which began in October
2001, and against Iraq, which began in March 2003. In addition to questions concerning the immorality of war and the critique of US militarism, wars have implications for some of the issues discussed in previous chapters. The huge expense of war makes it more difficult to fund
a wide variety of social programs geared toward poor and working people of all races and ethnicities. By the middle of 2010, the wars in
Afghanistan and Iraq had cost more than $1 trillion. Until 2010, more
money was spent on occupying Iraq than in Afghanistan. Now, the
reverse is true.

The National Priorities Project (2010) looked at what else could be
funded if the $170.5 billion proposed for the wars in FY2010 had been
spent on other domestic programs. This money could have funded 22.4
million Head Start slots for poor children, the salaries of 2.6 million
elementary school teachers or 3 million fire fighters, or 30.7 million
Pell grants (at $5,500 each) for college students. When politicians claim
there isn't enough money to spend on these and other programs, the
money that goes to war is one of the main reasons.

The movement to oppose the war in Iraq began before the invasion.
There was a national demonstration on October 26, 2002, and international demonstrations followed on January 18, 2003. After the invasion,
the protests continued. More than 100,000 people protested the war on
October 25, 2003. Between 400,000 and 500,000 people marched outside the Republican National Convention on August 29, 2004.

Two national groups organized these large-scale national demonstrations and are active in local communities: International Act Now
to Stop War and End Racism (www.internationalanswer.org) and
United for Peace and Justice (www.unitedforpeace.org). In addition
to opposing the war, coalition members support the rights of women
and people of color in the United States. The websites of both groups
list hundreds of local activist organizations. The American Friends
Service Committee (www.afsc.org) and the War Resisters League
(www.warresisters league.org), two pacifist organizations, and Not in
Our Name (www.notinourname.net) also participate in antiwar activ-

ities and have local offices throughout the country. Amnesty International (www.amnesty usa.org) focuses on human rights around the world.

Although it was formed in 1998, MoveOn (www.moveon.org) really took off in 2002 with online petitions and calls for activism. In 2004, MoveOn organized a serious of house parties in concert with the opening of Michael Moore's film *Fahrenheit 911.* After typing in your zip code on the MoveOn website, you would click on a home near you to reserve a seat. People then gathered in small groups to discuss the film and participate in a national conference call with Moore. A few months later, this same process was repeated with the showing of *Outfoxed,* a blistering critique of the conservative bias of the Fox News Network. Before Covid (and we hope afterward), these house parties provided huge potential to mobilize people at the local level.

Left-Wing Political Formations

Several organizations are working to build a socialist, rather than a capitalist, society. The Democratic Socialists of America (DSA; www.dsausa .org) is explicitly anticapitalist but does not want to repeat the authoritarian errors of countries such as the former Soviet Union and China. Senator Bernie Sanders and Representative Alexandria Ocasio-Cortez are two of the most prominent members.

The DSA is calling for a democratic form of socialism wherein the government would own a greater portion of the economy and ordinary people would have a much larger say in political decisions than they now have. Their model society is closer to Scandinavian social democracy than to Chinese Communism. The DSA employs a wide range of tactics, including trying to push the Democratic Party to the left.

DSA membership grew rapidly after the election of President Trump. On election day, 2016, DSA had about 8,500 members. The day after the election, 1,000 new members joined. By the spring of 2020, membership had jumped to 66,000. The DSA website lists more than 200 chapters across the country, including Young Democratic Socialists of America.

The Green Party of the United States (www.gp.org), in contrast, does field candidates and sees itself as a third political party. Focusing on "environmentalism, non-violence, social justice, and grassroots organizing," Green Party candidates have participated in federal, state, and local political races since 1996. In November 2010, 136 Green Party members held elected office in twenty-three states and the District of Columbia.

Our Revolution (www.ourrevolution.com) and Indivisible (www .indivisible.org) both formed as a result of the 2016 presidential election. Our Revolution is largely made up of those who supported Bernie Sanders for president in 2016 and 2020. Both groups have local chapters and support progressive political candidates.

We end this chapter with a brief word about Antifa, which stands for "anti-fascist." The fact that Antifa doesn't seem to have a website is indicative of its loose network of small groups around the country. Their stated goal is to confront, sometimes physically, White nationalist groups who hold outdoor rallies and marches (Bray 2017). In spite of Trump conflating Antifa with other Black Lives Matter protesters, they are a tiny group most other protesters shun. One of the most absurd accusations by conservatives is that Antifa infiltrated and was responsible for the right-wing attack on the Capitol on January 6, 2021.

* * *

As this chapter shows, there are numerous ways to become an activist to achieve a more just world. Many of the national organizations we mention have chapters or affiliates in your city, possibly even on your campus. There are also thousands of local organizations working on the issues raised in these pages. Get involved! Remember, if you are not part of the solution, you are probably part of the problem.

Key Terms

Ableism is the system of oppression based on disability status.

Bisexual refers to individuals sexually, physically, and emotionally attracted to both same- and opposite-sex partners.

Cisgender refers to people whose gender identity matches their physiological sex.

Cissexism is a system of oppression against transgender and nonbinary individuals.

Coming out refers to someone who has revealed his or her LGBTQ sexual orientation to others.

Conflict diversity refers to understanding how different groups exist in a hierarchy of inequality in terms of power, privilege, and wealth.

Conservative: see page 30.

Counting diversity refers to empirically enumerating differences within a given population.

Culture diversity refers to the importance of understanding and appreciating the cultural differences between groups.

Disability is a social exclusion, disadvantage, or restriction of activity caused by a contemporary social organization that takes little or no account of people who have physical impairments and thus excludes them from participation in the mainstream of social activities.

Discrimination refers to actions that deny equal treatment to people perceived to be members of some social category or group.

Diversity means "the condition of having or being composed of differing elements: variety; especially: the inclusion of different types of people (such as people of different races or cultures) in a group or organization." Synonyms include "assortment, diverseness, heterogeneity, heterogeneousness, manifoldness, miscellaneousness, multifarious-ness, multiplicity, variety, variousness."

A **dominant group** is a social group that controls the political, economic, and cultural institutions in a society.

The **essentialist perspective** argues that reality exists independent of our perception of it; that is, there are real and important (essential) differences among categories of people.

An **ethnic group** is a social group that has certain cultural characteristics that set it off from other groups and whose members see themselves as having a common past.

Exploitation means that the dominant group uses the subordinate group for its own ends, including economic profit and a higher position in the social hierarchy.

Feminism is a movement to end sexist oppression.

Gay usually refers to homosexual males, although it is also used as an umbrella term for homosexuals in general.

Gender refers to the behavior culturally defined as appropriate and inappropriate for males and females.

Gender nonconforming/gender nonbinary/genderqueer refer to people whose gender expression does not fully conform to sex-linked gender expectations.

Good-for-business diversity refers to the argument that businesses will be more profitable, and government agencies and not-for-profit corporations will be more efficient, with diverse labor forces.

Hegemonic ideologies are those ideas so influential that they dominate all other ideologies.

Heteronormativity is the worldview that promotes heterosexuality and the gender binary as the normal or default pattern of behavior. People wrongly assume that everyone else is a heterosexual, cis-gender man or woman unless told differently.

Heterosexism refers to a system of oppression against the LGBTQ population.

Heterosexual refers to people sexually, physically, and emotionally attracted to people of the opposite sex.

Homophobia refers to fear and hatred against those who love and sexually desire people of the same sex.

Homosexual refers to persons sexually, physically, and emotionally attracted to people of the same sex.

Ideology is a body of ideas reflecting the social needs and aspirations of an individual group, class, or culture.

Immigrants are people moving from one country to another to settle there.

Impairment refers to physical or mental limitations.

In the closet refers to someone who has not revealed his or her LGBTQ sexual orientation to others.

Income is the amount of money a person or family earns from wages and salaries, interest, dividends, rent, gifts, and transfer payments.

Intentional individual discrimination refers to the behavior of individual members of one group/category intended to have a differential and/or harmful effect on members of another group/category.

Intentional systemic discrimination refers to the policies of dominant group institutions, and the behavior of individuals who implement these policies and control these institutions, intended to have a differential and/or harmful effect on subordinate groups. It is also called *institutional or structural discrimination.*

Intergenerational mobility is a child's class position relative to the child's parents.

Intersectionality is a theoretical approach that asserts the existence of parallel systems of oppression (gender, race, sexual orientation, etc.) that sometimes reinforce each other and sometimes contradict each other.

Intersexed refers to a person having physical attributes of both males and females.

Intragenerational mobility is the degree to which a young worker who enters the labor force can improve his or her class position within a single lifetime.

Lesbian refers to homosexual females.

LGBTQ stands for lesbian, gay, bisexual, transgender, and queer people.

Liberal: see page 32.

A **master status** has a profound effect on one's life and dominates or overwhelms the other statuses one occupies.

Meritocracy is a stratified society wherein the most skilled people have the better jobs, and the least skilled people have the lowest-paying jobs, regardless of race, gender, age, and so on.

Microaggressions are commonplace verbal or behavioral indignities, intentional or unintentional, that communicate hostile, derogatory, or negative attitudes toward a subordinate group.

Monopoly capitalism refers to an economic system where there is a lack of competition and when a few corporations own and control most or nearly all the goods or services within a particular industry.

Technically, economists refer to this as an oligopoly, but the term monopoly has been widely used.

Nationalism exalts one nation above all others and places primary emphasis on promotion of its culture and interests.

Net worth is the value of the wealth and assets that a person or family owns minus the value of what they owe.

Occupational sex segregation refers to the differential distribution of men and women into sex-appropriate occupations in the labor force.

Oppression is a dynamic process by which one segment of society achieves power and privilege through the control and exploitation of other groups, which are burdened and pushed down into the lower levels of the social order.

The "other" is viewed as being unlike the dominant group in profoundly different, usually negative, ways.

Passing refers to a subordinate-group member who successfully pretends to be a dominant-group member.

Patriarchy is a hierarchical system that promotes male supremacy.

Political asylum is a legal status for immigrants offered government protection because they left their countries as political refugees.

Politics refers to any collective action intended to support, influence, or change social policy or social structures.

Prejudice refers to negative attitudes toward a specific group of people.

Privilege means that some groups have something of value denied to others simply because of the groups they belong to; these unearned advantages give some groups a head start in seeking a better life.

Queer, a former slur, has been reclaimed as an umbrella term for the LGBTQ community.

A **racial group** is a social group socially defined as having certain biological characteristics that set it apart from other groups, often in invidious ways.

Racial ideology is a body of ideas used by the dominant racial group to explain and justify oppression against the subordinate racial group(s).

Racism is a system of power and oppression that provides, on the one hand, economic, political, or psychological advantages and privileges for the White (i.e., dominant) racial group, and, on the other hand, discriminates against and disadvantages the non-White (i.e., subordinate) racial groups.

Radical: see page 34.

Refugees are forced to leave their country in order to escape war, persecution, or natural disasters.

Role specifies expected behavior that goes along with a specific status.

Sex refers to the physical and biological differences between the categories of male and female.

Sexism is a system of oppression based on gender.

Sexual behavior refers to whom we have sex with.

Sexual identification refers to what people call themselves.

Sexual orientation is determined by to whom we are attracted sexually, physically, and emotionally.

The **social constructionist** perspective argues that reality cannot be separated from the way a culture makes sense of it—that meaning is "constructed" through social, political, legal, scientific, and other processes.

Social mobility refers to individuals moving up or down in terms of their class level.

Status refers to a position one holds or a category one occupies in a society.

Stereotypes are cultural beliefs about a particular group that are usually highly exaggerated and distorted, even though they might have a grain of truth.

Stigma is an attribute for which someone is considered bad or unworthy because of the category he or she belongs to.

Straight refers to heterosexual people.

Stratification refers to the way in which societies are marked by inequality, by differences among people regarded as being higher or lower.

A **subordinate group** is a social group that lacks control of the political, economic, and cultural institutions in a society.

Transgender people feel that their gender identity doesn't match their physiological body.

Transphobia refers to the fear and hatred of transgender people and gender nonconformity more generally.

Transsexuals are people who have had sex change operations.

Undocumented immigrants moved to the United States and are here without the necessary legal documents.

Unintentional individual discrimination refers to the behavior of individual members of one group/category not intended to have a differential and/or harmful effect on members of another group/category but that has a negative effect.

Unintentional systemic discrimination refers to policies of dominant-group institutions, and the behavior of the individuals who implement these policies and control these institutions, that are neutral in intent—in terms of race, class, gender, and sexuality—but that have a differential or harmful effect on subordinate groups.

Wealth refers to the assets people own and is often expressed in terms of net worth.

Xenophobia is the fear and/or hatred of foreigners or anything that seems foreign.

References

Akom, A. A. 2000. "The House That Race Built: Some Observations on the Use of the Word *Nigga,* Popular Culture, and Urban Adolescent Behavior." In *Construction Sites: Excavating Race, Class, and Gender Among Urban Youth,* edited by Lois Weis and Michelle Fine. New York: Teachers College Press.

Albert, Judith Clavira, and Steward Edward Albert. 1984. *The Sixties Papers: Documents of a Rebellious Decade.* New York: Praeger.

Alexander, Michelle. 2012. *The New Jim Crow: Mass Incarceration in the Age of Colorblindness.* New York: New Press.

Allegretto, Sylvia, and Michelle M. Arthur. 2001. "An Empirical Analysis of Homosexual/Heterosexual Male Earnings Differentials: Unmarried and Unequal?" *Industrial and Labor Relations Review* 54, no. 3 (April): 631–646.

Alon, Titan, Matthias Doepke, Jane Olmstead-Rumsey, and Michele Tertilt. 2020. "Impact of the Covid-19 Crisis on Women's Employment." www.econofact .org/impact-of-the-covid-19-crisis-on-women's-employment.

American Community Survey. 2020. "Table 1: National Employment and Labor Force Characteristics for Same-Sex and Opposite-Sex Married Householders and Their Spouses: 2019." www.census.gov/data/tables/2019/demo/labor-force /same-sex-employment-characteristics.html.

American Federation of Labor-Congress of Industrial Organizations (AFL-CIO). 2019. "Highest-Paid CEOs." www.aflcio.org/paywatch/highest-paid-ceos.

Americans with Disabilities Act. 1990. Public Law No. 101-336, 42 U.S.C. 12101-213.

Anderson, Margaret L. 2003. *Thinking About Women: Sociological Perspectives on Sex and Gender.* Boston: Allyn and Bacon.

Anderson, Sarah, John Cavanagh, Chuck Collins, Sam Pizzigati, and Mike Lapham. 2008. *Executive Excess 2008.* Washington, DC: Institute for Policy Studies/ United for a Fair Economy.

Anti-Defamation League. 2019. "Murder and Extremism in the United States in 2019." February. www.adl.org/media/14107/download.

Antonak, Richard F., and Hanoch Livneh. 2000. "Measurement of Attitudes Towards Persons with Disabilities." *Disability and Rehabilitation* 22, no. 5: 211–224.

Associated Press. 2003. "DeShawn Might Be Less Employable Than Cody, Research Shows." *Baltimore Sun,* September 28, 4A.

———. 2004. "Texas Texts Won't Have 'Married Partners.'" *Baltimore Sun,* November 6, 5A.

Astor, Maggie. 2020. "Facing a 'Double Bind' or Racism and Sexism." *New York Times,* October 10, A13.

Babcock, Linda, and Sara Laschever. 2003. *Women Don't Ask: Negotiation and the Gender Divide.* Princeton, NJ: Princeton University Press.

Bach, Natasha. 2018. "American Women Face More Discrimination Than Europeans, Report Finds." *Fortune,* December 7.

Badgett, M. V. Lee. 2000. "The Myth of Gay and Lesbian Affluence." *Gay and Lesbian Review Worldwide* 7, no. 2 (Spring): 22–26.

Baird, Vanessa. 2001. *The No-Nonsense Guide to Sexual Diversity.* London: Verso.

Ballotpedia. 2020. "Timeline of Federal Policy on Immigration, 2017–2020." www .ballotpedia.org/timeline-of-federal-policy-on-immigration-2017-2020.

Barroso, Amanda. 2020a. "Most Black Adults Say Race Is Central to Their Identity and Feel Connected to a Broader Black Community." Pew Research Center.

———. 2020b. "61% of U.S. Women Say 'Feminist' Describes Them Well; Many See Feminism as Empowering, Polarizing." Pew Research Center. www.pew researchcenter.org/fact-tank/2020/07/07/61.

Beeghley, Leonard. 2005. *The Structure of Social Stratification in the United States,* 4th ed. Boston: Allyn and Bacon.

Bennett, Jessica. 2020. "Trump (Tough Guy), Biden (Nice Guy) and the Politics of Manliness." *New York Times,* November 2, A22.

Bhutta, Neil, Andrew C. Chang, Lisa J. Detting, and Joanne W. Hsu, with the assistance of Julia Hewitt. 2020. "Disparities in Wealth by Race and Ethnicity in the 2019 Survey of Consumer Finances." Washington, DC: Federal Reserve. www.federalreserve.gov/econres/notes/feds-notes/disparities-in-wealth-by -race-and-ethnicity-in-the-2019-survey-of-consumer-finances-20200928.htm.

Bilefsky, Dan. 2008. "Old Custom Fades in Albania: Woman as Man of Family." *New York Times,* June 25, A1, A12.

Black Futures Lab. 2019. "Beyond Kings and Queens: Gender and Politics in the 2019 Black Census." www.blackcensus.org/wp-content/uploads/2019/11 /Beyond-Kings -and-Queens-Gender-and-Politics.pdf.

Blauner, Robert. 1972. *Racial Oppression in America.* New York: Harper and Row.

———. 1992. "Talking Past Each Other: Black and White Languages of Race." *American Prospect* 10 (Spring): 55–64.

Blazina, Carrie Elizabeth, and Drew DeSilver. 2021. "A Record Number of Women Are Serving in the 117th Congress." Pew Research Center, January 15. https:// www.pewresearch.org/fact-tank/2021/01/15/a-record-number-of-women-are -serving-in-the-117th-congress/

Blumenfeld, Warren J., and Diane Raymond. 2000. "Prejudice and Discrimination." In *Readings for Diversity and Social Justice,* edited by Maurianne Adams, Warren J. Blumenfeld, and Rosie Castaneda et al. New York: Routledge.

Bonilla-Silva, Eduardo. 2003. *Racism Without Racists: Color-Blind Racism and the Persistence of Racial Inequality in the United States.* Lanham, MD: Rowman and Littlefield.

———. 2018. *Racism Without Racists: Color-Blind Racism and the Persistence of Racial Inequality in the United States,* 5th ed. Lanham, MD: Rowman and Littlefield.

Bowman, Karlyn H. 2004. "Attitudes About Homosexuality and Gay Marriage." American Enterprise Institute Studies in Public Opinion. www.aei.org.

Boylan, Jennifer Finney. 2003. *She's Not There: A Life in Two Genders.* New York: Broadway.

Bray, Mark. 2017. *Antifa: The Anti-Fascist Handbook.* New York: Melville House.

Brenan, Megan. 2020. "New Low 35% in U.S. Satisfied with Treatment of Black People." Gallup. www.news.gallup.com/poll/317327/record-satisfied-treatment -black-people.aspx?version=print.

Brockway, Claire, and Carroll Doherty. 2019. "Growing Share of Republicans Say U.S. Risks Losing Its Identity If It Is Too Open to Foreigners." Pew Research Center. www.pewresearch.org/fact-tank/2019/07/17.

Buchanan, Larry. 2020. "Black Lives Matter May Be the Largest Movement in U.S. History." *New York Times,* July 3.

Budiman, Abby, Anthony Cilluffo, and Neil G. Ruiz. 2019. "Key Facts About Asian Origin Groups in the U.S." www.pewresearch.org/fact-tank/2019/05/22/key -facts-about-asian-origin-groups-in-the-u-s/.

Cameron, Chris. 2020. "Trump Advances Limits for Transgender Rights." *New York Times*, July 25, A16.

Caron, Christina. 2018. "Teacher Marries Her Girlfriend, and Then Catholic Schools Fires Her." *New York Times,* February 17.

Carroll, Joseph. 2007. "Most Americans Approve of Interracial Marriage." Gallup News Service, August 16.

Center for American Women in Politics. 2019. "Women in the U.S. Congress 2019." www.cawp.rutgers.edu/women-us-congress-2019.

Churchwell, Sarah. 2018. www.smithsonianmag.com/history/behold-america-american -dream-slogan-book-sarah-churchwell-180970311/.

Cohen, Adam. 2020. *Supreme Inequality: The Supreme Court's Fifty-Year Battle for a More Unjust America.* New York: Random House.

Cohen, Patricia. 2009. "Rethinking Gender Bias in Theater." *New York Times,* June 24: C1.

———. 2019. "Country Is Full? It's News to Us, Employers Say." *New York Times,* August 23, A1, 14.

Collins, Chuck. 2020. "U.S. Billionaire Wealth Is Up $850 Billion Since March 18th." Institute for Policy Studies, October 8. www.ips-dc.org/u-s-billionaire -wealth-up-850-billion/.

———. 2021. "660 Billionaires See Wealth Rise 40 Percent." Portside, January 26.

Community Marketing Inc. (CMI). 2019. "13th Annual LGBTQ Community Survey." www.communitymarketinginc.com/documents/temp/CMI-13th_LGBTQ _Community_Survey_US_Profile.pdf.

Compton, D'Lane R., and Amanda K. Baumle. 2018. "Demographics of Gay and Lesbian Partnerships and Families." In *International Handbook on Gender and Demographic Processes,* edited by N. E. Riley and J. Brunson. Springer Science + Business Media.

Connor, Phillip, and Abby Budiman. 2019. "Immigrant Share in U.S. Nears Record High but Remains Below That of Many Other Countries." Pew Research Center. www.pewresearch.org/fact-tank/2019/01/30.

Covert, Bryce. 2019. "Nearly Two Decades Ago, Women Across the Country Sued Walmart for Discrimination. They're Not Done Fighting." *Time,* May 9. www .time.com/5586423/Walmart-gender-discrimination.

Cramer, Maria. 2020. "Barbie Tries to Reinvent Herself." *Baltimore Sun,* February 1, 6.

Crenshaw, Kimberlé. 1989. "Demarginalizing the Intersection of Race and Sex: A Black Feminist Critique of Antidiscrimination Doctrine, Feminist Theory, and

Antiracist Politics." *University of Chicago Legal Forum.* Chicago, IL: University of Chicago Law School, 139–168.

Cyrus, Virginia. 2000. *Experiencing Race, Class, and Gender in the United States,* 3rd ed. Mountain View, CA: Mayfield.

Dang, Alain, and Somjen Frazier. 2004. "Black and Same-Sex Households in the United States: A Report from the 2000 Census." New York: National Gay and Lesbian Task Force Policy Institute/National Black Justice Coalition.

D'Arcy, Janice. 2005. "Religious Houses Stand Divided on Gay Marriage Debate." *Baltimore Sun,* January 30, 1A, 6A.

Darling, Rosalyn Benjamin. 2003. "Toward a Model of Changing Disability Identities." *Disability and Society* 18, no. 7: 881–895.

Dayen, David. 2020. *Monopolized: Life in the Age of Corporate Power.* New York: New Press.

de Tocqueville, Alexis. 1994. *Democracy in America.* New York: Random House.

Deal, Mark. 2003. "Disabled People's Attitudes Toward Other Impairment Groups." *Disability and Society* 18: 897–910.

Denvir, Daniel. 2020. "The Deep Roots of Trump's Anti-Immigrant Policies." *Jacobin Magazine.* www.jacobinmag.com/2020/02.

DeParle, Jason. 2020. "With Aid Spent, Poverty Traps Millions More." *New York Times,* October 16, A1, A20.

Despres, Cliff. 2020. "Study: Since Trump, Latino Youth Anxiety over Immigration Has Skyrocketed." Salud America, March 10. https://salud-america.org/study -since-trump-latino-youth-anxiety-over-immigration-has-skyrocketed/.

Diangelo, Robin. 2018. *White Fragility: Why It's So Hard for White People to Talk About Racism.* Boston: Beacon Press.

Disability Rights Advocates. 2009. "Deaf and Hearing-Impaired Employees Settle Class Action Lawsuit with UPS." Press release, June 16.

Disability Rights Online News. 2008. "University of Michigan Agrees to Improve Accessibility at Football Stadium." April. www.ada.gov/disabilitynews.htm.

———. 2009. "Walmart to Improve Access for People with Disabilities Nationwide." April.

Diversity Insight. 2008. "Walmart Agrees to Pay $300,000 to Rejected Applicant to Settle Disability Discrimination Lawsuit." July 21.

Doan, Long, Annalise Loehr, and Lisa R. Miller. 2014. "Formal Rights and Informal Privileges for Same-Sex Couples: Evidence from a National Survey Experiment." *American Sociological Review* 79, no. 6: 1172–1195.

Domhoff, G. William. N.d. "Power, Politics, and Social Change." whorulesamerica .ucsc.edu.

D'Souza, Dinesh. 1995. *The End of Racism: Principles for a Multiracial Society.* New York: Free Press.

Du Bois, W. E. B. 1990. *The Souls of Black Folk.* New York: Vintage.

Dunn, Amina. 2018. "Partisans Are Divided over the Fairness of the U.S. Economy—and Why People Are Rich or Poor." Pew Research Center, October 4.

Eagly, A. H., C. Nater, D. I. Miller, M. Kaufman, and S. Sczesny. 2019. "Gender Stereotypes Have Changed: A Cross-Temporal Meta-Analysis of U.S. Public Opinion Polls from 1946 to 2018." *American Psychologist.* doi: 10.1037 /amp0000494.

Economist. 2004. "Ever Higher Society, Ever Harder to Ascend." www.economist .com/world/na/PrinterFriendly.cfm?Story_ID.

Edwards, Cliff. 2003. "Coming Out in Corporate America: Gays Are Making Huge Strides Everywhere but in the Executive Suite." *Business Week.* December 15: 64–72.

Eisler, Riane, and Allie C. Hixson. 2001. "The Equal Rights Amendment: What Is It, Why Do We Need It, and Why Don't We Have It Yet?" In *Issues in Feminism: An Introduction to Women's Studies*, edited by Shelia Ruth. Mountain View, CA: Mayfield.

Ellis, Lee. 1996. "Theories of Homosexuality." In *The Lives of Lesbians, Gays, and Bisexuals: Children to Adults*, edited by Ritch C. Savin-Williams and Kenneth M. Cohen. Fort Worth, TX: Harcourt Brace.

Epstein, Joseph. 2020. "Is There a Doctor in the White House? Not if You Need an M.D." *Wall Street Journal,* December 11. https://www.wsj.com/articles /is-there-a-doctor-in-the-white-house-not-if-you-need-an-m-d-116077 27380.

Equal Employment Opportunity Commission. 2010. "Walmart to Pay More Than $11.7 Million to Settle EEOC Sex Discrimination Suit." Press release, March 1.

———. 2020a. "Americans with Disabilities Act of 1990 (ADA) Charges (Charges Filed with EEOC) (Includes Concurrent Charges with Title VII, ADEA, EPA, and GINA) FY 1997–FY 2019." www .eeoc.gov/statistics/americans-disabilities -act-1990-ada-charges-charges-filed-eeoc-includes-concurrent.

———. 2020b. "National Origin-Based Charges (Charges Filed with EEOC) FY 1997–FY2019." www.eeoc.gov/statistics/national-origin-based-charges-charges -filed-with-eeoc-fy-1997-fy-2019.

———. 2020c. "Sex-Based Charges (Charges Filed with EEOC) FY1997– FY2019." www.eeoc.gov/statistics/charge-statistics-charges-filed-eeoc-fy-1997 -through-fy-2019?renderforprint=1.

———. 2020d. "Race-Based Charges (Charges Filed with the EEOC) FY1997– 2019." https://www.eeoc.gov/statistics/race-based-charges-charges-filed-eeoc -fy-1997-fy-2020.

Equal Pay Day. 2020. http://www.equalpaytoday.org/equalpaydays.

Espiritu, Yen Le. 1992. *Asian-American Panethnicity: Bridging Institutions and Identities.* Philadelphia, PA: Temple University Press.

Esterberg, Kristin Gay. 1996. "Gay Cultures, Gay Communities: The Social Organization of Lesbians, Gay Men, and Bisexuals." In *The Lives of Lesbians, Gays, and Bisexuals: Children to Adults,* edited by Ritch C. Savin-Williams and Kenneth M. Cohen. Fort Worth, TX: Harcourt Brace.

"Fact Sheet: Women in Service Review (WISR) Implementation." 2020. www.dod .defense.gov/Portals/1/Documents/pubs/Fact_Sheet_WISR_FINAL.pdf.

Faludi, Susan. 2020. "Trump's Thoroughly Modern Masculinity." *New York Times,* October 30, A31.

Farley, Robert. 2018. "Is Illegal Immigration Linked to More or Less Crime?" www.factcheck.org/2018/06/.

Fausto-Sterling, Anne. 1993. "The Five Sexes: Why Male and Female Are Not Enough." *Sciences* 33, no. 2 (March–April): 20–26.

———. 2000. "The Five Sexes Revisited." *Sciences* 40, no. 4 (July–August): 18–24.

Feagin, Joe R. 2000. *Racist America: Roots, Current Realities, and Future Reparations.* New York: Routledge.

———. 2010. *Racist America: Roots, Current Realities, and Future Reparations,* 2nd ed. New York: Routledge.

Federal Bureau of Investigation. 2020. "Hate Crime Statistics, 2018." www.justice .gov/hatecrimes/hate-crime-statistics.

Feminist News. 2010. "Orthodox Rabbis Issue Statement Supporting Gays and Lesbians." August 3.

Feuerherd, Peter. 2017. "St. Augustine, the First Real European Settlement in America?" *Jstor Daily,* April 15. https://daily.jstor.org/st-augustine-the-real-first-european-settlement-in-america/.

Files, John. 2005. "Ruling on Gays Exacts a Cost in Recruiting, a Study Finds." *New York Times,* February 24, A16.

Fischer, Marc. 2016. "Donald Trump: 'I am the least racist person.'" *Washington Post,* June 10. www.washingtonpost.com/politics/donald-trump-i-am-the-least-racist-person/2016/06/10/eac7874c-2f3a-11e6-9de3-6e6e7a14000c_story.html.

Flores, Andrew R., Jody L. Herman, Gary J. Gates, and Taylor N. T. Brown. 2016. "How Many Adults Identify as Transgender in the United States?" Los Angeles: Williams Institute. www.williamsinstitute.law.ucla.edu/publications/trans-adults-united-states/

Forbes. 2020. The World's Billionaires List: The Richest in 2020." www.forbes.com/billionaires.

Fortune. 2010. "Annual Ranking of America's Largest Corporations."

Freeman, Jo, and Victoria Johnson, eds. 1999. *Waves of Protest: Social Movements Since the Sixties.* Lanham, MD: Rowman and Littlefield.

Freiberg, Fred. 2019. "Prove It!" *Poverty and Race Research Action Council* 28, no. 3 (September–December): 1–7.

Fruscione, Joseph. 2014. "When a College Contracts 'Adjunctivitis,' It's the Students Who Lose." July 25, *PBS News Hour.* www.pbs.org/newshour/nation/when-a-college-contracts-adjunctivitis-its-the-students-who-lose.

Frye, Marilyn. 1983. *The Politics of Reality: Essays in Feminist Theory.* Freedom, CA: Crossing.

Gallup. 2019. "Gay and Lesbian Rights." www.news.gallup.com/poll/1651/gay-lesbian-rights.aspx?version=print.

Gao, George. 2015. "Most Americans Now Say Learning Their Child Is Gay Wouldn't Upset Them." Pew Research Center. www.pewresearch.org/fact-tank/215/06/29.

Gay and Lesbian Alliance Against Defamation. 2020. "Where We Are on TV Report—2019." www.glaad.org/publications/where-we-are-tv-report-2019-0.

Gay, Lesbian, and Straight Education Network (GLSEN). 2012. "The 2011 National School Climate Survey." www.glsen.org/news/2011-national-school-climate-survey.

Gee, Alastair. 2017. "Facing Poverty, Academics Turn to Sex Work and Sleeping in Cars." *Guardian,* September 28. www.theguardian.com/us-news/2017/sep/28/adjunct-professors-homeless-sex-work-academia-poverty.

General Accounting Office (GAO). 2003. "Women's Earnings: Work Patterns Partially Explain Difference Between Men's and Women's Earnings." GAO-04-35, October. Washington, DC: General Accounting Office.

General Social Survey (GSS). 2018. "Data Explorer: Subjective Class Identification." www.gssdataexplorer.norc.org/variables/568/vshow.

Gerstenfeld, Phyllis B. 2004. *Hate Crimes: Causes, Controls, and Controversies.* Thousand Oaks, CA: Sage.

Gibbons-Neff, Thomas. 2020. "Barrier Falls as a Woman Becomes a Green Beret." *New York Times,* July 10, A13.

Gibbs, Nancy. 2009. "What Women Want Now: A *Time* Special Report." *Time* 174, no. 16 (October 26): 24–35.

Gilbert, Dennis. 2008. *The American Class Structure: In an Age of Growing Inequality,* 7th ed. Belmont, CA: Wadsworth.

Glenn, David. 2003. "The *Economist* as Affable Provocateur." *Chronicle of Higher Education,* December 5, A10–A11.

Goffman, Erving. 1963. *Stigma: Notes on the Management of Spoiled Identity.* Englewood Cliffs, NJ: Prentice-Hall.

Gonyea, Don. 2017. "Majority of White Americans Say They Believe Whites Face Discrimination." National Public Radio. www.npr.org/2017/10/24/559604836 /majority-of-white-americans-think-theyre-discriminated-against/.

Gould, Elise, and Jon Kandra. 2021. "Wages Grew in 2020 Because the Bottom Fell Out of the Low-Wage Labor Market." Economic Policy Institute. February 24.

Greenhouse, Steven. 2009. "Labor Fight Ends in Win for Students." *New York Times,* November 17.

Griffith, Janelle, Laura Strickler, and Gabe Gutierrez. 2020. "City of Louisville Reaches $12 Million Settlement with Breonna Taylor's Family." NBC News, September 15. https://www.nbcnews.com/news/us-news/city-louisville-reaches -settlement-breonna-taylor-s-family-n1240115.

Grothaus, Michael. 2020. "Walmart Is Giving 165,000 Employees a Pay Raise Between $15 and $30 Per Hour." MSN, September 18. www.msn.com/en -us/money/companies/walmart-is-giving-165000-employees-a-pay-raise -between-dollar15-and-dollar30-per-hour/ar-BB19aHW4.

Gupta, Alisha Haridasani. 2020. "Why Did Hundreds of Thousands of Women Drop Out of the Workforce?" *New York Times,* October 3.

Handwerker, Elizabeth Weber, Peter B. Meyer, Joseph Piacentini, Michael Schultz, and Leo Sveikauskas. 2020. "Employment Recovery in the Wake of the COVID-19 Pandemic." *Monthly Labor Review*, January 20. https://www.bls .gov/opub/mlr/2020/article/employment-recovery.htm.

Harder, Jenna A., Victor N. Keller, and William J. Chopik. 2019. "Demographic, Experiential, and Temporal Variation in Ableism." *Journal of Social Issues* 75, no. 3: 683–706.

Harrington, Anne. 2019. "Psychiatry, Racism, and the Birth of *Sesame Street*." May 17. www.undark.org/2019/05/17/psychiatry-racism-sesame-street/.

Harrington, Michael. 1997. *The Other America: Poverty in the United States*. New York: Touchstone.

Harriot, Michael. 2020. "Segregation, Reparations, and Cultural Appropriation: Maryland Passes Legislation Settling HCU Lawsuit." *Root*, March 16.

Harrison, Lawrence E. 1992. *Who Prospers? How Cultural Values Shape Economic and Political Success*. New York: Basic.

Hauck, Grace, and N'dea Yancey-Bragg. 2021. "Minneapolis Reaches $27M Settlement with George Floyd's Family in Wrongful Death Lawsuit." *USA Today*, March 12.

Hawkins, Stephen, Daniel Yudkin, Miriam Juan-Torres, and Tim Dixon. 2018. "Hidden Tribes: A Study of America's Polarized Landscape." New York: More in Common.

Healy, Jack. 2020. "For Tribe in Oklahoma, Ruling Sparks Emotion Over 'A Promise Kept.'" *New York Times,* July 13, A16.

Hegewisch, Ariane, Hannah Liepmann, Jeffrey Hayes, and Heidi Hartmann. 2010. "Separate and Not Equal? Gender Segregation in the Labor Market and the Gender Wage Gap." Institute for Women's Policy Research Briefing Paper C377.

Herbenick, Debby, Michael Reece, Vanessa Schnick, Stephanie Sanders, Brian Dodge, and J. Dennis Fortenberry. 2010. "Sexual Behavior in the United States: Results from a National Probability Sample of Men and Women Ages 14–94." *Journal of Sexual Medicine* 7: 255s–265s.

Hernandez, Brigida, Christopher Keys, and Fabricio Balcazar. 2000. "Employer Attitudes Toward Workers with Disabilities and Their ADA Employment

Rights: A Literature Review." *Journal of Rehabilitation* (October–December): 4–16.

Heyl, Barbara Sherman. 2003. "Homosexuality: A Social Phenomenon." In *The Meaning of Difference: American Constructions of Race, Sex, and Gender, Social Class, and Sexual Orientation,* 3rd ed., edited by Karen E. Rosenblum and Toni-Michelle C. Travis. Boston: McGraw-Hill.

Hofmann, Sudie. 2005. "Framing the Family Tree: How Teachers Can Be Sensitive to Students' Family Situations." *Rethinking Schools* 19 (Spring): 20–22.

hooks, bell. 2000. "Feminism: A Movement to End Sexist Oppression." In *Readings for Diversity and Social Justice: An Anthology on Racism, Antisemitism, Sexism, Heterosexism, Ableism, and Classism,* edited by Maurianne Adams, Warren J. Blumenfeld, and Rosie Castaneda et al. New York: Routledge.

Hopkins, Daniel J., and Samantha Washington. 2020. "The Rise of Trump, the Fall of Prejudice? Tracking White Americans' Racial Attitudes via a Panel Survey, 2008–2018." *Public Opinion Quarterly* 84, no. 1 (Spring): 119–140.

Horowitz, Juliana Menasce. 2019a. "Americans See Advantages and Challenges in Country's Growing Racial and Ethnic Diversity." Pew Research Center.

———. 2019b. "Most Americans Say the Legacy of Slavery Still Affects Black People in the U.S. Today." Pew Research Center.

Horowitz, Juliana Menasce, Anna Brown, and Kiana Cox. 2019. "Race in America 2019." Pew Research Center. www.pewsocialtrends.org/2019/04/09/race-in -america-2019/?utm_source=link_newsv9&utm_campaign=item_312590&utm _medium=copy.

Horowitz, Juliana Menasce, and Ruth Igielnik. 2020. "A Century After Women Gained the Right to Vote, Majority of Americans See Work to Do on Gender Equality." Pew Research Center. www.pewsocialtrends.org/2020/07/07/.

Horowitz, Juliana Menasce, Kim Parker, Anna Brown, and Kiana Cox. 2020. "Amid National Reckoning, Americans Divided on Whether Increased Focus on Race Will Lead to Major Policy Change." Pew Research Center. www.pewsocial trends.org/2020/10/06/amid-national-reckoning-americans-divided-on-whether -increased-focus-on-race-will-lead-to-major-policy-change/.

Horowitz, Juliana Menasce, Kim Parker, and Renee Stepler. 2017. "Wide Partisan Gaps in U.S. over How Far the Country Has Come on Gender Equality." Pew Research Center. www.pewsocialtrends.org/2017/10/18.

Hout, Michael. 2019. "State of the Union: Social Mobility." The Poverty and Inequality Report. *Pathways: A Magazine on Poverty, Inequality and Social Policy.*

Human Rights Campaign. 2009. "Equality from State to State 2009." www.hrc.org.

———. 2019. "Faith Positions." www.hrc.org/resources/faith-positions.

———. 2020. "Corporate Equality Index 2020." www.hrc.org/resources/corporate -equality-index.

Ibe, Peniel. 2020. "Trump's Attacks on the Legal Immigration System Explained." American Friends Service Committee. www.afsc.org/blogs/news-and-commentary /trumps-attacks-on-the-legal-immigration-system-explained.

Igielnik, Ruth, and Kim Parker. 2019. "Most Americans Say the Current Economy Is Helping the Rich, Hurting the Poor and the Middle Class." Pew Research Center, December 11.

Institute for Women's Policy Research. 2020. "The Gender Wage Gap by Occupation 2019 and by Race and Ethnicity." IWPR no. C490. March. Washington, DC: Institute for Women's Policy Research.

Ipsos. 2020. "Glossary of Gender Terms." www.future.ipsos.com/?p=10521& preview=true.

Johfre, Sasha Shen, and Aliya Saperstein. 2019. "Racial and Gender Identities." *Pathways: A Magazine on Poverty, Inequality and Social Policy*: 7–10.

Johnson, Allan. 2001. *Privilege, Power, and Difference*. Mountain View, CA: Mayfield.

Johnston, David Cay. 2020. "The Super Rich—You Know, People Like the Trumps—Are Raking in Billions." December 19. DCReport.org. www.dc report.org/2020/09/15/the-super-rich-you-know-people-like-the-tumps-are -raking-in-billions/.

Jones, Bradley. 2019. "Majority of Americans Continue to Say Immigrants Strengthen the U.S." Pew Research Center. www.pewresearch.org/fact -tank/2019/01/31.

Jones, Camara P. 2014 "Systems of Power, Axes of Inequality: Parallels, Intersections, Braiding the Strands." *Medical Care* 52, no.10, Supplement 3: S71–S75.

Jones, James M. 1997. *Prejudice and Racism*, 2nd ed. Hightstown, NJ: McGraw-Hill.

Jones, Jeffrey M. 2020. "Black, White Adults' Confidence Diverge Most on Police." Gallup. https://news.gallup.com/poll/317114/black-white-adults -confidence-diverges-police.aspx.

———. 2021a. "LGBT Identification Rises to 5.6% in Latest US Estimate." https://news.gallup.com/poll/329708/lgbt-identification-rises-latest-estimate .aspx.

———. 2021b. "One in 10 LGBT Americans Married to Same-Sex Spouse." https://news.gallup.com/poll/329975/one-lgbt-americans-married-sex -spouse.aspx.

Jordan, Bryant. 2010. "Booted Gays Consider Life After DADT." Palmcenter.org.

Kahn, Robert. 2004. "Scholarships Reach Out to Gays in College." *Baltimore Sun*, October 5, 1C, 5C.

Kalleberg, Arne L. 2011. *Good Jobs, Bad Jobs: The Rise of Polarized and Precarious Employment Systems in the United States, 1970s to 2000s*. New York: Russell Sage Foundation.

Kallman, Davi. 2017. "Integrating Disability: Boomerang Effects When Using Positive Media Exemplars to Reduce Disability Prejudice." *International Journal of Disability, Development and Education* 64, no. 6: 644–652.

Kamdar, Mira. 2020. "Why I'm Glad I Left America." *Atlantic*, October 14. www.theatlantic.com/ideas/archive/2020/10/american-emigre/616705/.

Katz, Jonathan Ned. 1995. *The Invention of Heterosexuality*. New York: Dutton/Penguin.

Kaufman, Cynthia. 2003. *Ideas for Action: Relevant Theory of Radical Change*. Cambridge, MA: South End.

Kauffman, L. A. 2018. *How to Read a Protest: The Art of Organizing and Resistance*. Berkeley: University of California Press.

Keeter, Scott. 2015. "From Telephone to the Web: The Challenge of Mode of Interview Effects in Public Opinion Polls." Pew Research Center.

Kelly, Christine, and Joel Lefkowitz. 2003. "Radical and Pragmatic: United Students Against Sweatshops." In *Teamsters and Turtles? US Progressive Political Movements in the Twenty-First Century*, edited by John C. Berg. Lanham, MD: Rowman and Littlefield.

Kendi, Ibram X. 2019. *How to Be an Antiracist*. New York: Random House.

Kerbo, Harold R. 2009. *Social Stratification and Inequality: Class Conflict in Historical, Comparative, and Global Perspective,* 7th ed. Boston: McGraw-Hill.

Kimmel, Michael S. 2004. "Inequality and Difference." In *Oppression, Privilege, and Resistance: Theoretical Perspectives on Racism, Sexism, and Heterosexism,* edited by Lisa Heldke and Peg O'Connor. Boston: McGraw-Hill.

King, J. L. 2004. *Living on the Down Low: A Journey into the Lives of "Straight" Black Men Who Sleep with Men.* New York: Broadway.

Kinsey, Alfred C., Wardell B. Pomeroy, Clyde E. Martin, and Paul H. Gebhard. 1948. *Sexual Behavior in the Human Male.* Philadelphia, PA: W. B. Saunders.

———. 1953. *Sexual Behavior in the Human Female.* Philadelphia, PA: W. B. Saunders.

Kohut, Andrew. 2019. "From the Archives: In '60s, Americans Gave Thumbs-Up to Immigration Law That Changed the Nation." Pew Research Center. www.pewresearch.org/fact-tank/2019/09/20.

Kolata, Gina. 2020. "Race Factors into Medical Decision-Making." *New York Times,* June 18, 4A.

Krogstad, Jens Manuel, Mark Hugo Lopez, and Jeffrey S. Passel. 2020. "A Majority of Americans Say Immigrants Mostly Fill Jobs U.S. Citizens Do Not Want." Pew Research Center. www.pewresearch.org/fact-tank/2020/06/10.

Ladd, Everett Carll, and Karlyn H. Bowman. 1998. *Attitudes Toward Economic Inequality.* Washington, DC: American Enterprise Institute for Public Policy Research.

Lane, Randall. 2017. "The Age of Amazon." *Forbes*, September 30, 80.

Lappe, Frances Moore. 2019. "Blood on Our Hands: How We Help Drive Immigration North." Portside, July 23.

Laster, Jill. 2010. "Unlike Men, Female Scientists Have a Second Shift: Housework." *Chronicle of Higher Education,* January 20, A10.

Lauzen, Martha M. 2019a. "Boxed In 2018–19: Women on Screen and Behind the Scenes in Television." San Diego: Center for the Study of Women in Television and Film.

———. 2019b. "It's a Man's (Celluloid) World: Portrayals of Female Characters in the Top Grossing Films of 2019." San Diego: Center for the Study of Women in Television and Film.

Leisenring, Mary. 2020. "Women Still Have to Work Three Months Longer to Equal What Men Earned in a Year." www.census.gov/library/visualizations/interactive/men-women-earnings-gap.html.

Levitt, Daniel. 2018. "State of Pay: Tennis Has Huge Gender Gap in Earning Power." *Guardian.* www.google.com/search?client=firefox-b-1-d&q=guardian+sport.

Libowsky, Sarah, and Krista Oehlke. 2021. "President Biden's Immigration Executive Actions: A Recap." Lawfare, March 3. https://www.lawfareblog.com/president-bidens-immigration-executive-actions-recap.

Lloyd, Camille. 2020. "Black Adults Disproportionately Experience Microaggressions." Gallup, June 15. https://news.gallup.com/poll/315695/black-adults-disproportionately-experience-microaggressions.aspx.

Lorber, Judith. 1998. *Gender Equality: Feminist Theory and Politics.* Los Angeles: Roxbury.

Lottes, Ilsa, and Eric Grollman. 2010. "Conceptualization and Assessment of Homonegativity." *International Journal of Sexual Health* 22: 219–233.

Markovits, Daniel. 2019. *The Meritocracy Trap: How America's Foundational Myth Feeds Inequality, Dismantles the Middle Class, and Devours the Elite.* New York: Penguin.

Marso, Andy. 2011. "Funeral Protesters Vow to Fight Picketing Curbs." *Baltimore Sun,* March 5, 7.

Mascaro, Lisa, and James Oliphant. 2010. "Senate Votes to Repeal 'Don't Ask, Don't Tell.'" *Los Angeles Times,* December 18.

Meem, Deborah T., Michelle A. Gibson, and Jonathan F. Alexander. 2010. *Finding Out: An Introduction to GLBT Studies.* Thousand Oaks, CA: Sage.

Metz, Cade. 2020. "When Data Lacks Diversity, Black Voices Are Muffled." *New York Times,* March 24, A16.

Meyer, David S. 2003. "How Social Movements Matter." *Contexts* 2, no. 4 (Fall): 30–35.

Miller, Claire Cain. 2019. "Women Did Everything Right. Then Work Got 'Greedy.'" *New York Times,* April 28, Business, 1–6.

Minkin, Rachel 2020. "Most Americans Support Gender Equality, Even if They Don't Identify as Feminists." Pew Research Center. www.pewresearchcenter.org/fact-tank/2020/07/04.

Mishel, Emma. 2016. "Discrimination Against Queer Women in the U.S. Workforce: A Resume Audit." *Socius: Sociological Research for a Dynamic World:* 1–13.

Mishel, Lawrence, Jared Bernstein, and Sylvia Allegretto. 2005. *The State of Working America, 2004–2005.* Ithaca, NY: ILR Press.

Mishel, Lawrence, and Jori Kandra. 2020. "CEO Compensation Surged 14% in 2019 to $21.3 Million." Economic Policy Institute, August 18.

Moore, Mignon R., and Michael Stambolis-Ruhstorfer. 2013. "LGBT Sexuality and Families at the Start of the Twenty-First Century." *Annual Review of Sociology* 39: 491–507.

Moreau, Julie. 2020. "Anti-LGBTQ Hate Groups on the Rise in U.S., Report Warns." www.nbcnews.com/feature/nbc-out/anti-lgbtq-hate-groups-rise-u-s-report-warns-n1171956?cid=googlenews-usnews.

Morin, Rich. 2015. "Exploring Racial Bias Among Biracial and Single-Race Adults: The IAT." Pew Research Center. www.pewsocialtrends.org/2015/08/19/exploring-racial-bias-among-biracial-and-single-race-adults-the-iat/.

Morrison, Melanie A., and Todd G. Morrison. 2002. "Development and Validation of a Scale Measuring Modern Prejudice Toward Gay Men and Lesbian Women." *Journal of Homosexuality* 43: 15–37.

Mueller, Carlyn O., Anjali J. Forber-Pratt, and Julie Sriken. 2019. "Disability: Missing from the Conversation of Violence." *Journal of Social Issues* 75, no. 3: 707–725.

Mulcahy, Diane. 2016. *The Gig Economy: The Complete Guide to Getting Better Work, Taking More Time Off, and Financing the Life You Want.* New York: AMACOM.

Mystal, Elie. 2021. "The Massacre in Atlanta Was as Predictable as White Supremacy." *The Nation,* March 18.

National Institute of Justice. 2019. *Women in Policing: Breaking Barriers and Blazing a Path.* www.nij.ojp.gov.

National Organization on Disability/Harris Poll. 2004. "The NOD/Harris 2004 Survey of Americans with Disabilities." New York: Harris Interactive.

National Priorities Project. 2010. www.nationalpriorities.org.

National Public Radio, Robert Wood Johnson Foundation, Harvard T. H. Chan School of Public Health. 2017. "Discrimination in America: Experiences and Views of American Women." Cambridge, MA: Authors.

Navarro, Vicente. 2007. "The Worldwide Class Struggle." In *More Unequal: Aspects of Class in the United States,* edited by Michael D. Yates. New York: Monthly Review Press.

Neel, Joe. 2017. "Poll: Most Americans Think Their Own Group Faces Discrimination." National Public Radio. https://www.npr.org/sections/health-shots/2017 /10/24/559116373/poll-most-americans-think-their-own-group-faces -discrimination.

Ness, Immanuel. 2003. "Unions and American Workers: Whither the Labor Movement?" In *Teamsters and Turtles? US Progressive Political Movements in the Twenty-First Century,* edited by John C. Berg. Lanham, MD: Rowman and Littlefield.

Newport, Frank. 2013. "In US, 87% Approve of Black-White Marriage, vs. 4% in 1958." Gallup, July 25. https://news.gallup.com/poll/163697/approve-marriage -blacks-whites.aspx.

———. 2016. "Americans' Identification as Middle Class Edges Back Up." Gallup News Service, December 15. news.gallup.com/poll/199727/americans -identification-middle-class-edges-back.aspx.

———. 2018a. "In U.S., Estimate of LGBT Population Rises to 4.5%." news .gallup.com/poll/234863/estimate-lgbt-population-rises.aspx?version =print.

———. 2018b. "Looking Into What Americans Mean by 'Working Class." https://news.gallup.com/opinion/polling-matters/239195/looking-americans -mean-working-class.aspx?version=print.

———. 2021. "American Public Opinion and the Equality Act." March 18. https://news.gallup.com/opinion/polling-matters/340349/american-public -opinion-equality-act.aspx?version=print.

New York Times. 2017. "Economic Diversity and Student Outcomes at Harvard University." www.nytimes.com/interactive/projects/college-mobility/harvard -university.

New York Times/CBS News. 2005. "Class Project Poll."

———. 2010. "Poll: National Survey of Tea Party Supporters."

Nguyen, Janet. 2020. "Americans on Shaky Ground Financially, Speaking Out More on Racism, Poll Shows." Marketplace Morning Report. www.market place.org/2020/10/15/americans-on-shaky-ground-financially-speaking-out -more-on-racism-covid-19-pandemic/.

Noe-Bustamante, Lauren Mora, and Mark Hugo Lopez. 2020. "About One-in-Four U.S. Hispanics Have Heard of Latinx, but Just 3% Use It." https://www.pew research.org/hispanic/2020/08/11/about-one-in-four-u-s-hispanics-have-heard -of-latinx-but-just-3-use-it/.

Nowrasteh, Alex. 2019. "Illegal Immigrants and Crime: Assessing the Evidence." CATO Institute. www.cato.org/blog/illegal-immigrants-crime-assessing -evidence.

O'Brien, Eileen. 2001. *Whites Confront Racism: Anti Racists and Their Paths to Activism.* Lanham, MD: Rowman and Littlefield.

Ollenberger, Jane C., and Helen A. Moore. 1998. *A Sociology of Women: The Intersection of Patriarchy, Capitalism, and Colonization,* 2nd ed. Upper Saddle River, NJ: Prentice Hall.

"Outsourcing Is Breaking Out of the Back Office." 2007. *New York Times.*

Pager, Devah. 2003. "The Mark of a Criminal Record." *American Journal of Sociology* 108 (March): 937–975.

Palm Center. 2009. "Countries That Allow Military Service by Openly Gay People." Palmcenter.org.

Parker, Kim, Juliana Menasce Horowitz, and Monica Anderson. 2020. "Amid Protests, Majorities Across Racial and Ethnic Groups Express Support for the

Black Lives Matter Movement." Pew Research Center. www.pewsocialtrends
.org/2020/06/12.

Parker, Kim, Juliana Menasce Horowitz, and Renee Stepler. 2017a. "Americans See
Different Expectations for Men and Women." Pew Research Center. www
.pewsocialtrends.org/2017/12/05.

———. 2017b. "On Gender Differences, No Consensus on Nature vs. Nurture."
Pew Research Center. www.pewsocialtrends.org/2017/12/05.

Parolin, Zachary, Megan Curran, Jordan Matsudaira, Jane Waldfogel, and Christo-
pher Wimer. 2020. "Monthly Poverty Rates in the United States During the
Covid-19 Pandemic." *Poverty and Social Policy Working Paper*, October 15.
Povertycenter.columbia.edu.

Pascoe, C. J. 2011. *Dude You're a Fag: Masculinity and Sexuality in High School*,
2nd ed. Berkeley: University of California Press.

Passel, Jeffrey S., and D'Vera Cohn. 2019. "Mexicans Decline to Less Than Half
the U.S. Unauthorized Immigrant Population for the First Time." Pew Research
Center. www.pewresearchcenter.org/fact-tank/2019/06/12.

Pedulla, David S. 2019. "Discrimination." *State of the Union 2018.* Palo Alto, CA:
Stanford Center on Poverty and Inequality.

Pedulla, David S., and Devah Pager. 2019. "Race and Networks in the Job Search
Process." *American Sociological Review* 84, no. 6.

Perry, Andre. 2020. *Know Your Price: Valuing Black Lives and Property in America's Black Cities.* Washington, DC: Brookings Institution.

Perryundem Research Communication. 2017. "The State of the Union on Gender
Equality, Sexism, and Women's Rights." www.plannedparenthoodaction.org
/uploads/filer_public/c9/ba/c9ba8d51-2719-4267-8784-ada24f047adc/perry
undem_gender_equality_report_1.pdf.

Peterson, Anne M., and Ronald Blum. 2020. "Women's Team, US Soccer Settle Part
of Their Lawsuit." December 1. https://apnews.com/article/international-soccer
-soccer-womens-soccer-lawsuits-courts-19b5599494006be69d6162ecd350
58a3.

Pew Research Center. 2010. "Gay Marriage Gains More Acceptance." https://
www.pewresearch.org/2010/10/06/gay-marriage-gains-more-acceptance/.

———. 2017. "Top Frustrations with Tax System: Sense That Corporations,
Wealthy Don't Pay Fair Share." April 4.

———. 2018a. "Majorities Say Government Does Too Little for Older People, the
Poor, and the Middle Class." January 30.

———. 2018b. "Shifting Public Views on Legal Immigration into the U.S."
www.people-press.org/2018/06/28.

———. 2019. "Remittance Flows Worldwide in 2017." www.pewresearch.org
/global/interactives/remittance-flows-by-country/.

———. 2020. "Most Americans Point to Circumstances, Not Work Ethic, for Why
People Are Rich or Poor." www.pewresearch.org/politics/2020/03/02.

Pfeffer, Fabian T., and Alexandra Killewald. 2015. "How Rigid Is the Wealth Struc-
ture and Why? Inter- and Multi-Generational Associations in Family Wealth."
Population Studies Center: University of Michigan Institute for Social
Research, Report 15-845, September.

Piketty, Thomas. 2013. *Capital in the Twenty-First Century.* Cambridge, MA: Bel-
knap Press.

Pilkington, Ed. 2020. "Covid Death Rate Among African Americans and Latinos
Rising Sharply." *Guardian,* September 8. https://www.theguardian.com

/world/2020/sep/08/covid-19-death-rate-african-americans-and-latinos
   -rising-sharply.
Pinkus, Susan, and Jill Darling Richardson. 2004. "Americans Oppose Same-Sex
   Marriage, but Acceptance of Gays in Society Grows." *Los Angeles Times*
   Poll/Gay Issues Survey, Study 501.
Potok, Mark. 2010. "Gays Remain Minority Most Targeted by Hate Crimes." *Intelligence Report* 140 (Winter).
Price, Barbara Raffel, and Natalie J. Sokoloff, eds. 2004. *The Criminal Justice System and Women: Offenders, Prisoners, Victims, and Workers,* 3rd ed. Boston:
   McGraw-Hill.
ProsperityNow.Org. 2018. "Financial Stability of People with Disabilities."
   www.prosperitynow.org/sites/default/files/resources/Financial-Stability-of
   -People-with-Disabilities.pdf.
Public Broadcasting System. 2003. "Indentured Servants in the US." History Detectives. PBS.org.
PYMNTS. 2021. "Amazon and Walmart Are Nearly Tied in Full-Year Share of
   Retail Sales." https://www.pymnts.com/news/retail/2021/amazon-walmart-
   nearly-tied-in-full-year-share-of-retail-sales/.
Radford, Jynnah, and Jens Manuel Krogstad. 2019. "Recently Arrived U.S. Immigrants, Growing in Number, Differ from Long-Term Residents." Pew Research
   Center: www.pewresearchcenter.org/fact-tank/2019/06/03.
Radford, Jynnah, and Luis Noe-Bustamante. 2019. "Facts on U.S. Immigrants,
   2017." Pew Research Center. www.pewresearch.org/hispanic/2019/06/03.
Rauch, Jonathan. 2020. "It's George Wallace's World Now." *Atlantic,* April 26.
   www.theatlantic.com/ideas/archive/2020/04/george-wallace-donald-trump
   /607336/.
Renzetti, Claire M., and Daniel J. Curran. 1999. *Women, Men, and Society,* 4th ed.
   Boston: Allyn and Bacon.
Rim, Christopher. 2018. "Can You Buy Your Way into Harvard?" *Forbes,* October
   24. www.forbes.com/sites/christopherrim/2018/10/24/can-you-buy-your-way
   -into-harvard/?sh=5836dec42206.
Robert, Pamela M., and Sharon L. Harlan. 2006. "Mechanisms of Disability in
   Large Bureaucratic Organizations." *Sociological Quarterly* 47: 599–630.
Robertson, Campbell, and Robert Gebeloff. 2020. "When It Comes to 'Essential,'
   It's a Woman's World Today." *New York Times,* April 19.
Rooney, Caitlin, Charlie Whittington, and Laura E. Durso. 2018. "Protecting Basic
   Living Standards for LGBTQ People." Center for American Progress:
   www.americanprogress.org/issues/lgbtq-rights/2018.
Rosenblum, Karen E., and Toni-Michelle C. Travis, eds. 2003. *The Meaning of Difference: American Constructions of Race, Sex, and Gender, Social Class, and
   Sexual Orientation,* 3rd ed. Boston: McGraw-Hill.
Roth, Byron. 1994. "Racism and Traditional American Values." *Studies in Social
   Philosophy and Policy* 18: 119–140.
Rothenberg, Paula S., ed. 2004. *Race, Class, and Gender in the United States,* 6th
   ed. New York: Worth.
Rupp, Leila J., and Verta Taylor. 2016. "Straight Girls Kissing." *Contexts* 19, no. 2:
   28–32.
Saad, Lydia. 2007, "Tolerance for Gay Rights at High-Water Mark." Gallup News
   Service. https://news.gallup.com/poll/27694/tolerance-gay-rights-highwater
   -mark.aspx.

————. 2020. "Black Americans' Preferred Racial Label." Gallup Vault, July 13. news.gallup.com/vault/315566/gallup-vault-black-americans-preferred-racial -label.aspx.

Salinas, Sara. 2018. "Amazon Raises Minimum Wage to $15 for All US Employ-ees." CNBC, October 2. www.cnbc.com/2018/10/02/amazon-raises-minimum -wage-to-15-for-all-us-employees.html.

Sassen, Saskia. 1999. "America's Immigration Problem." In *Race and Ethnic Conflict*, edited by Fred L. Pincus and Howard J. Ehrlich. Boulder, CO: Westview Press, 229–238.

Scarborough, William J., Ray Sin, and Barbara Risman. 2019. "Attitudes and the Stalled Gender Revolution: Egalitarianism, Traditionalism, and Ambivalence from 1977 Through 2016." *Gender and Society* 33, no. 2 (April): 173–200.

Schaeffer, Katherine. 2021. "Racial, Ethnic Diversity Increases Yet Again with the 117th Congress." Pew Research Center, January 28. https://www.pew research.org/fact-tank/2021/01/28/racial-ethnic-diversity-increases-yet-again -with-the-117th-congress/.

Scholarship.com. 2021. "Scholarships for Gay and Lesbian Students." https://www.scholarships.com/financial-aid/college-scholarships/scholarships -by-type/scholarships-for-gay-or-lesbian-students/.

Seid, Judith. 2001. *Good Optional Judaism*. New York: Citadel.

Sentencing Project. 2013. "Ending Mass Incarceration: Charting a New Justice Reinvestment." www.sentencingproject.org/wp-content/uploads/2015/12 /Ending-Mass-Incarceration-Charting-a-New-Justice-Reinvestment.pdf.

Shakespeare, T. 2006. "The Social Model of Disability." In *The Disability Studies Reader*, 2nd ed., edited by Leonard J. Davis. New York: Routledge.

Shapiro, Thomas M., Tatjana Meschede, and Laura Sullivan. 2010. "The Racial Wealth Gap Increases Fourfold." Research and Policy Brief, Institute on Assets and Social Policy.

Shepard, Benjamin. 2003. "The AIDS Coalition to Unleash Power: A Brief Reconsideration." In *Teamsters and Turtles? US Progressive Political Movements in the Twenty-first Century*, edited by John C. Berg. Lanham, MD: Rowman and Littlefield.

Shyong, Frank. 2020. "'It's just too much': Asian Americans Confront Xenophobia, Economic Devastation, and the Coronavirus." *Los Angeles Times*, March 23. www.latimes.com/california/story/2020-03-23/coronavirus-devastation -immigrants.

Sincavage, Jessica R., Carl Haub, and O. P. Sharma. 2010. "Labor Costs in India's Organized Manufacturing Sector." *Monthly Labor Review* 132 (May): 3–22.

Small, Mario Luis, David J. Harding, and Michele Lamont. 2010. "Reconsidering Culture and Poverty." *Annals of the American Academy of Political and Social Science* 629 (May): 6–29.

Sneiderman, Paul M., and Edward G. Carmines. 1997. *Reaching Beyond Race*. Cambridge, MA: Harvard University Press.

Snyder, Thomas D., Cristobal de Brey, and Sally A. Dillow. 2020. *Digest of Education Statistics, 2019*. Washington, DC: National Center for Education Statistics.

Sokoloff, Natalie J. 2008. "Expanding the Intersectional Paradigm to Better Understand Domestic Violence in Immigrant Communities." *Critical Criminology* 16: 229–255.

Southall, Ashley. 2010. "Senate Approves Payment of Black Farmers' Claims." *New York Times*, November 20.

Southern Poverty Law Center. 2004. "Center Responds to Hate and Bias on Campuses." *SPLC Report* 34 (March): 1, 5.

Spence, J. T., R. Helmreich, and J. Stapp. 1973. "A Short Version of the Attitudes Toward Women Scale (AWS)." *Psychology of Women Quarterly* 2: 219–220.

Steinbuch, Yaron. 2020. "White Supremacists Reportedly Urge Members to Infect Cops, Jews with Coronavirus." *New York Post*, March 23. www.nypost.com /2020/03/23/white-supremacists-reportedly-urge-members-to-infect-cops-jews -with-coronavirus/.

Stepp, Laura Sessions. 2003. "In La. School, Son of Lesbian Learns 'Gay' Is a 'Bad Wurd.'" *Washington Post,* December 3, C1, C10.

Sumerau, J. E., and Eric Anthony Grollman. 2018. "Obscuring Oppression: Racism, Cissexism, and the Persistence of Social Inequality." *Sociology of Race and Ethnicity* 4, no. 3: 322–337.

Sumerau, J. E., Eric Anthony Grollman, and Ryan T. Cragun. 2017. "'Oh My God, I Sound Like a Horrible Person': Generic Processes in the Conditional Acceptance of Sexual and Gender Diversity." *Symbolic Interaction* 41, no. 1: 62–82.

Svokos, Alexandra. 2019. "After World Cup Win, U.S. Women Pivot to Gender Discrimination Lawsuit." ABC News. www.abcnews.go.com/Sports/world-cup-us -women-gender-discrimination.

Swarns, Rachel L. 2004. "Hispanics Debate Racial Grouping by Census." *New York Times,* October 24, A1, A18.

Swim, Janet K., and Bernadette Campbell. 2001. "Sexism: Attitudes, Beliefs, and Behaviors." *Blackwell Handbook of Social Psychology: Intergroup Processes.* Malden, MA: Blackwell.

Tatum, Beverly Daniel. 2003. *Why Are All the Black Kids Sitting Together in the Cafeteria? And Other Conversations About Race.* New York: Basic.

Taylor, Danielle M. 2018. "Americans with Disabilities: 2014." *Current Population Reports*, P70-152.

Thomas, Lauren. 2021. "Walmart to Hike Wages for 425,000 Workers to Average Above $15 an Hour." CNBC, February 18.

Tilcsik, Andras. 2011. "Pride and Prejudice: Employment Discrimination Against Openly Gay Men in the United States." *American Journal of Sociology* 117: 586–626.

Timmons, Heather. 2010. "Outsourcing to India Draws Western Lawyers." *New York Times,* August 4.

United for a Fair Economy. 2012. "New Report: *Forbes* 400 Reinforces Flawed 'We Built It' Claims." September 24.

US Bureau of Labor Statistics. 2010. "Current Employment Statistics: Highlights February 2010." Press release, March 5. www.bls.gov.

———. 2020a. "Union Membership Summary." News Release USDL-20-0108, January 22. www.bls.gov/news.release/union2.nr0.htm.

———. 2020b. "Most New Jobs: 20 Occupations with the Highest Projected Numeric Change in Employment." *Occupational Outlook Handbook.* www.bls .gov/ooh/most-new-jobs.htm.

———. 2020c. "Fastest-Growing Occupations: 20 Occupations with the Highest Percent Change of Employment Between 2019–2020." *Occupational Outlook Handbook.* www.bls.gov/ooh/fastest-growing.htm.

———. 2020d. "Employed Persons by Detailed Occupation, Sex, Race, and Hispanic or Latino Ethnicity." www.bls.gov/cps/cpsaat11.pdf.

———. 2020e. "Employed Persons by Occupation, Race, Hispanic or Latino Ethnicity, and Sex." Household Data Annual Averages. Labor Force Statistics from the Current Population Survey, Table 10.

———. 2020f. "Civilian Labor Force Participation Rate by Age, Sex, Race, and Ethnicity." www.bls.gov/emp/tables/civilian-labor-force-participation-rate.htm.

———. 2020g. "Persons with a Disability: Labor Force Characteristics—2019." News Release USDL-20-0339.

———. 2021. "Employment Status of the Noninstitutionalized Civilian Population." Tables 3–5. https://www.bls.gov/cps/cpsa2020.pdf.

US Census Bureau. 2017a. "Percent Distribution of Household Net Worth, by Amount of Net Worth and Selected Characteristics." Wealth, Asset Ownership, and Debt of Households Detailed Tables: Table 4.

———. 2017b. "Percent Distribution of Families, by Selected Characteristics Within Income Quintile and Top 5 Percent." Current Population Survey and Annual Social and Economic Supplement: Table FINC-06.

———. 2018a. "America's Family and Living Arrangements: 2018." Table A3. www.census.gov/data/tables/2018/demo/families/cps-2018.html.

———. 2018b. "ACS Demographics and Housing Estimates." American Community Survey. Table DP05.

———. 2018c. "Disability Characteristics." www.data.census.gov/cedsci/table?q=S1810&tid=acsst1y2018.s1810.

———. 2019. "Race and Hispanic Origin of Householder—Families by Median and Mean Income." Historical Income Tables: Families. Table F-5.

———. 2020a. "Household Pulse Survey: Measuring Social and Economic Impacts During the Coronavirus Pandemic." Household Pulse Survey.

———. 2020b. "Full-Time, Year-Round All Workers by Median Income and Sex: 1955 to 2019." Table P-38.

———. 2020c. "Poverty Status of People by Family Relationship, Race, and Hispanic Origin, 1959–2019." Table B5. www.census.gov/data/tables/2020/demo/income-poverty/p60-270.html.

———. 2020d. "Current Population Survey Tables for Household Income." Table HINC-05.

US Commission on Civil Rights. 2019. "In the Name of Hate: Examining the Federal Government's Role in Responding to Hate Crimes." www.usccr.gov/pubs/2019/11-13-in-the-name-of-hate.pdf.

Vandenburgh, Reid. 2005. Personal communication.

Vought, Russell. 2020. "Memorandum for the Heads of Executive Departments and Agencies." www.whitehouse.gov/wp-content/uploads/2020/09/M-20-34.pdf.

Walker, Andrea K. 2008. "Target Settles Lawsuit with Advocates for Blind." *Baltimore Sun,* August 28, 20.

Walmart. 2010. "Corporate Facts: Walmart by the Numbers." March.

Watanabe, Teresa. 2019. "Women's STEM Programs Under Fire." *Baltimore Sun,* August 26, 4.

Weinberg, Daniel. 2004. "Evidence from Census 2000 About Earnings by Detailed Occupation for Men and Women." CENSR-15, May. www.census.gov/newonsite.

Werschkul, Misha, and Jody Herman. 2004. "New IWPR Report Addresses Women's Employment Equity and Earnings: How Many More Years Until Equality?" *Institute for Women's Policy Research Quarterly Newsletter* (Winter/Spring): 1, 7.

West, Paul. 2010. "A New Law to Protect the Disabled." *New York Times,* October 9, A1, A12.

White House. 2020. "Immigration." www.whitehouse.gov/issues/immigration.

230   *References*

Wilkerson, Isabel. 1989. "African American Favored by Many of America's Blacks." *New York Times*, January 31, A1.

Williams, Claire. 2021. "With Congressional Stimulus Fight Looming, 76 Percent of Voters Back $1.9 Trillion Plan, Including 60 Percent of Republicans." https://morningconsult.com/2021/02/24/covid-stimulus-support-poll/.

Williams, David R., Jourdyn A. Lawrence, and Brigette A. Davis. 2019. "Racism and Health: Evidence and Needed Research." *Annual Review of Public Health* 40 (April): 105–125.

Williams Institute. 2019. "LGBT People in the U.S. Not Protected by State Nondiscrimination Statues." Los Angeles: University of California–Los Angeles, Williams Institute.

Wilson, Michelle Clare, and Katrina Scior. 2014. "Attitudes Towards Individuals with Disabilities as Measured by the Implicit Association Test: A Literature Review." *Research in Developmental Disabilities* 35: 294–321.

Wilson, William Julius. 2012. *The Truly Disadvantaged: The Inner City, the Underclass, and Public Policy*, 2nd ed. Chicago, IL: University of Chicago Press.

Wise, Tim. 2002. "Honkey Wanna Cracker?" *Z-Net Daily Commentary*, June 10.

Witters, Dan. 2020. "Life Ratings Among Black Americans Erode During Trump Era." Gallup, September 24.

World Inequality Database. 2020. "Income Inequality, USA, 1913–2019." www.wid.world/country/usa/.

Wright, Erik Olin. 1997. *Class Counts: Student Edition*. New York: Cambridge University Press.

Yaffe-Bellany, David. 2019. "Employers Are Wringing Their Hands." *New York Times,* August 23, B1, 4.

Yarrow, Andrew L. 2018. *Man Out: Men on the Sidelines of American Life*. Washington, DC: Brookings Institution Press.

Yates, Michael D. 2005. "A Statistical Portrait of the US Working Class." *Monthly Review* 56 (April): 12–31.

Yuan, Oscar. 2020. "Gender Means More Than You Think It Does." Ipsos. www.future.ipsos.com/gender/gender-means-more-than-you-think-it-does.

Zinn, Howard. 2003. *A People's History of the United States: 1492–Present*. New York: Perennial.

Zurawik, David. 2005. "Despite Denunciation, 'Buster' Episode to Air." *Baltimore Sun,* February 1, 1A, 6A.

Zweig, Michael. 2000. *The Working-Class Majority: America's Best Kept Secret*. Ithaca, NY: Cornell University Press.

Index

Able-bodied people, 13, 18
Ableism, 169
Abolitionists, 187
Accessibility, 177–178
Acquired immunodeficiency syndrome (AIDS), 202–203
ACT UP, 202–203
Actions, political, 30, 180, 203; collective social, 10, 181–182, 185, 187–196. *See also* Protests
Active Minds, 204
Activism, 155–156, 182, 190–191, 196–197, 202
ADAPT (organization), 203
Addams, Jane, 201
Adjunct faculty, 58
Affirmative action, 3, 19, 30, 50–51
Affordable Care Act (2010), 33
Afghanistan, war in, 30, 163, 204
African Americans, 18–19, 100, 159, 175, 186, 189; civil rights movement by, 190–192; confidence in US institutions by, 89–90; educational attainment for, 86–87, 86*tab*; equal rights for, 91–92, 92*tab*; on issues of race, 92–93, 92*tab*; median household net worth for, 83, 83*tab*; median incomes for, 79–82, 80*tab*, 81*tab*, 82*tab*, 88*tab*; men, 73–74, 96; "N word" use by, 4, 75; occupations of, 78–79, 79*tab*; people with disabilities as, 170, 170*tab*, 172*tab*;

poverty rates for, 84–86, 84*tab*, 85*tab*; stereotypes about, 21–22, 99; unemployment rates for, 76–78, 77*tab*, 78*tab*; unintentional systemic discrimination against, 28–29
Africans, 75
Age, 12, 108, 110, 134, 150, 180; paid labor force participation by, 122–123, 122*tab*; people with disabilities by, 170–171, 170*tab*, 171*tab*, 172*tab*; unemployment rates by, 77*tab*, 78*tab*
Albania, 118
Alexander, Michelle, 100
Ali, Muhammad, 193
Allegretto, Sylvia, 152
Alt Right. *See* White nationalism
Amazon, 62, 63–64
American Coalition of Citizens with Disabilities, 194
American Community Study (ACS), 168–169
American dream, 52–53, 55
American Federation of Labor (AFL), 188–189
American Federation of Labor-Congress of Industrial Organizations (AFL-CIO), 196, 197
American Friends Service Committee (AFSC), 204–205
American Indian Movement, 198
American Psychiatric Association, 143

240   *Index*

About the Book

What is diversity? How does prejudice show itself? What are the societal consequences of discrimination? Has anything changed over the past fifty years? These are just some of the questions addressed in *Understanding Diversity*, an introduction to the issues and controversies surrounding concepts of class, race, ethnicity, gender, sexual orientation, and disability.

This new edition has been thoroughly updated, as well as expanded to include a chapter on immigration, discussion of the varied impacts of the Covid-19 pandemic, and a section on gender diversity. The student-friendly structure of the book, however, remains unchanged. Accessible and practical, yet theoretically rich, *Understanding Diversity* is the perfect companion to the diversity anthology of your choice.

Fred L. Pincus is professor emeritus of sociology at the University of Maryland, Baltimore County. **Bryan R. Ellis** is senior lecturer in the Irvin D. Reid Honors College at Wayne State University.